Gottfried Keller in old age.

Etching by Karl Stauffer-Bern, 1887

J. M. LINDSAY

GOTTFRIED KELLER

Life and works

DUFOUR

1969

PRINTED IN GREAT BRITAIN

CONTENTS

PREFACE

WHILE there is no shortage of books and articles in German on Gottfried Keller, the English-speaking student will search in vain for a general introduction in English to Keller. The present book aims to fill the gap.

The extent of my indebtedness to my predecessors, particularly Professor Ermatinger and Dr Ackerknecht, will be clear to the reader. Ermatinger's book will probably remain the authoritative guide to Keller's works for a long time. However, for the foreign student something shorter and yet reasonably comprehensive is required.

The method I have chosen has advantages and disadvantages. The first part of this work consists of a short biography, the second and longer part of a consideration of Keller's works in the chronological order of their first appearance. I am well aware that many users will prefer to look only at the second, critical part, and I hope that they will find it a convenience not to have to read through what they may regard as irrelevant, biographical material. On the other hand, my method does lead occasionally to repetition in the second part of those biographical facts which are essential for the understanding of a particular work. I regard such repetition as the lesser evil, as compared with dealing with the works within the context of the biography.

I have thought it worth while to consider again in some detail Feuerbach's influence on Keller. While Keller was clearly deeply affected by Feuerbach as a young man in Heidelberg and for some years thereafter, the evidence of his later works suggests that he was less completely convinced by Feuerbach at the end of his life. I hope that what I have in mind is made clear in the following pages.

I offer one or two new emphases of interpretation which I think can fittingly be made in a work by an author who is neither German nor Swiss. The special, rather hallowed place of the

Bildungsroman within the German literary tradition has tended to cause *Der grüne Heinrich* to be overrated as a work of art. I prefer to regard *Das Sinngedicht* as Keller's crowning achievement for reasons which are set down in detail in the appropriate chapter of this study.

I have been able to view Keller not only from outside the German-speaking world, but also from a point sufficiently far removed in time for his work to appear in a rather different perspective from that in which he was seen by his contemporaries and immediate successors. I have tried to see him within the wider literary context of European rather than German prose fiction. Even against this background Keller remains a considerable figure, although of course his weaknesses as well as his strength stand more fully revealed when one looks at him in the light of the technical advances which have occurred with Zola, Thomas Mann, Henry James, James Joyce, Virginia Woolf, Kafka and others.

I should like to thank Dr Paul Stauffer, the Cultural Attaché at the Swiss Embassy in London, who read my manuscript and has shown unfailing courtesy, patience and kindness in all his dealings with me. Professor L. W. Forster of Cambridge read my manuscript, made numerous suggestions for improvements and helped greatly to smooth the path to publication. I am especially grateful to him. Professor Emil Staiger of Zurich showed great interest in my project, gave freely of his time and helped me to clarify my ideas about Keller as well as to find my way among the vast secondary literature on Keller. Professor Max Zollinger of Zurich also advised me during the early stages of planning the book. My colleagues Mr E. V. K. Brill, Mr P. J. Branscombe, Professor C. T. Carr and Dr James Trainer all read part of my manuscript and made valuable suggestions Miss R. C. Harvey of St Anne's College, Oxford, read the chapter on Keller's poetry. Professor Edgar Dickie of St Andrews helped me to understand Feuerbach and offered bibliographical guidance. The staffs of the St Andrews University Library, the *Zentralbibliothek* in Zurich and the Zurich *Stadtarchiv* could not have been more helpful. My friend Dr Hans Rudolf Faerber assisted me both with scholarly advice, and repeatedly in the practical matter of finding accommodation in

Zurich. Miss Christine Paterson, the Modern Languages Secretary in St Salvator's College, St Andrews, typed a large part of my manuscript. My wife typed parts of the manuscript, read all of it, and has uncomplainingly offered practical and moral support during the years I have spent on this task. The Travel Fund Committee of the University of St Andrews have repeatedly made it possible for me to visit libraries in Switzerland and Germany. To all these people and others not mentioned who have helped me I should like to express my sincere gratitude. I also wish to thank Dr Oswald Wolff for undertaking the publication of this book.

St Andrews
Christmas 1967

I am very greatly indebted to the "Pro Helvetia" Foundation for providing the financial support which has made possible the publication of this book.

PART I

KELLER'S LIFE

CHAPTER ONE

CHILDHOOD AND ADOLESCENCE

GOTTFRIED KELLER's father Rudolf Keller (born 1791) returned in 1816 to his native Switzerland as a master of the woodturner's craft from extensive travels in Germany and Austria. As well as considerable technical skill, he possessed a lively and eager mind and some artistic ability. He married Elisabeth Scheuchzer, the doctor's daughter from his native village of Glattfelden, and soon afterwards set up business in the Zurich *Rindermarkt*. There were six children of the marriage, of whom only two, Gottfried (born 19th July 1819) and his sister (born 1822) survived early childhood. Rudolf Keller was a man of rare integrity, industry and intelligence, of whom Gottfried preserved an almost hallowed memory.

Elisabeth Scheuchzer had a more practical bent. If Rudolf Keller gave his son his artistic imagination, his political idealism, his wide intellectual interests and his somewhat unpredictable temper, Gottfried's legacy from his mother was more down to earth. After her husband's early death Frau Keller filled the rambling old house in the *Rindermarkt* with tenants and boarders to provide for her children. Although she and her son were very undemonstrative towards one another, they were united by a bond of deep affection. She was sustained by a strong faith in God the Provider, but her religion had no great devotional intensity.

From the "Armenschule zum Brunnenturm" Gottfried progressed to the "Landknabeninstitut", where the boys learned German, French and Italian, book-keeping and scripture.

A brief visit to the Zurich Altstadt still gives a good impression of the background against which Keller grew up. There have been few changes in the outward aspect of the narrow streets and tall, ramshackle old houses with their dingy back yards. From upstairs windows one still enjoys the splendid prospect of lake and Alps. In the 1820s, Zurich was still mainly a cantonal capital, whose population retained in many respects a rural outlook on life.

At the *Landknabeninstitut* Keller's poetic and artistic talents began to emerge. He wrote dramas for his own puppet stage, and composed some rather indifferent verses, which give no indication at all of the future greatness of their author, though clearly he was an imaginative child with a certain talent for caricature.

At thirteen Keller moved to the Zurich *Industrieschule* whose pupils were mostly the sons of well-to-do citizens. Keller seems to have made an enemy in the Deputy Headmaster, Prorektor Meyer. At any rate, the evidence available suggests that his expulsion from the *Industrieschule* after a little over a year was too harsh a punishment for an episode for which he was not mainly to blame. He had taken part in a procession to molest an unpopular and inefficient master, and the school authorities made an example of him, though he claimed to have been a late and reluctant participant in the affair.

Keller now had to educate himself, which in the long run proved to be no disadvantage. Yet he often looked back on the years following his expulsion and regretted his wasted youth. Certainly his immediate surroundings offered little encouragement to his higher aspirations. On the face of it, for an adolescent to spend months on end desultorily reading and painting in his mother's attic scarcely seemed an adequate preparation for life.

In the summer of 1834, Keller went as usual to stay with his uncle, Dr Scheuchzer, in his parents' native village of Glattfelden. He was very responsive to scenic impressions that year, and perhaps in a fit of foolish bravado, took the decision to become a landscape painter. His mother and uncle did their best to make him change his mind. When he refused to do so, Frau Keller tried to discover how a young man could learn the art of landscape painting. Her enquiries proved fruitless; no landscape artist of repute then lived in Zurich.

In the *Predigerhof*, near Frau Keller's house, Peter Steiger copied, coloured and peddled Swiss views. Gottfried was sent to Steiger to be trained as a proper artist ("zum eigentlichen Künstler herangebildet"). He soon picked up a slickly superficial technique. He was too early allowed to give free rein to his fertile imagination and undoubted gift for original composition. Before long, he was again spending most of his time reading at home.

From 1834 onwards he regularly attended the recently opened theatre in Zurich.

Though Keller was not deeply affected by his confirmation as a member of the Zwinglian church, his mind was not altogether closed to religious impressions. He liked reading books of a mystical or pantheistic character, and the ecstatic nature worship of Jean Paul found in him a willing disciple. In *Eine Nacht auf dem Uto* he tells how he approaches a mountain summit at sunset, falls asleep and dreams how a kindly old man leads him to the mountain top, which has turned into an altar. From it streams a brilliant light, which warms and refreshes every thing and creature, and round about in attitudes of veneration the whole of mankind is congregated. From amid the bright light the Creator manifests Himself to the dreamer and exhorts him to see God in His works. We should notice the dual nature of Keller's belief in God at this stage. Part of him would like to enjoy mystical union with his Creator and all creation, would gladly be free from the ordinary human bondage of space and time; another part of him is content to see God in His works. In time Keller accepts more and more realistically man's limitations, no longer expecting super-human insights but satisfied to use his normal powers of thought and perception to the full. He forsakes the vague romanticism of his youth with its unrealisable transcendental aspirations for an empirical realism which aims simply at reproducing and interpreting human experience as it is actually known to him. A corresponding metamorphosis takes place in his style, which is purged of the imitative romantic exuberance so reminiscent of Jean Paul and Novalis.

In 1837 he thought he had found a teacher and intellectual confidant in Rudolf Meyer, a sensitive but mentally unstable painter in water colours. In the latter part of 1837 Keller took lessons from Meyer, whose painstaking attention to detail and rigid insistence on the exact imitation of nature came as a wholesome revelation to his pupil. Meyer introduced Keller to Homer and Ariosto. This promising relationship was rudely interrupted by Meyer's sudden and unexplained departure from Zurich, perhaps in a fit of madness.

Keller's first experience of love was rather saddening. Henriette Keller lived with her mother, brother and two sisters in Frau Keller's house, although they were not related to Gottfried and

his mother. Henriette, a delicate girl one year older than Gottfried, used to spend summer holidays at Glattfelden where he saw
her as well as at home. She died of tuberculosis in May 1839.
Keller's poem *Das Grab am Zürichsee*, records a deeply felt
grief, despite its obvious indebtedness to Heine. The last lines,
which Keller omitted from his collected poems, run as follows:

> Und wenn ich das Grab erblicke
> will es mir das Herz zerreißzen
> Meiner Jugend schönstes Hoffen
> Hat der Tod hineingelegt.

> And when I see the grave
> It seems to rend my heart:
> Death has laid in it
> The fairest hope of my youth.

These words belie the older Keller's statement that this early
love was a very superficial affair. He could not have portrayed
Anna so memorably in *Der grüne Heinrich* if it had not meant a
great deal to him. His statement in the *selbstbiographie* that he
had "as it were from a mere nothing built up hundreds of verses"
certainly does less than justice to his younger self.

A letter to a friend well conveys the gloomy and unsettled state
of his mind. "Now I am a full twenty years old, and can still do
nothing and am still stuck in the same old rut and see no means
of getting away and have to bumble about in Zurich while others
at this age have already begun their careers." Though it was his
birthday he had neither money to spend nor friends to brighten
the day for him; on the point of weeping from self pity, he suddenly noticed that the "Föhn" was blowing up, clouds were
already masking the sun and he knew there would soon be a
thunderstorm. He dashed from the house to the top of the
Ütliberg, from which he enjoyed a grandstand view of the celestial performance. The sight of the great mountains and the
populous valleys in the reddish, flickering light of the storm, the
noise of trees cracking and falling when struck by lightning, the
spectacle of the great rocks near which he sat, brilliantly but fit-
fully illuminated, not only cured his feeling of boredom and
depression, but actually made that birthday memorable and
enjoyable.

Several of Keller's friends had gone to Munich to study art, and he decided to go there, too. Even had he realised that landscape painting was neither practised nor taught by the leading painters in Munich at that time, he might well still have gone there to escape from the constricting atmosphere of his petty bourgeois home. He persuaded his uncle to secure payment for him by the competent authority of part of his little patrimony. Frau Keller consoled herself for not being able to stop him from leaving home by giving him exhaustive instructions how to look after his clothes. His uncle did his best to dissuade him from going to Munich, but Gottfried was determined to go.

CHAPTER TWO

THE ART STUDENT

DURING the journey to Munich in May 1840 Keller wrote to his mother in affectionate terms:

> I thank you once again, mother dear, for everything you have done for me, and ask you not to think that I do not appreciate it... I only hope to be able to repay you for everything one day.

In a later letter he made some characteristic observations about the behaviour of Bavarian women:

> If one comes in contact with the ordinary people they are courteous and agreeable, only the middle class women are uncommonly rude. They curse and swear like the stable boys at home and sit in the pubs every evening and swill beer. Even the most refined ladies go to the coffee house and drink there not coffee—but, just for fun, a pint or even two pints of beer.

The matter of fact tone of this letter contrasts sharply with the colourful account of Heinrich's arrival in the *Kunststadt* in the first edition of *Der grüne Heinrich*:

> Glowing in the last light of evening were Greek gables and gothic towers; pillars of the most various kinds still raised their ornamental capitals in the rosy light, bright, freshly cast statues, gleaming new, shimmered in the chiaroscuro of the twilight, while brightly painted open halls were already lit by lantern light, and women wearing their best finery walked about in them. Stone statues towered in long rows from high columns, royal castles, palaces, theatres and churches formed large groups together, here one saw united buildings of all possible styles of architecture, while yonder old, blackened domes, council chambers and burghers' houses formed a sharp contrast. All was life and excitement in the streets and squares.

From churches and great hostelries came the sound of music,
bell-ringing, organ and harp; from chapel doors, covered with
all manner of mystical symbols, clouds of incense came surging
out into the street; artists both handsome and grotesque passed
in hordes, students in braided coats and silver-embroidered
caps walked past, armoured horsemen with gleaming steel
helmets rode nonchalantly and proudly across a square, volup-
tucus harlots with bare white shoulders made their way to
illuminated dance-halls, from which resounded the noise of
drums and trumpets; fat old women bowed before thin black
monks, who circulated in large numbers; in the open front
halls of their houses sat well nourished burghers behind roast
geese and mighty tankards and enjoyed the mild spring evening; shiny coaches with blackamoors and footmen drove past
and were held up by an enormous knot of soldiers and
apprentices who were battering one another over the head.
There was everywhere an unending hum of noise.

Keller's resolution to practise strict economy did not last long;
in a few weeks he was living a sociable and rather extravagant
life. While he knew roughly how to set about becoming a landscape painter, he fell far short of carrying out his own good
intentions or applying his own best insights to the practice of his
art. If his life had ended during his Munich days he would merely
have been a colourful but unimportant figure of the student
Bohemia in the Bavarian capital.

Keller found serious and unexpected obstacles to his progress
as a painter. The tone of the Munich Academy was set by its
Director, Peter von Cornelius, who favoured allegorical and
historical subjects. The cold intellectualism of Cornelius' inventions was not calculated to help Keller to find his own style.
Guidance from a more experienced man might still have saved
him as a painter; without this, progress was impossible. In painting Keller was never able to resolve successfully the conflict between romantic and realistic tendencies, which also preoccupied
him for part of his literary life. Unfortunately no person of
distinction or real authority, whether in the field of painting or
any other, crossed Keller's path in Munich.

Paul Schaffner[*] has shown how the paintings of the Munich

[*] In *Gottfried Keller als Maler*, Zurich, Atlantis, 1942.

period reflect the unsettled state of Keller's mind. Traditional motifs jostle with the inventions of his own imagination. Incapable of the self-discipline of selection, he could not control his own exuberant fancy. The *Ossianic Landscape* of 1841 contains several extremely effective motifs, though the wild rocks and boulders in the foreground bear little resemblance to any rock-formation found in nature.

Other works of the period are either too derivative or too extravagantly romantic to be taken seriously, although they do offer evidence of a talent which might have been developed.

Before long his money had run out, and an attack of typhoid fever nearly cost him his life in the summer of 1840. His mother wrote in August:

A little while ago I dreamt about you that you had come home in torn clothes and so thin and pale that I took quite a turn at seeing you look so awful! Do be careful and particular about your health and clothes, so that I do not have to experience anything of the kind.

At the time when Frau Keller wrote he was actually at the height of his illness. Although Keller and his mother were undemonstrative they were linked by a deep affection and intuitive understanding.

When he had recovered she tried to persuade him to come home, at least for a time, but he refused:

I have started out on my way and will pursue it to the end, even if it were to mean eating cats in Munich.

Some deep-seated inner compulsion kept him in Munich. He told himself that he had to complete and exhibit this or that painting, but if this had been the real reason he would surely have succeeded in producing more completed work and attained some modest commercial success. From his letters we gain a lively impression of his reckless, convivial way of life in Munich, although he had a certain underlying seriousness:

The only thing that causes me anxiety is the fear of becoming a worthless, idle and ruined character, and I have to struggle very hard to prevent this in face of my never-ending bad luck; and it is only by good reading that I have managed

Gottfried Keller, Ossianic Landscape.

Oil, Munich, 1842

Gottfried Keller, Landscape with Painter.

Water-colour, Munich, about 1840

to keep myself above water up to now. (Letter to Hegi, April 1841.)

Later in the same year he began to contemplate the possibility of abandoning landscape painting, "for only an ass would want to be a martyr to painting". Keller's intellectual release from the false bondage of painting was now complete, and very soon he would also attain the emotional detachment from this enthusiasm that would allow him to give it up. Yet before he did so he had persuaded his mother to mortgage her house and send him the proceeds so that he might prolong his stay in Munich. It was all to no avail. He could seldom complete any work, and when he did, he failed to sell it.

By the latter part of 1842 things had come to a head. Keller had had to sell all his paintings and personal effects for a song, and gratefully accepted employment painting blue and white spirals on flagstaffs for a royal wedding. His credit was exhausted, and he even had to ask his mother to send him the money for the journey. In November Frau Keller did so, and by the end of that month he was back in Zurich. The triumphant summer homecoming of Pankraz in the *Novelle** is Keller's artistic compensation for the humiliation and dejection of his own return from Munich.

Clearly he derived no material advantage from his exile. He did not even return a much better painter than he went away. For long stretches of his two and a half years in Munich he was the victim of his own irresolution. He claimed that he could not afford to go into the country to paint from nature, yet he was willing enough to do the things which appealed to him, even if they cost more than he could afford, like his trips to Augsburg to speed on their way home to Switzerland friends who would easily have managed to return unassisted.

Keller had no genius as a painter, but he did have a modest competence, and several smaller works of his are extremely pleasing, particularly the luminous and unpretentious water colours he painted for his friends after he had resigned himself to the role of dilettante. Not to put too fine a point on it, he was a mediocre painter striving for effects which lay beyond his grasp. He might paint a landscape with moderate success, but he could

* *Pankraz der Schmoller.*

not introduce the single figure which would give purpose and cohesion to the whole. It was an admission of weakness that he had to ask other people to help when it came to placing human figures in his landscapes. His poetic imagination—the word has slipped out—made unrealisable demands on his technical ability. He was working in the wrong medium and still did not know it. He had come to an end of his material resources in Munich; perhaps he also sensed that he was straining at the limits of his artistic powers. Time for clarification, to explore his own abilities and limitations was what Keller now required. It had been necessary for him to go to Munich, even if the whole enterprise was misconceived. He now needed to recover from that mistake.

CHAPTER THREE

THE BIRTH OF A POET

AFTER returning from Munich Keller wrote few letters, and the biographer turns gratefully to the autobiographical sketch of 1876. He still hoped to become a painter, and rented a studio in Zurich, which, however, proved so cold that he had to use his studies for "poetic landscapes" as draught screens. He read a great deal, and even contemplated writing a "melancholy little novel" about the tragic cutting short of a young artist's career; by letting both the artist and his mother die he planned to mete out poetic justice to himself for the worry he had caused his mother. This first germ of *Der grüne Heinrich* was conceived when Keller was twenty-three. The book would be at once lyrical and elegiac, though relieved by brighter episodes. The ending would be "cypress-dark", and he planned to bury everyone.

Before Keller had written down more than the bare plan of his novel, he was stirred to emulation by the sudden discovery of Georg Herwegh's and Anastasius Grün's political poetry. He was hard pressed to learn enough of the poet's craft to discipline and polish the abundance of half-formed verses that poured from him, and it went without saying that he supported the radical and anti-clerical political interests. There is no mistaking the elemental force of the new poet's utterance. Even as an old man Keller could write:

> I still do not regret that it was the call of the living age which awoke me and determined the direction of my life.

In a diary kept in the summer of 1843 Keller mentions the possibility of telling his life story, but does not explicitly refer to *Der grüne Heinrich*; as far as we know he put no part of the work on paper before 1846. The diary calls his life "a succession of grey, hopeless days, which often pass in dull idleness and disappear into the darkling past". He considers communism "a problem of the times which is becoming important" and which had forced itself on his attention through his chance acquaintance with the Zurich communist, Wilhelm Weitling (1808–71). While Keller applauds the communists' professed desire to provide equality of educational opportunity and full employment and to assume responsibility for those members of society who are incapable of earning their own living, he deplores the revolutionary tendency of the movement and foresees that it will overthrow "the whole order of things not only in an outward sense, but also in our innermost soul".

The diary gives a good idea of the life Keller was leading. He read and greatly admired Jean Paul's *Hesperus*. He tells of a walk on a fine day in August when ideas for poems came tumbling into his mind in unmanageable profusion. He could not think one train of thought to the end before it was crowded out by a new series of ideas. The sudden access of poetic inspiration was transforming his drab, unsatisfying and unhappy life, giving it substance, direction and meaning. He seems aware of his own superior gifts and becomes impatient with ordinary people. Then the diary breaks off; we can only conclude that the poetic impulse had become so powerful that Keller no longer needed to commit his frustrations to paper.

In August 1843 Keller wrote to one of his old masters in the *Industrieschule* asking him to give an opinion on some poems. Fröbel—the educationist's nephew—was a publisher who specialised in publishing works by the victims of the traditional German distaste for political non-conformists. The first book which he published was Georg Herwegh's *Lieder eines Lebendigen*, which earned their author an enviable reputation. Herwegh's example quickly loosened Keller's tongue.

Fröbel soon replied that he had read the poems. It had delighted him to see a young Swiss moving with the times instead of wallowing in obscurantism and political reaction like Gotthelf. This stricture on the author of *Uli der Knecht* betrays a narrow outlook, and Keller must have realised that Fröbel liked his work largely for the wrong reason.

Fröbel recommended Keller to August Adolf Ludwig Follen, a picturesque and lively member of the Zurich German émigré society who taught German literature at the Aarau *Gymnasium*. Follen enjoyed the friendship of a large circle of poets, artists and scholars. A gifted literary dilettante, Follen deserves well of posterity for having taken Keller under his wing and helped to shorten the painful process of the birth and launching of a new poet.

Keller's first poems left much to be desired from the technical point of view. Follen taught him to apply exacting standards of craftsmanship to his work, to eliminate impure rhymes and jarring rhythms or ruthlessly to sacrifice an unsuitable image. Sometimes he emasculated Keller's virile verses in his anxiety to smooth the rough edges. Later on Keller sometimes deliberately restored to their original form poems which he had amended at Follen's suggestion, and when fully formed, his taste surpassed Follen's. Yet Follen taught him a great deal about the mechanics of versification, to say nothing of enlarging his mental horizons by introducing him to the clever and distinguished people who frequented his house.

At the end of 1844, in the *Deutsches Taschenbuch* for 1845, forty-one poems by Keller were printed under the title *Lieder eines Autodidakten*, the poet's name being given in the index as "Gottfried Keller von Glattfelden bei Zürich". Follen read the proofs and promised to make Keller's wellbeing his concern.

In later life Keller spoke slightingly of his early poems. Compared with his later work the collection of 1845–46 is immature and uneven in quality. Yet the poems he wrote in the 1840s were the fruits of genuine poetic inspiration, and some of them are still generally agreed to be among his best. Unfortunately, Keller's judgements of his own early work are sometimes accepted by his readers at their face value. Among the well-known poems included in this first collection are: *Stille der Nacht, Morgen, Frühlingsglaube, Der Nachtfalter, Rosenwacht, Goethe-Pedanten.* His autobiography of 1876 is misleading in its offhand, deprecating treatment of the whole collection.

Keller's poems were favourably received by the critics when they were noticed at all. Wilhelm Schulz declared in a review in Cotta's *Morgenblatt* that Keller was "the most significant lyrical talent which has raised its voice in Switzerland". Other reviewers though impressed said so more cautiously than Keller's old friend. Keller's circle of acquaintances now included Ferdinand Freiligrath, the Russian revolutionary Michael Bakunin and Wilhelm Weitling. Follen's friends opened Keller's eyes to what was going on in the rest of Europe. The unknown love of whom Keller writes to his friends in 1845 was probably Marie Melos, Ferdinand Freiligrath's sister-in-law.

One result of Keller's democratic political affiliations was his involvement in the *Freischaren* movement, which represented a reaction of the Zurich liberals against the decision in Canton Lucerne to entrust the teaching of theology in the cantonal seminar to the Jesuits. No official action was taken by the Protestant cantons, but some irregular military units were formed by Protestants who thought they would teach their Catholic neighbours a lesson. Keller marched with one such band in December 1844 and with another in March 1945. Both campaigns ended in fiasco. In *Frau Regel Amrain* such escapades are regarded as examples of the kind of folly to which young men are subject. The older Keller viewed these matters rather like Fritz Amrain:

> He did not exactly decide never to go on any more campaigns, since events can not be calculated in advance and no one can command his blood to stand still when it flows quicker, but he was now safe from any merely outward and ill-considered urge to fight.

He came to believe that a human life should not be sacrificed to an abstract idea, that even in the name of liberalism and democracy it is indefensible to attempt to enforce political conformity on one's neighbours by the use of armed might.

In 1845 Cotta's *Morgenblatt* published a selection of the twenty-one *Liebeslieder* inspired by Henriette Keller. The poet was irritated that the cycle had not been published in its entirety; he informed the editor that he would shortly have the whole cycle printed together, which he did.

A visit to Glattfelden that summer proved less exciting than those memorable boyhood visits; since the death of his Aunt Regula in 1844 his uncle's household seemed a dreary place, especially since all his cousins except one had left home. After returning to Zurich he spent boisterous convivial evenings with his boon companions:

> We laugh and make such bad jokes that the boots under the table are ashamed.

Yet in his moving poem *Bei einer Kindesleiche* Keller shows a fitting awe of the wonders of childhood and death; the unnamed child had given him strength, comfort and refreshment like the blue sky or the sea; by all those things he had been reminded of fairer pastures, and had risen above the burdens of his existence.

In fairness to those who misjudged Keller at this time, he often gave his acquaintances a completely different impression from that conveyed by the poem. Many people regarded him as an idle, irresponsible young man, who wasted his talents in unprofitable artistic aspirations and neglected his duty towards his mother and sister. Keller showed that he appreciated this point of view in the first version of *Der grüne Heinrich* where the hero is so overcome with remorse at his neglect of his mother that after her death he sinks into a decline and dies.

At the end of 1845 *Das Deutsche Taschenbuch* published the *Einundzwanzig Liebeslieder* and the *Feueridylle*. These, along with poems published the preceding year, formed the substance of Keller's first collection in 1846. Interestingly enough, two poems written in opposition to the Pomeranian atheist Arnold Ruge and his supporters, *Die Zweifellosen*, were retained by Keller in the *Gesammelte Gedicht* of 1876. His atheism never became unequivocal enough to make him repudiate the half-formed religious opinions of his youth.

The 1846 collection was published by Winter in Heidelberg at Follen's request. An unexpectedly handsome payment of 700 Gulden (about £100) enabled Keller to pay the debts incurred in Munich and enjoy a good summer holiday.

This book was welcomed by Wilhelm Schulz, who in the *Jahrbücher der Gegenwart* acclaimed Keller's poetry as comparable with Germany's best and rejoiced that once again a real poet was writing in German. While praising Keller's politics he said that he did not owe his poetic success to his political soundness. Keller had steered a middle course between a watery and characterless internationalism and Swiss smugness. He retained his national identity but avoided intellectual provincialism. "He is a Swiss poet of the German nation", writes Schulz, "and at the same time a warm Swiss republican."

Other reviewers were less kind to Keller, notably Wolfgang Menzel, the reactionary editor of the *Literaturblatt*. However, a cordial letter arrived from Varnhagen von Ense, the leading German literary connoisseur of the day. While recognition by

Fröbel and Follen meant something, a bouquet from Varnhagen was better. He lived in the leading centre of German cultural life, Berlin, at that time not yet given over to the worship of military power and wealth as it was to be a generation later. From being an obscure and eccentric young Swiss, eking out a precarious and parasitical existence and obstinately refusing to conform to a bourgeois manner of life, he had within a few months won self-assurance, public acclaim and some knowledge-able and influential friends. Though his fellow countrymen were more prepared to praise him than to pay him, he now knew that he was on the right road.

In addition to previously published material, the *Gedichte* of 1846 contained the now famous patriotic poem, *An das Vater-land*, the rhythmically vigorous *Waldlieder* and three sensitive poems of times and seasons, *Regen-Sommer, Winterabend* and *Morgenwache*. One poem replies to Justinus Kerner, who viewed with anticipatory horror the desecration of the atmosphere which the invention of flying machines was bound to bring. Keller faced the future unafraid, prepared to accept inevitable changes in the pattern of human existence. The success of *An das Vaterland* may be at least partially attributed to Wilhelm Baumgartner's spirited musical setting. This composer, now almost forgotten, was in his lifetime a friend of both Keller and Richard Wagner.

In 1846 Keller began *Der grüne Heinrich* in earnest. Certainly what he actually wrote down that year amounted to far less and resembled the finished novel less than the vague plan of the whole work which he had mentioned in his diary in 1843. But the romantic description of Heinrich's home town and of his depar-ture to seek the fulfilment of his aspirations in German lands re-presents the first fumbling attempt to give concrete form to the half-considered plan of 1843. Keller told Freiligrath (letter of 5th February 1847) that he would soon finish *Der grüne Heinrich*. He consistently underestimated the time it would take him to complete his works. While the letter mentions the title *Der grüne Heinrich* for the first time, this need not imply that he had any detailed conception of what the book would be like. He still required time to gain distance from his material, and in particular he could not yet view his disheartening experiences in Munich with sufficient detachment. Even in 1854–55 Keller was still obsessed with the problem of his guilt towards his mother, which he had to some extent renewed by his second long visit to Germany. He could not yet see what these long absences would lead to, and thus in his own eyes he was completely without justification. A few years later he would not have felt it imperative to make his hero die; Heinrich does not die in the revised version. In 1846 he could not even see as far ahead as he could when he completed the first version, in which Heinrich dies without adequate motivation. Almost everything in the first *grüne Heinrich* is an organic growth except the ending, which is violently superimposed on the rest of the work. In 1846 Keller could not even take his hero as far as he does in the first completed version. Whether or not Keller chose to reproduce real life directly he always needed it as a basis.

In 1846 Keller made visible progress towards his eventual artistic vocation, but in the following year his love for Luise Rieter dominated his existence. He met Luise at the house of a Professor Orelli-Breitinger in the spring of that year. She reported to her mother on the meeting as follows:

> Keller does not say much and seems to be of rather phlegmatic temperament. He has very small, short legs, which is a pity, for his head would not be bad, his extraordinarily high brow being particularly noticeable. He did not seem altogether comfortable, let us hope that it wasn't me that distressed him, and he soon left us again.

Luise Rieter, the tall, graceful daughter of a well-to-do Winterthur family, could draw agreeably and write passable verses, as well as possessing great personal charm. She won Keller's heart by the naturalness of her behaviour. But he did not dare tell her so, and his very revealing *Traumbuch* (written between 15th September 1847 and the following spring) testifies to his feeling of utter inadequacy. His poetic gifts did not compensate for his other shortcomings:

> My poor poetry disappeared and shrank into nothing before my inward eye. I despaired of myself, as often happens to me. I do not know what is wrong, but my merit always seems to me insufficient to hold a good woman.

The *Traumbuch* records both dreams and waking imaginations, all of which display the same lurid, nightmarish quality.

He is oppressed by the ballast of his soul, stuffed crocodiles and horrible sea monsters, tigers and hyenas, as he calls his own bad qualities. Despite his dissatisfaction with himself and his desire to be worthy of Luise he still takes refuge in alcohol, sometimes for days on end. His sister's illness during that summer provoked the following reflection:

> I am the useless decorative plant, the scentless tulip, which absorbs all the juices of this little heap of noble clay, the life of mother and sister. If God helps me past this warning example, then things shall be different.

In October, Luise again came to stay with the Orellis, and Keller met her unexpectedly in an art exhibition. He was so taken aback that he ran away, which must have disconcerted Luise. A little later that month, however, he wrote her this letter:

Dear Fräulein Rieter,

Do not be alarmed that I should write you a letter, and even a love letter, forgive me for its unseemly and irregular form, for I am at the moment in such confusion that I cannot possibly compose a well phrased letter, and I must write more or less as I should speak. I am still a mere nobody and have still to become what I hope one day to be, and in addition I am a poor, inconsiderable young man; and so I have no right to offer my heart to such a beautiful and splendid young lady as you, but if I had to think one day that you had been truly well disposed towards me and that I had said nothing, then that would be very great unhappiness for me and I don't think I could bear it. And so I owe it to myself to put an end to this state of affairs; for just imagine, I have spent this whole week running from one public house to the next, because I am anxious and afraid when I am alone. Will you please be so kind as to tell me in a note, in two words, before you go away, whether you are fond of me or not? Only so that I can have some certainty; but for Heaven's sake do not pause to consider whether you might become so in time. No, if you do not already love me definitely, then simply say no quite cheerfully, and have a good laugh at me; for I would hold nothing against you, and it is no disgrace to me that I should love you as I do.

I can tell you now, I am most passionately in love at this time, and have no idea where all the stuff that is going through my head is coming from. You are the very first girl to whom I have declared my love, though several have appealed to me before; and if you had not treated me in such a friendly fashion, then I would perhaps not have dared to say anything this time either. I am very eager to have your reply, I should be very surprised at myself if I were to win such a gracious lady overnight. But do not hesitate to throw a good, rough, outspoken No in the letter box, if you can be nothing to me; for later on I will get over it. Even now I have a feeling of lightness and relief, since I am writing direct to you and know that in a few hours you will be holding this paper in your dear hands. I should like to say so many good and beautiful things to you, that at this very moment I could write a whole book of them, but when I meet you face to face, then I will again be the old, awkward fool, and I will have nothing to say to you.

It has just occurred to me that I might be open to reproach. I should not have assumed on account of our free and easy relationship and the kindness you have shown me that I had the right to think of such an association immediately; but I have been silent long enough and spent a miserable and idle summer, and I must at last return to being myself again. When something gets hold of me, then I yield myself to it quite unreservedly, and I am not a friend of newfangled half measures. But I must close. Once again I ask you, dear lady, not to take exception to the confusion of this letter : it is certainly not due to a lack of a sense of fitness or respect, but merely my emotional state. If things turn out well I will then certainly write a sensible and clear letter, for as a rule I am really quite sensible. Will you be so good then as to send me a note with a couple of words, and that as soon as possible; and, as I say, without having the least hesitation if you think you are uncertain; the rest will attend to itself. Goodbye, and give dear Mrs Orelli my greetings, and make some allowances for a poor poet.

Yours sincerely,
Gottfried Keller.

Hottingen, October 1847

The gentle play of flirtation was foreign to Keller's nature. At twenty-eight he remained as shy and helpless with the other sex as an adolescent boy. He could not subordinate all other interests to the supreme end of winning Luise. Instead of simulating a confidence which he did not feel, he made it easy for her to refuse him. Small wonder that Luise replied that she was sorry if her conduct had seemed to encourage him, since that had never been her intention.

Shortly afterwards Keller wrote to Frau Orelli in terms which remind one of Grillparzer and other congenital bachelors. A revealing phrase describes his reluctance in the past to expose himself by declaring his love. "It was my healthy tact," he writes. Keller was never prepared to pay the price of seeking normal relations with the other sex. Twice previously he had been a little in love but had not declared himself. To see in Keller's poverty and his shortness of stature the complete answer to his inconclusive love life is not good enough. The main reason why Keller never succeeded in his relations with women was that he did not want to. Keller could never become completely absorbed by his love for a woman for more than a very short time. Less than a week after Luise refused him, he wrote to Frau Orelli that he could already view the whole affair fairly objectively. He would like to remember Luise "in a tranquil soul", but he considers that "it would be childish and unreasonable of me to assert in advance that the memory of this love will never fade". A man thus capable of assessing and analysing his own emotions is not likely to be overcome by them for long.

Keller's diaries composed during the following autumn and winter show a gain in judgement and maturity. In politics he had progressed from a doctrinaire democrat to a man of predominantly liberal views who liked to weigh every case on its merits. Yet he was still working at only a fraction of his full capacity. A few poems, a very slight story, *Die mißlungene Vergiftung,* and a handful of reviews represented his literary harvest since the collected poems, and he had neither continued work on his novel nor undertaken the systematic reading which he knew to be necessary. He was only now beginning to realise what his expulsion from school had meant. He saw that his intellectual growth had become stunted, that every schoolboy knew things which he ought to know but did not. Once again he longed to seek outside Switzerland the means of supplementing his piece-meal education. But he was without money, having spent almost the whole proceeds of his poetry on paying the debts incurred in Munich.

Then suddenly Keller's financial fortunes were redeemed by an imaginative stroke of generosity on the part of the Zurich government. His poems had made such a favourable impression that the cantonal authorities unexpectedly offered him the opportunity of studying in Germany at the public expense for a year. Keller hoped at this time to become a dramatist, and his sponsors wanted him to visit the East to accumulate impressions for use in his plays. First of all, however, he thought he should study history for a year. He decided to go to Heidelberg for this period.

He left for Heidelberg in the autumn of 1848, a thrilling year for European Liberals. Keller wrote to a friend:

> Things are going on in the world that one must study pro-perly while they are still fresh (*kuhwarm*), so that one day, when one is an old man and has children, one may have some-thing to tell them.

The events of the spring and summer of 1848 alternately delighted and horrified Liberals. By May after some vicissitudes the forces of reaction were rallying in Austria and Prussia. Keller felt himself to be thoroughly involved in the happenings of the time, as can be seen from his *Traumbuch*. His generation still thought that their lives could be radically altered by the granting of constitutions, and that political liberty in itself was a suffi-ciently worthy end to engage all mankind's aspirations. Keller uses in the *Traumbuch* language akin to that of the Old Testa-ment to express his thoughts on the political future of Europe. Even before he went to Heidelberg religious experience had to take second place to the secular satisfaction of seeing thrones totter and a society of free, equal and dignified men arise. Since Keller had at least implicitly abandoned the religion of his child-hood, the atheistic philosopher Ludwig Feuerbach should at most be given credit for clearing away a certain amount of lumber from Keller's mind. Keller was inclined to give Feuerbach credit for his own thoughts, simply because he found ideas of his own reproduced in Feuerbach. At the time when he met the German he was probably overcome by the autodidact's feeling of inferiority in face of the professional philosopher. But we are here anticipating the most important intellectual experience of Keller's second sojourn in Germany.

CHAPTER FOUR

GERMANY

KELLER arrived in Heidelberg on 22nd October 1848, having stopped in Strassburg on the way to see the cathedral. A week later he wrote giving his mother his first impressions of the town:

> Altogether the people here are a ragged, squalid lot, they all live entirely off the students, half or three-quarters of the population are students' bastards and they run about in rags.

He was now feeling very lukewarm about going on a journey to the East. This information delighted his mother, who had not liked the sound of the project at all.

As in Munich years before Keller mingled mainly with his fellow countrymen. People knew he was writing a novel, though he rarely spoke of it. He attended duels, and even took up fencing in a mild way himself. Professor Henle of Heidelberg wrote years later to Vieweg, who had sent him a copy of *Der grüne Heinrich*:

> I have for years been out of touch with the author, who was recommended to me in Heidelberg by friends in Zurich. There he visited me at first, but he soon got tired of our chatter, and he used to spend his days in the company of a large dog behind a beer glass in the public house—not that he actually boozed. Nobody would have thought to look at him what splendid thoughts go on in his head.

Keller attended lectures on anthropology and law. He was not much interested in the historical studies which he could have pursued in Heidelberg, but in general he tried to fill up the gaps left by his incomplete schooling. His principal interest was in philosophy and theology. Hermann Hettner's lectures on Spinoza fascinated him. Keller once described Hettner as "this perfect blossom of our modern intellectual culture". Hettner was equally at home in literature, the fine arts and philosophy.

Keller also went to hear Ludwig Feuerbach, the exponent of a view of life diametrically opposed to his own. For years Feuerbach wielded an important influence on Keller, who had barely considered Feuerbach's point of view before going to Heidelberg. It had not occurred to him that a man might be completely honest with himself and benevolently disposed towards his fellows, yet remain an atheist. Keller had regarded atheism as a wicked perversion, a deliberate rejection of known truth about God and man by people who ought to know better. Ermatinger* suggests that Keller was inconsistent in being prepared to believe in a monarch of the universe while holding strongly republican political views. The present writer fails to see why the governmental hierarchy of heaven need necessarily correspond to that with which we are familiar on earth. Although Keller could see that one should try to reach some considered view of the universe and man's role in it, he had not yet done this himself. He had not thought seriously about the existence of God or human immortality, so that he was naturally at a disadvantage. He was the poet arguing with the professional philosopher, the weak Christian contending with a man who had made a lifetime's study of cutting the ground from under the feet of unconvinced Christians.

Ludwig Feuerbach's career as an anti-religious philosopher began with his *Thoughts on Death and Immortality* (1830), in which he views the preoccupation with immortality as a canker sapping the full enjoyment and use of this life. As soon as we abandon unfruitful theorising about the life to come, of which we know nothing, and devote ourselves wholeheartedly to the creation of a better and fuller life on this earth, the better it will be for us. Despite excellent professional qualifications Feuerbach could not gain a foothold on the academic ladder. Nevertheless he remained productive, writing a *Critique of Hegel's Philosophy* (1839) and in 1841 a work on the philosophy of religion, *The Nature of Christianity*. Attempts to have him installed in a professorship in Heidelberg met with no success. The lectures which Keller heard in 1848–49 were delivered at the invitation of the Heidelberg students in the *Rathaus*.

The gist of Feuerbach's teaching was as follows. Man knows

* *Gottfried Kellers Leben,* 3rd and 4th impression, Berlin 1919, pp. 196–97.

nothing of God except what he discovers either from within himself or from the speech and writings of others. His own conscience is a principal source of information about God. In proportion as his own life becomes more civilised and his sense of right and wrong more highly developed, his conception of God becomes more sophsticated. From demon worship he progresses to the idea of an avenging deity who will espouse his cause regardless of his own behaviour towards his fellows. From this still crude and barbarous conception he advances by degrees to the stage where God lays down the laws of civilised social behaviour, or where he becomes the ultimate authority, capable of enforcing the rule of law. The Hebrew patriarchs were not on the whole remarkable for their moral rectitude. A man like Jacob prospers whereas his brother Esau, seemingly with right on his side, is condemned to be an outcast. By the time of the Mosaic law, God will not tolerate idolatry or theft or adultery or shady dealings with one's fellows or behaviour contrary to the dictates of hygiene or good neighbourliness. In the later books of the Old Testament a high degree of sophistication in the writers' conception of God mirrors their advancing civilisation. The God-Man of the New Testament, according to Feuerbach, represents the ultimate self-deception; Man, having projected his highest aspirations, his noblest moral insights, his best judgements as to the purpose and value of life into a being outside himself, wishes to re-establish the connection between himself and that being, who is now separated from him by the natural gulf between his ideal aspirations and his actual conduct. This is conditioned by the painful and often demoralising circumstances of daily life. Therefore he has to bring God back to earth, though without sacrificing any of His divine attributes. He does this in such a way as to boost the credit of his ordinary human family relationships, by attributing to God, who is a mere projection of the best that is within himself, the same typical family relationships to which he is accustomed in his own life; from the strict monotheism of Old Testament times he moves fairly quickly to the position where the godhead comprises Father and Son; the Holy Spirit, an invention of the misogynist Paul intended to discredit the role of the female in the celestial family, is quickly replaced, particularly in Roman Catholic religious practice, though not yet in theology, by the Mother of God and Queen of Heaven. Belief in

God is nothing but *"the belief in human dignity, the belief in the divine significance of the human being"* (*Wesen des Christentums*, Leipzig, Otto Wigand, 1849, p. 154).

Everything else in Christian theology is reduced by Feuerbach to terms of Man's attempt to glorify himself in his creature, God. Thus, for instance, when we talk of the Creation :

> We are dealing with the personality of God; but the personality of God is simply the personality of Man freed from all the local characteristics and limitations of Nature.

It is for this reason that Man upholds the traditional doctrine of the Creation from nothing; Man's dislike of pantheistic cosmogonies can be explained in this way :

> ... the creation is a *personal matter*, not an object of the *free intelligence*, but of emotional interest; for what matters about the creation is merely its guarantee, the ultimate thinkable confirmation of the personality or subjectivity as a quite separate entity standing above and outside the universe, and having nothing at all in common with Nature ... *Man distinguishes himself from Nature. This differentiation of himself is his God —the differentiation between God and Nature is nothing other than the distinction between Man and Nature.*

From all this it follows that the reader should concede :

> that your personal God is nothing but your own personal nature, that in believing in and proving the existence of your God above and outside Nature, you believe in and prove nothing but the existence above and outside Nature of your own self.

Every Christian dogma is taken and ruthlessly turned outside in by this atheistic philosopher, and he always comes back to the same conclusion—one might almost call it a foregone conclusion—all religion is merely an expresson of Man's narcissistic admiration for himself, sometimes, it is true, an inverted admiration that plays curious verbal gymnastics of self-abasement and self-negation, but that unmistakably leads back in the end to self-assertion and self-glorification.

It would be tedious and irrelevant to follow Feuerbach through all the intricacies of his anti-religious arguments. It is sufficient to

say that he proves to his own satisfaction that the basis of all
religion is simply the desire to enjoy a life which differs from this
life by the absence of the restraints and limitations to which we
are subject in this world of time, space and death; it would be
more courageous, he says, to accept this life as it is, and not chafe
at the conditions it imposes, not to look for any personal immortality, but to regard each day with its tasks and enjoyments as
sacred; we can have no certainty about the hereafter.

Even as God, according to Feuerbach, is merely a wish image
of ourselves, free from all the constraints which limit and inhibit
our existence, so the desire for immortality merely reflects our
dissatisfaction with this world, coupled with a lively disinclina-
tion to leave it:

> Just as God is nothing else but the Nature of Man, cleansed
> of that which appears as a constraint or evil to the human
> individual, whether emotionally or intellectually, so the here-
> after is nothing else but this world, freed of that which appears
> to be a limitation or evil. . . . The other world is the emotion,
> the idea of freedom from *those limitations* which here impair
> the pride in self, the very existence of the individual.

Belief in the hereafter is merely the belief in the freedom of
the human personality from the barriers to which we are subject
in this natural life; belief in God is merely Man's belief in his
own infiniteness and immortality. To sum up the whole argument; Man is the beginning, middle and end of all religion.

In the second part of *Das Wesen des Christentums* Feuerbach
attacks Christian dogma unsparingly. He skilfully seizes on the
seemingly weakest elements in the Christian creed. He mocks
at the willingness of Christians to believe that things happened
in the distant past which they would not believe could happen
today. Belief in miracles is the height of egoism; the man who
believes that the course of natural law will be altered by his
prayers is deluding himself, he flatters himself that he, poor, weak
human individual has power to influence the whole world of
Nature. Religion knows nothing, says Feuerbach, of the pride
in achievement of the human collectivity, of the whole human
race, but prefers to seek consolation in God, that is, in a projection of the self, for all the disappointments and imperfections of
life. He says that the dogmatists are willing to turn into a dogma

anything, however far-fetched, that happens to suit their purpose, anything that happens to fulfil a need of theirs at a given time:

Belief in revelation not only destroys moral sense and taste, the aestheticism of virtue; it poisons and even kills the most divine sense in Man—the sense of truth, the feeling for truth. The revelation of God is a definite revelation in time. God revealed Himself once and for all in such and such a year, and *nota bene* not to Man of all times and places, to human reason, to the whole species, but to definite, limited individuals. Limited as it was by place and time this revelation had to be preserved in writing, so that the enjoyment of it might come down to others unimpaired. Belief in revelation is therefore at least for later ages belief in a written revelation; the *necessary* consequence and effect of a faith, however, in which an *historical* book, one necessarily composed under all the *conditions of temporality and finiteness* has the significance of an eternal, absolute, universally valid Word—is superstition and sophistry.

The authority of the Bible is then relentlessly attacked:

A book which imposes on me the necessity of discrimination, the necessity of criticism, to separate the divine from the human, the eternal from the temporal, is not a divine book, nor a reliable book free from deception, it is cast out into the category of profane books: for every profane book has the same quality, that it contains in addition to or within its human content the divine, that is in addition to or within the individual universal and eternal elements. A truly good or rather divine book is, however, only one in which there is not some good and some bad, some eternal elements and other temporal, but one in which everything is of equal quality, everything is eternal, everything true and good.

The foregoing summary of Feuerbach's position helps to point the contrast between the two very different types of mind represented by Feuerbach and Keller. The arid, doctrinaire, atheistic philosopher seems to the modern reader distressingly sure of himself; Keller's humble agnosticism is more endearing. Feuerbach fails to provide satisfactory answers to several questions which it is his business as an atheistic philosopher of religion to answer. A man who denies the existence of God and then cannot supply an explanation for the existence of the world and his own existence is hardly in a stronger position than the theologians he affects to despise.

Keller completely remoulded his religious thinking along the lines suggested by Feuerbach. He found himself conceding point after point of Feuerbach's case, at first reluctantly, and then with increasing readiness, until by the end of the course of lectures he could accurately be described as a pupil of Feuerbach's. Yet like every pupil worth his salt, he was not content to regard his master's teaching as the last word on the subject. Even in the letter to Baumgartner (28th January 1848) in which Keller tells of the intellectual excitement of those months, he sounds a cautious note, and by no means claims to have found a final answer to his religious difficulties:

I shall make a clean sweep (or rather it has already happened) of all my earlier religious views until I am on Feuerbach's level. The world is a republic, he says, and cannot have either an absolute or a constitutional God (rationalist). For the time being I cannot counter this claim. For a long time my God had been only a kind of president or first consul, who did not enjoy a great reputation, I had to depose him. But I *cannot* swear that *my* world will not again elect an imperial sovereign one fine morning. Immortality is involved in the business, too. Beautiful and moving as the thought is—turn your hand round in the right way, and its opposite is equally affecting and profound. At least for me they were very solemn and thoughtful hours, when I began to become used to the thought of real death. I can assure you that one pulls oneself together and does not exactly become a worse person.

All this, my dear Baumgartner, did not take place as easily in reality as it seems to have done here. I let the ground be won from me step by step. At first I even indulged in systematic criticism of Feuerbach's lectures. Although I conceded the acuteness of his thought, I always had a parallel series of my own ideas running at the same time, I thought I needed only to press little levers and springs differently to use his whole machine for my own ends. But that gradually ceased at the fifth or sixth hour, and in the end I began to work for him myself. Objections which I had been harbouring were sure enough produced by him and often removed in a way that I had already half foreseen and made use of myself. I have never yet seen a man who is so free of all school dust, of all the scholar's conceit as this Feuerbach. He has nothing but Nature and Nature again, he apprehends it with his every fibre and in all its depth and does not let himself be torn away from it by God or devil.

For me the principal question is this: Does the world, and does life become more prosaic and common after Feuerbach? Up till now I must answer most decidedly, No, on the contrary, everything becomes clearer, sterner, but also more brilliant and sensual. The rest I must leave to the future, for I shall never be a fanatic and *shall consider the mysterious beautiful world capable of anything, if it seems reasonably plausible to me.*

This then was Keller's point of view in 1849; although he provisionally accepted Feuerbach's opinions, he might change his mind at any time that he felt like restoring the deposed monarch of his universe. While the thought of human immortality was attractive, the thought that there was nothing more than this life also had a certain austere appeal; the chances lost in this world would never recur, and one must make a supreme effort to fulfil one's task properly. He writes in this sense to Baumgartner two years later:

How trivial the view seems to me that with the abandonment of so-called religious ideas all poetry and every mood of exaltation disappear from the world! On the contrary! The world has become infinitely more beautiful and profound for me, life is more valuable and intensive, death more serious and thought-provoking, and challenges me now properly for the first time to fulfil my task and cleanse and satisfy my consciousness, since I have no prospect of catching up on what I have neglected in some other corner of the universe. . . . Anyway I am far from being intolerant and regarding as a complete ass anyone who believes in God and immortality, as the Germans generally do as soon as they are over the Rubicon themselves.

Keller goes on to discuss the consequences of his changed beliefs for his art:

... for art and poetry there is from now on no salvation without perfect intellectual freedom and total burning apprehension of Nature without any secondary considerations or arrière-pensées, and I am firmly convinced that no artist has any future before him now who is not prepared to be wholly and exclusively a mortal man. And so my recent development and Feuerbach are far more important for my dramatic plans and hopes than in any other way, for I feel clearly that I am now in a position to sound human nature more deeply and to apprehend it. Every dramatic work will therefore be the purer and the more consistent, since now the last *deus ex machina* is banished, and the worn out tragic muse will gain through real and final death a new germ of life.

Thus for many years Keller made himself free of religious ties; he did not regard the issue as finally decided, but merely saw that his art was the first thing in his life and that he could not afford to allow anything a place in it which might distort his artistic vision and make him involuntarily break the highest law that he knew. The urge to artistic creation was so strong in him and his artistic conscience so important that he felt he could carry no lumber in the shape of a set of religious beliefs which might turn out to be false. Herein lies the difference between Feuerbach's position and Keller's. Feuerbach was sure that traditional Christian religious teaching was wrong and harmful; Keller was afraid that it might be, and that if he had a falsehood at the centre of his life his art would suffer. "One fine morning" he might feel like reinstating the monarch of his universe, but he would certainly beware of anything which might make him, the artist, create in a tendentious, unworthy manner. Feuerbach had given him the courage and supplied the impetus which made him act on his own doubts. The Christianity he was forsaking (which had not taken him back to church in fifteen years since his confirmation) could not have meant a great deal to him; but under Feuerbach's instruction Keller saw that even a nominal adherence to a faith which he did not take very seriously might be harmful to his art.

From the point of view of social intercourse Keller spent his time more profitably in Heidelberg than in Munich. His two years in the Bavarian capital had been of value more in the sense of a character-building ordeal than in the ways in which a sojourn in a foreign country under good conditions may be expected to benefit a talented young man. Part at least of the reason for his failure as a painter lay in the absence of stimulus, supervision and encouragement from people whom he could respect.

In Heidelberg Keller enjoyed the entrée into several houses where he was esteemed as a poet even if his manners were found a little odd. He was no longer content to live in a Bohemian world of young students and artists. He deliberately sought the company of older men of assured standing. He no longer relied exclusively on the public house society with which he had been content in Munich.

An amusing light is shed on Keller's life in Heidelberg by a letter written to his mother in March 1849. He had made a point of living modestly in simple rooms with poor people. However, the first family he lived with proved quite impossible:

> At the moment I am completely on my uppers and I am taking another room, for the people that I am with are a very disreputable lot. Yesterday the woman of the house, an old person, ordered the maid, who still wanted to mend her petticoat, to go to bed, for she needed the light to catch fleas by, whereupon the maid scolded and was cross. Then the woman took the chamber-pot and flung it at the maid's head, and she in turn got hold of the woman and flung her behind the stove, whereupon the man sprang out of bed and began to beat the pair of them together. This kind of thing goes on every day, and I should not like to stay here any longer.

The actual course of the 1848–49 Revolution in Baden interested Keller less than might have been expected in view of his liberal sympathies. He found that the Revolution upset his finances and proved a noisy and unpleasant interruption of his ordinary routine:

> . . . once or twice the enemy (the Prussian troops) approached close to the town, so that we could see them running about on the mountain. They fired into our streets, from 2,000 paces' distance, and a soldier fell down dead, not far from me, on the bridge. Hereupon we, who had nothing to do there, considered it advisable to withdraw for a little.

Despite the brave resistance of the Baden soldiers Heidelberg was occupied by the Prussians on 23rd June 1849.

Keller had meantime again fallen in love. Johanna Kapp, the daughter of a liberal professor, lived just across the Neckar from Keller's lodgings near the bridge. Before long she was being shown his sketch books, his *Traumbuch* and new poems. Keller hinted in a letter to his mother that he was forming a new attachment. After some weeks he could bear the suspense no longer and resolved to declare himself, which he did by letter early in November. Johanna destroyed the letter, but he preserved her answer :

7 November 1849

Dear, dear friend,

I am so deeply moved that I hardly know how I am to write to you, and yet I feel compelled to do it. Your dear letter has made me fearfully sad, although you forbid me to be sad. I should like to thank you, and do it from a full heart; but it seems to me frightfully sad that I cause so much misery. It is often quite incomprehensible to me. In the last few days I have certainly felt that you were fond of me; but I thought it was pure human interest, and should have been afraid to think anything more. But now the riches of your beautiful heart lie spread before me in a new splendour, and I had to breathe a deep sigh ! I told you yesterday that I am at once happy and unhappy, because I am in love, but separated from my lover ! When I gave you my poems a week ago, then I planned in my own mind to tell you the name of him, in whom my being is completely absorbed. But it seemed to me that to tell even you would be a profanation. But today I feel differently; differently even from yesterday, when I would have been glad for you to know, but couldn't at any price have told you. But now you are certainly worthy of it, and I feel I owe it to you, so that you may understand me completely and also comprehend how after such bitter tortures of the heart a life has nevertheless remained possible for me, which up to now has united me only for brief periods with my lover. It is certainly a profoundly tragic happiness when moments have to compensate for long separation; but even if my last hope of attaining lasting union were to disappear, I think I retain enough strength to grasp and enjoy the short moments as moments which brighten my agitated life. You have yourself uttered the well-loved name in your beautiful letter. The man who became for your mind what your noble heart found in me, this splendid man is he, and the curious coincidence that made you mention us both in the same breath seized me with tempestuous joy. . . .

Even in translation Johanna's personality emerges from this letter, with its mixture of sincerity and pose, its elements of self-dramatisation mingled with genuine sympathy, its flamboyant revelation of her personal emotional difficulties. She succeeds in implying that she is marked out by destiny for great unhappiness and that she must inevitably cause misery wherever she goes.

Keller took the disappointment very much to heart, as we see from a letter written to Johanna on 7th December 1849 but never dispatched.

My youth is now past, and with it the need for a youthful, poetic happiness will disappear; perhaps if things go well for me in the world in other respects I will yet become a merry fellow, who will enact this or that winter comedy. But to offer my heart now to a loving woman as current coin, for that purpose, it seems to me, I have worn it out too much already, and shall wear it out still more, before it is free from you.

Later on he came to regard Johanna with more detachment, and he once wrote to Hettner that she had encouraged him beyond the limits which should be observed by a woman who is not seriously interested in a man. In the *Landvogt von Greifensee*, however, she provided some traits for the character of the delightful Figura Leu, so we must conclude that Johanna remained on the whole a fragrant memory.

Keller's letters and diaries show an almost complete hiatus over the following winter. He probably spent Christmas in Heidelberg and may have devoted some time to his drama, *Theresa*, which was partly inspired by Johanna. *Der grüne Heinrich* was having to be revised in the light of his changed religious views. This re-casting took longer than he had hoped, but he had in any case written down very little of the book by the beginning of 1849. In March of that year he approached the publisher Vieweg with the request to have 1,400 copies of the novel printed. The volume would contain some poems as well as the novel, and he wanted an honorarium of 75 louis-dor. In December he sent on the poems, which Vieweg returned, since his firm did not usually publish verse. Vieweg asked for a plan of the whole novel, but Keller did not send it to him at this stage.

Before the affair with Johanna Kapp Keller had considered visiting Berlin, and later in 1849 he asked the Zurich authorities if he might do this. In October they made him a further grant of 1,000 francs, to last him another year, but at that time Keller was too preoccupied with his love affair to consider leaving Heidelberg. It was 6th April 1850 before he managed to tear himself away, although Johanna had gone to Munich several months before.

A letter from Freiligrath who was then living in Cologne invited Keller to visit him en route for Berlin. Freiligrath asked about Keller's present attitude to God and religious faith, whereupon Keller replied:

> When I renounced belief in God and immortality I thought at first I should become a better and more disciplined person, but I have become neither better nor worse, but in my good as well as in my bad ways have remained just as I was before. . . .

Although Keller occasionally still vigorously defended the atheistic position, as time progresses we find that such evidence of his religious beliefs as does exist tends to point in another direction altogether. Perhaps the Count's pronouncement in *Der grüne Heinrich* provides the key to his creator's mature outlook. The Count tells Heinrich that he does not care whether he believes in God or not; what matters is the kind of person he is:

> In any case, man goes to school all the days of his life, and no man can prophesy with certainty what he will believe in the evening of his life.

Keller's departure from Heidelberg marks the end of an important phase in his life. He had learned there the value of sustained intellectual discipline, and had for the first time since leaving school attended planned courses of instruction. He went to Heidelberg aware of the inadequacies of his formal education and determined to remedy them. In addition to the mental ferment caused by Feuerbach and the emotional disturbance caused by Johanna Kapp, Heidelberg gave Keller what a university education should give any man of sufficient talent—an unprejudiced curiosity about the universe and man's role in it and the best available information on some aspects of this problem. If one adds these assets to those which Keller possessed by nature, the gift of self-expression in words and the painter's keen eye, one realises that the elements of greatness were there. Only time was needed to bring them to fruition.

Three foreign cities served as the scenes of Keller's apprenticeship to life. In Munich he learned slowly and painfully what he was not and never could be; in Heidelberg, aware of where his true talent lay, he laboured to equip himself for the task that lay ahead; in Berlin he wrestled with native inertia, diffidence, poverty and the recalcitrance of the material he was working on to produce a masterpiece. He knew that he now needed to stand on his own feet. In Munich he had lived on his own patrimony and his mother's subsidies. In Heidelberg he had enjoyed the support of Canton Zurich. In Berlin he knew this could not continue much longer and that his sojourn there was a test of his ability and character. He had to succeed in his chosen career, or the Zurich authorities' generous confidence would be shown to have been misplaced.

When Keller arrived in Berlin he found that Fanny Lewald, through whom he had hoped to enter Berlin literary circles, was away on a prolonged absence. Keller did not make any other contacts: "Up to now I haven't seen a single literary louse." He expresses his intention of visiting Varnhagen: Werde nun aber doch den Harnwagen von Ense aufsuchen und mich bescheiden hinten aufsetzen. However, he did not venture to call on him for a long time.

Berlin was a cheerless enough place for the stranger in 1850. Following upon the suppression of the 1848 Revolution, the notorious *Treubund* had been formed, an alliance between Church and State against the dangers of democracy. In 1844 the king disfranchised some voters who had been enfranchised only a year earlier. The brutal Hinckeldey was in charge of the city police. All the apparatus of the police state was there, the close censorship, the purging of democratic elements from the population, the arrest of political suspects in the night, the strict control

of travellers by the police, who checked every train that entered
and left Berlin.

Keller wrote gleefully to Freiligrath: "The constables are
watching me like anything and think I am an agitator. . . ." But
he certainly did not mean to see the inside of a Prussian prison.
He had come to Berlin primarily so that he might study the
drama on the stage He attended theatrical performances regularly, and wrote long, closely argued letters to Hettner on the art
of the theatre. He was lavish with promises to write a tragedy,
yet he never finished his *Theresa*:

> I can easily finish the tragedy as soon as I want to; but I
> am not sure whether it is not too simple and too restrained
> for a theatrical début.

His doubts about the play prevailed, and it remained a frag-
ment.

Keller was slow to make friends with Berlin literary personalities. He always felt rather intimidated by the cosmopolitan veneer
of the literary men in the great city. The glibness of the Berlin
literati was completely alien to him, and he felt he could never
do himself justice in this milieu. Keller was conscious and proud
of his Swiss-ness. The qualities which he cherished and esteemed
were distasteful or even ridiculous to the Prussians. His view of
the Berliners was coloured by the peasant's suspicion of the men
from the city.

After about a year in Berlin Keller again became seriously
short of money. He had never learned to live economically, and
his income was still very slender. His naturally expansive temperament made it impossible for him to live within his means. A letter
written years later to Emil Kuh illustrates Keller's poverty in
1851:

> One evening I had only five silver groschen left, when a
> sculptor friend took me to Wagner's beer saloon, where various
> notables of the day were sitting . . . they did not know what to
> make of me, and kept saying to one another: What sort of a
> Swiss is that? What is that fellow doing here? and so on. I was
> only careful to see that I kept *one* groschen, thinking, with that
> you can buy yourself a roll tomorrow at lunchtime, that will
> help the day to pass! Sure enough the following midday I
> assure myself that the bloody thing is still there, go into a big

baker's shop in the neighbourhood and take a roll value one groschen and hand over the groschen. The tall, rather sour but elegant and respectable baker's daughter, who had certainly watched me pass every day, looks at the groschen: the waitress the preceding evening had given me an invalid, worthless groschen of some German robber state, which I had not known or understood. The baker's daughter says: "We can't take that one, it's a dud!" I haven't got another one and have to hand over the bread again and creep out of the shop with my raging hunger, while the creature surveys me from head to foot. I felt myself doubly wronged, by the waitress who had cheated me as well as by the narrow-minded baker's daughter, who didn't dream of thinking of my distress, and who was merely glad not to be the victim of a cunning rogue. Sure enough, I spent the day without eating, and then had to borrow money after all the following morning.

His financial misery made it more difficult for him to fulfil his obligations towards Vieweg. Despite assurances that he would finish the whole work in the early spring, he managed to complete only the first book by July. Vieweg at this stage was understanding and tolerant, although when the end of 1851 came and he still had not received the manuscript of Book Two, he began to feel annoyed. Keller also misled his friends, especially Baumgartner, telling him in March 1851 that his first volume was already printed, though it was not completed till four months later.

The appearance of the *Neue Gedichte* in 1852 delighted Frau Keller, who had not heard from her son for a year and a half. He wrote on 18th February giving a fairly full account of his life in Berlin. When his play had been accepted by a Berlin theatre he would come home, he said, but did not suggest that this might take years. Keller was sensible enough to send a copy of his poems to Varnhagen, who invited him to call, which he did on 4th March. The appearance of his poems was followed by an invitation to contribute poems to the *Deutscher Musenalmanach*. The payment for these poems must have been particularly welcome, for along with the next grant from Zurich came a note to say that it would be the last. Altogether Zurich had given him 2,900 francs, a large sum in those days.

He was vexed by the news later in the year that his mother

Gottfried Keller, Landscape with oak trees.

Water-colour, Berlin, 1885

Gottfried Keller, Circular water-colour of Lake Zurich.

About 1860

had sold her house "Zur Sichel" in the *Rindermarkt* and had taken a flat in the district known as the *Platte* on the slopes of the Zürichberg. He hoped to be home soon and to take over the expenses of the household :

> I am now thirty-three years old, and beginning where my father left off; but then life treats people very differently in this world.

Some gleams of hope and encouragement persisted during this depressing time. Early in 1853 Vieweg began to realise that *Der grüne Heinrich* was no ordinary novel and that it must be completed. He sent Keller a further advance and proposed that he should add a fourth book. He protested against Keller's plan to let Heinrich die at the end of the book, thus anticipating the criticism levelled against the first version by many readers.

We know now that Heinrich's death was Keller's way of administering poetic justice to himself for his conduct towards his mother and sister. But Vieweg, who did not understand all the circumstances, begged Keller to let Heinrich live on, and even suggested a fifth book of *Novellen*, connected in some way with the main narrative and rounding the work off on a cheerful note. Keller considered and rejected this proposal.

Until the first three volumes of *Der grüne Heinrich* appeared at Christmas 1853, one might easily have imagined that Keller's literary career was going to resemble his career as a painter only too closely. It scarcely looked as if he would ever be more than an able dilettante. Though he had written some good poems, he had been almost silent as a poet for years. None of his promised dramas had yet appeared and probably his generously conceived novel would remain unfinished.

Now the situation was completely changed. Keller had evidently not been vegetating during those bitter years in Berlin. The three volumes formed a quantitative measure of his industry, despite his loneliness, debts and unhappiness. They also proved convincingly that a new genius had arisen among the German Swiss, a novelist free from the emotional extravagances of a Jean Paul, with a deep knowledge of the childhood and adolescent mind. Keller established his position conclusively as a leading novelist with this work; no prose writing of this quality had appeared in Germany since Goethe's death.

In the summer of 1853 Keller informed Hettner that *Der grüne Heinrich* would soon be finished and that two collections of short stories would quickly follow. He would soon complete his *Heine-Romanzero-Geschichte*, i.e. the *Apotheker von Chamounix*, and he had an idea for a play, too. The two collections of stories subsequently became *Die Leute von Seldwyla* and *Das Sinngedicht*.

Although he had not performed all that he had promised by the end of 1853, the appearance of three volumes of *Der grüne Heinrich* would have enabled him to return home holding his head high. A curious doggedness of character kept him in Berlin; if he imagined that this would hasten the completion of the novel he was deluding himself.

Later in 1853 and 1854 Keller had a tussle with Vieweg, who had become tired of his endless delays in finishing the novel. To bring Keller to heel Vieweg simply refrained from answering his letters. When Keller sent him the beginnings of his Galatea stories and the first part of *Der Apotheker von Chamounix*, Vieweg remained silent. At the end of July 1854 Keller sent part of the manuscript of the last volume of *Der grüne Heinrich* and demanded the return of his other material. Vieweg waited till Keller wrote again more insistently, and then sent back the short story manuscripts and the *Apotheker,* with some caustic comments on Keller's dilatory behaviour. He did not object so much to the slowness of Keller's creative process as to his repeated failure to adhere to his self-imposed time limits. It is the old story of the artist's unwillingness to see the point of view of the man of affairs. When the book was finished, Keller offered an olive-branch, but Vieweg had been so sorely tried that he refused to accept it.

At the beginning of 1854 Keller sent Hettner a summary of the contents of his fourth volume. He endeavoured to justify Heinrich's death, just as he had earlier done with Vieweg. No amount of persuasion would have made him change his mind at this stage; only the need to record the essentials of his real life experience could make him alter his original plan, and he had not yet gained a sufficiently objective view of his own life. He was still obsessed by a feeling of guilt towards his own family.

In 1854 he was offered an unexpected opportunity to escape

from financial hardship in the shape of a Chair of Literature in the proposed new Federal Polytechnic at Zurich. Although Hettner urged him to accept, Keller refused, saying that he would rather be a passable poet than a bad professor. He declared that the chair would make demands on him which he could only fulfil by altering his whole manner of life in a way that would be foreign to his nature.

In February 1854 the following generous and wise appreciation of the first three volumes of *Der grüne Heinrich* arrived from Hettner:

I congratulate you sincerely on your creation. It undoubtedly assures you for all time of an outstanding place in our literature. What appeals to us so deeply and enduringly in your novel is the feeling that we are here concerned with a work which has *grown* of necessity, and has not been arbitrarily put together. Everywhere one feels the warmth of experience; we have here in the highest sense Poetry and Truth. Everyone who has enjoyed an inner cultural development finds his inmost nature reproduced here, only more clearly and deeply than he could have done it himself. I am certain that every thoughtful reader will willingly return to your book again and again; he will ever be able to comfort, edify and help himself through the contemplation of the rich and strong nature of the hero whom you represent. The more so, since truly the individual descriptions are permeated by the most wonderful freshness and poetry. Particularly the idyllic summers in the country, the pastor's family, the schoolmaster, the charmingly spiritual Anna and the healthily sensual Judith as well as the hero himself, naively and yet always firmly and tactfully picking his steps through all these various situations and complications, show an unsurpassed mastery of situation as well as of characterisation. Again there is the clear, simple, in the noblest sense Goethean language, which again is, however, only the inevitable expression of the measured clarity of conception. I tell you again in all honesty, the story of Heinrich's youth is a jewel; and I am proud to be allowed to call the hero and author of it my friend.

His book also earned for Keller the friendship of Varnhagen von Ense and his niece Ludmilla Assing. Despite his lack of social polish he became a regular and honoured guest at Varnhagen's house. Ludmilla made a bad pastel portrait of him, a sure sign of approval, and Varnhagen gave him as a keepsake his wife Rahel's copy of *Der cherubinische Wandersmann*. (Readers of *Der grüne Heinrich* will remember how this work receives a place of honour in the concluding chapters.) Keller esteemed Varnhagen as a prose writer of rare merit and a critic of unfaltering discernment, and long after he left Berlin he continued to correspond with Ludmilla.

Since the affair with Johanna Kapp, Keller had not been in love. In the winter of 1854–55 he was suddenly seized by a passion of unexampled intensity for Betty Tendering, the sister-in-law of Franz Duncker, one of his publishers. Betty was another of those beautiful Amazons towards whom the undersized Keller by some malicious freak of nature always felt himself irresistibly drawn. Orphaned at a tender age she had grown up in the homes of wealthy and cultured relatives and had received a good education. Keller's love reached its climax in May 1855. Once again he loved in vain; he does not even seem to have declared himself by letter. The main evidence of his state of mind during that winter and spring consists of two sheets of paper which he used to place under his manuscript when writing *Der grüne Heinrich*. The sheets are covered with the name Betty, written in letters large and small. There are also such revealing comments as the French sentence: La partie n'est pas égale, and we also find the equation: B.T. = Bella Trovata, Belle Trouvée, which leaves us in no doubt as to the real life original of Dortchen Schönfund. The paper tells plaintively of the inevitable renunciation: Abrenuncio, writes Keller in large letters, or again, after a whole series of Nein's, comes the hard pronouncement: Resignatio ist keine schöne Gegend. Then he draws himself in the form of a skeleton, sadly playing the 'cello, adding the caption: Der Tränenmeier—Herr Gottfried Tränensimpel and Gottfried Tränenberger-Tränenmeier.

While Keller tried to drown his sorrows in drink, Betty was in Switzerland. She even took it into her head that she would like to call on Frau Keller during her visit. Unfortunately Frau Keller was not at home. Keller wrote and told his mother about the incident the following October:

Last summer a young woman who was making a journey to Switzerland wanted to visit you, and I gave her a letter to the Schulzes, so that they should come over with her, for she is a pretty and distinguished-looking young woman, who might make people confused . . . . That she wanted to visit my mother was on the one hand an ordinary politeness, since I often see the lady in the house of friends, and she behaved as if she had a good opinion of me. On the other hand perhaps it was just a piece of roguery so that I should imagine goodness knows what; for she has played a whole lot of tricks like that on me, and she wasn't really interested in running out to Hottingen: but I hope she enjoyed herself! Of course I have been sitting long enough in Berlin. She is a tall, rich and beautiful girl, who has neither father nor mother, doesn't know what she wants, and especially can't bear it, if the whole world doesn't pay court to her.

Betty Tendering certainly never dreamed for one moment of marrying Keller. He was probably quite wrong in imputing motives of coquetry to her for trying to visit his mother. She merely wanted to see what sort of home the strange, gifted, uncouth little Swiss sprang from. Keller compensates himself for the disappointments of real life when he makes Dortchen Schönfund show Heinrich Lee unmistakable signs of her affection, which he is too shy to interpret at their face value.

At the beginning of 1855 *Der grüne Heinrich* still remained unfinished. Though Keller had promised Vieweg not to write anything else till he had finished the novel, he was full of ideas for new works, stories, dramas, essays and poems. He was reading avidly, too, Homer and Sophocles, Ariosto, Shakespeare and Rabelais, so that he was able to judge all he read or wrote by the highest standards. No wonder he felt dissatisfied with the earlier parts of *Der grüne Heinrich*, which he could not revise in accordance with his new and superior artistic standards. He repeatedly expresses regret in his correspondence that he is bound by the already printed part of the book. The radical revision of *Der grüne Heinrich* which he finally undertook as a middle-aged man had been on his mind before the work was even completed.

Keller finished *Der grüne Heinrich* after several weeks of fever-

ish activity between January and April 1855. He wrote to
Hettner :

> I scribbled down the last chapter of my novel on Palm
> Sunday with eyes full of tears : I will never forget the day.

The papers again contained enthusiastic criticisms of his book.
Hettner, however, in an otherwise appreciative letter, hinted that
he still did not see the need for the tragic ending. Keller replied
that "quite ordinary and uneducated readers had said that they
did not find this death edifying". Yet he obstinately believed
that if there were a weakness it lay simply in his failure to motivate Heinrich's death adequately. When Keller revised the book
twenty-five years later, he had reached the state of detachment
in judging his affairs of which other people were immediately
capable. That he found it necessary to let the hero die in the
1855 version shows how emotionally involved in the book he
still was at the time of writing. He had not yet had time to digest
inwardly some of the experiences which lay behind the novel.
Later on he wished to repudiate utterly the first version, which reminded him of times when raw and painful experience was
absorbed directly into his writing without an interval for recollection in tranquillity. This is the most important difference between
the first version and the later one; the first version records directly, the second more artistically and selectively the significant
experiences of half a lifetime. Even in the first version *Der grüne
Heinrich* was one of the greatest works of German Literature
since Goethe's *Faust* more than twenty years earlier. Keller's later
works are indeed more polished, but none of them is so comprehensive in scope, none shows an honest and courageous human
individual grappling one by one with so many of the universal
and inescapable problems of mankind and reaching at least a
provisional clarity about them, learning through the frustrations
and disappointments of life, as well as through its occasional
moments of triumph, something of the laws and limitations to
which he, in common with the rest of us, is subject.

Keller's letters say little about the progress of his love for Betty
Tendering. In May 1855 he told Hettner that he was "at that
moment experiencing something which seems to resemble a
fair and lovely star". By November, however, he says that the
devil has sent him "an awkward passion", which has made his

life a misery for the last three quarters of a year. He still cherished hopes in May which by the end of the year he had bitterly abandoned. Keller's letters to Betty Tendering have all been lost, so we do not know whether he ever told her of his love. The letters to his mother and Hettner, together with the pathetic evidence of his *Schreibunterlage* and the story of Pankraz's vain love for Lydia, form the main sources of information about Keller's passion for Betty Tendering.

Now that his novel was finished and he could clearly hope no further as far as Betty was concerned, Keller longed for release from the "Pennsylvanian Prison" which Berlin represented for him. He had to borrow money again for the journey home. "I absolutely must get away from here and the sooner the better." By mid-November Frau Keller had sent him the desired sum, and within a month he was back in Zurich.

The years in Berlin had brought him more loneliness, misery and poverty than he had yet known. He had on the whole disliked the people there, and even the Berliners whom he liked had enough North German and foreign characteristics to irritate him often and get on his nerves. Keller was so beset by tribulations that his naturally inflammable temper became more explosive than ever. Yet during this time he first disciplined himself to compose a major work. In the last summer and autumn in Berlin he had pitted all his creative energy against the outward and inward ills that beset him and had triumphantly secured the splendid booty of the first volume of Seldwyla stories, an achievement in its way as remarkable as the completion of the novel. The Galatea stories, too, had been well pondered, and he needed only time and leisure to set them down on paper. If he did not return home rich and prosperous like Pankraz at least he did not come home feeling himself to be a failure. Whatever hardships the future might hold he was following his true vocation, and outward recognition and financial success could not be delayed indefinitely. He could face his family and his Swiss benefactors with a good conscience.

CHAPTER FIVE

HOMECOMING

UNLIKE Heinrich Lee Keller returned home to find his mother and sister both in good health. His letters give the impression of relief, wellbeing and relaxation after a long period of tension, misery and hard endeavour. His mother and sister were glad to have him home again, although before he had been home a month Regula had to rebuke him for shouting at his mother.

Switzerland was now undergoing a rapid social transformation. Railways connected the main towns, and communications with the outside world were improving. Industrialisation was proceeding apace, and silk manufacturers in particular were prospering. Banks were being founded, a thriving cotton industry was establishing itself, and the foundations of the engineering industry were being laid. From being a predominantly pastoral community with a few small towns on the main European trade routes Switzerland was emerging as a country with commercial and industrial wealth out of all proportion to its size. Along with the optimism born of material prosperity the unpleasant qualities associated with a sudden access of worldly wellbeing were also in evidence, and Keller complained in his letters that people now thought only of the accumulation of wealth.

His mother now lived in the suburb of Hottingen, which still retained something of a rural aspect. Writing to Ludmilla Assing in April 1856 Keller describes the beauty of the garden in spring, and says that woods and meadows lie just beyond it. A little farther away he can be on a green hillside, with splendid prospects of the Alps and Lake Zurich. The joy of experiencing spring in these surroundings acted like a restorative on Keller's jaded nerves; he loved walking on the wooded hills about the town.

Soon after his return to Zurich he wrote to Lina Duncker. He speaks with evident pleasure of his mother and sister, and gives this account of his routine in Zurich:

Here in Zurich things have been going well with me so far,
I mix with the best society, and see all sorts of people who
wouldn't live so conveniently close to one another in Berlin.
There is a Rhenish family called Wesendonck, originally from
Düsseldorf, but they were in New York for a time. She is a
very pretty woman, by name Mathilde Luckemeier, and these
people keep up an elegant establishment; they are building a
magnificent villa in the neighbourhood of the town, and they
have welcomed me into their circle. Then there are fine suppers
at the house of an elegant *Regierungsrat*, where Richard
Wagner, Semper, who built the Dresden Theatre and Museum,
Vischer from Tübingen and a few Zurich people forgather
and where one gets at two in the morning after some moderate
dissipation a cup of hot tea and a Havanna cigar. Sometimes
Wagner gives very decent lunch-parties, where there is some
hearty drinking, so that I, who thought I had got away from
the materialism of Berlin, seem to have fallen out of the frying
pan into the fire.

Before going to Heidelberg Keller had been merely the clever
and rather odd protégé of a handful of influential men in Zurich
literary and political circles. He had returned as a mature man,
with firm views and a secure literary reputation. He mingled as
of right with Wagner and the Wesendoncks, with Friedrich
Theodor Vischer and Gottfried Semper. Formerly a gifted out-
sider, he now took his place as a leader in his chosen sphere.

The composer Wilhelm Baumgartner was almost the only
one of his former friends with whom he still associated regularly.
He now mainly sought his friends among the leading personalities at the University and the new Polytechnic. Vischer taught
the history of literature and aesthetics at both institutions from
1855 till 1866. Semper taught architecture at the Polytechnic.
The presence of such men made its impact on the town; it became fashionable to attend evening lectures on the most diverse
subjects: Semper discoursed on the nature and function of
decoration in architecture, and Vischer lectured on Macbeth.

Keller had a good opinion of Richard Wagner:

Wagner is a very talented and entertaining man, highly
cultured and profoundly perceptive. His new opera-text, the
Nibelung trilogy, is a work of poetry in its own right, full of

fire and rich in poetic blossoms, and made a far deeper impression on me than any other poetic work that I have read for a long time.

Keller might now have been expected to write the second volume of *Die Leute von Seldwya* and the Galatea stories, which he had promised to complete soon. Yet none of these works appeared within fifteen years of the time promised. The dramas of which he constantly spoke were never written at all. His income was consequently very small indeed.

He was still capable of behaving in a devastatingly primitive way. Once in Wesendonck's villa Keller became so enraged about the failings of a fellow author that he smashed with his fist a precious little ornament of Japanese porcelain. No doubt his friends learned to bear with these primeval eruptions, but they must have been upsetting for strangers.

When the first volume of *Die Leute von Seldwyla* was published in 1856 the stories enjoyed an excellent reception, largely because of Berthold Auerbach's favourable opinion of them. People who had never read and never would read Keller's works began to greet him respectfully in the street because Auerbach had praised him. Keller wrote politely to Auerbach on 2nd June 1856 to thank him for reviewing the book so sympathetically, but between the lines one can tell that Keller wished he were not under an obligation towards him. Later on when Auerbach again did him a similar service Keller sad he would soon be known as "Auerbach's Keller".

When Varnhagen and Ludmilla visited Zurich in the summer of 1856 they asked Keller to spend an afternoon and evening with them. They went on a tour of the town, sailed on the Lake and spent the evening on the terrace of the Bellevue Hotel. Varnhagen solemnly noted in his diary afterwards: "Keller is genuine and solid and deserves every encouragement."

Not only was 1856 an unfruitful year, so were all the years between his return from Berlin and his appointment as *Staatsschreiber*. *Das Fähnlein*, *Der Apotheker von Chamounix* and a few poems represented a very small harvest for this period. He was fertile in excuses for himself; it was too soon to publish his new volume of stories for Franz Duncker (which subsequently became *Das Sinngedicht*), when *Die Leute von Seldwyla* had not had time to become known. His literary development might not be apparent if two works appeared simultaneously which had been conceived and written at completely different times.

In 1856, when war with Prussia over the possession of Neuchatel threatened, Keller appealed in the *Eidgenössische Zeitung* to the Federal Assembly in these words:

> Elected representatives of the Fatherland! You may come together at a time that has been spoken of among the Swiss people since it renewed its Federation; it is the hour of testing and trial for this federation ... if a solitary man stands alone in the darkness and feels that opponents are creeping up round him ready to strike, he wishes for a single ray of light, so that he can see where he can use his hand most effectively to defend his body. This is the kind of situation in which the Swiss nation finds itself, and it asks you, its governors, to give it that ray of light, inasmuch as you will do everything that lies in your power, so far as the true honour and perfect independence of the whole Fatherland allow, to keep the peace. Only in so far as you proclaim in the name of the Swiss nation an unmistakably peaceful attitude and accordingly offer the utmost concession that is possible for the honourable and loyal Swiss citizen do you shine that ray of light in the face of those foreign powers, their true intentions stand revealed, and from that moment, when your efforts prove to be in vain we shall know that we need pay no more heed to the words of others, but have to resort to action. ... Calmly and in good heart the stout army marches from all directions towards the frontiers, while those who still wait behind are full of concern, wherever the eye looks. But it is not the concern of timidity, but honourable and well-armed prudence, the mother of the best deeds, of the only just courage in warfare.

Surprisingly, war was averted, thanks to the pressure of the other European powers on Prussia. In 1856 as at every time of testing since, the essential strength and cohesion of the Swiss nation were evident. On this occasion Keller had without fuss or self-advertisement acted as the mouthpiece of all his German Swiss fellow-countrymen.

The summer of 1857 brought various visitors to Zurich, including Paul Heyse. Keller, Heyse and Burckhardt in a convivial evening together laid the foundation of a long-lasting friendship. The Dunckers came later to Zurich, and Keller accompanied them on excursions around the town, which must have been good for him, because he was growing fat and lazy.

In 1857 various attempts were made by Keller's friends and well-wishers to provide him with a regular livelihood. These would certainly have succeeded if Keller had himself shown the slightest initiative in the matter. But a deep-seated fear of being tied down prevented him from taking positive steps to end his poverty.

Every now and again a sentence in his letters shows that Keller was not so pleased with his way of life as he might seem to the superficial observer. With his good wishes to Ludmilla at the beginning of 1858 came the following confession:

> I had a little thunder shower this morning, for it is an old superstitious heathen custom with me that I have to begin every New Year's morning with a vehement fit of weeping, and I don't know whether this will ever stop.

Surprisingly, Keller's share in the Zurich festivities for the centenary of Schiller's birth in 1859 was not very great. He sat on the committee in charge of these celebrations, but the main public addresses were given by others. Keller was a very small man and his speech was not remarkable for its mellifluousness or elegance of articulation. He may have been passed over for these reasons. The Berne *Musikgesellschaft*, however, invited him to contribute a Prologue to their Schiller celebrations, and this work has achieved a lasting place in the literature which has grown up around Schiller.

In March 1860 Keller wrote to Ludmilla on a cheerful and confident note. After the long period of flagging productivity he had again managed to get under way:

> I am marvellously busy all the time, and all my fingers are covered in inkspots. At the same time, I am enjoying myself almost as much as when I was twenty years old and did my writing secretly instead of attending to my duty.

The story which was then engaging his attention was *Das Fähnlein der sieben Aufrechten*. Berthold Auerbach had asked for a contribution for his *Volkskalender*, perhaps a Swiss short story or an account of the homecoming of a Swiss from abroad. Keller replied (25th February 1860), stressing that Switzerland could never have a separate cultural existence from Germany, no matter what political divisions might exist. In the first part of *Die Leute von Seldwyla* Keller had shown his awareness of the positive qualities and failings of the Swiss people. This work ruthlessly exposes the parochialism to which the less enlightened among them are prone and castigates the smugness found in small and comparatively isolated communities. Yet the work is not cruelly satirical; the essential justice, kindness and self-respect towards which most German Swiss aspire prevent them from being merely figures of fun.

Das Fähnlein der sieben Aufrechten (Auerbach supplied the title) was completed by June 1860. In the letter of 25th February Keller gave Auerbach a fairly full summary of the story, which shows that the work was complete in his mind before he put pen to paper.

Keller realised that *Das Fähnlein* gives a somewhat rosy picture of Swiss life. He wrote to Auerbach in June that there was something to be said for writing about the Swiss in such a way that they felt encouraged to live up to the rather idealised picture of them which he had presented. In his autobiographical sketch of 1889 he calls *Das Fähnlein* "an expression of satisfaction with the state of affairs in the Fatherland, a rejoicing over the possession of the new federal constitution. It was the fair moment when one is not yet conscious of the inexorable consequences which all things bring after them and regards the world as good and quite perfect."

Baron Georg von Cotta, the German publisher, was so impressed by *Das Fähnlein* that he asked Keller to write articles for his journals on the Schiller centenary celebrations at Brunnen. In the essay *Am Mythenstein*, Keller gracefully and modestly acknowledges the Swiss nation's indebtedness to the German poet; Keller carries his learning lightly, and makes bold suggestions for the future of poetry.

In 1859 and 1860, when Napoleon III managed to secure for France the sovereignty over Savoy, which the Swiss regarded as lying within their sphere of influence, Switzerland was divided between those like Keller who wanted war with France and those who thought that such a gesture would only be quixotic.

Public dissatisfaction over the Savoy affair coincided with more general irritation with the government, which was felt to be excessively commercial in outlook. Keller belonged to a committee which protested against the government's policies, in particular against its conciliatory attitude towards France. In newspaper articles he condemned the administration for allowing economic considerations to weigh more heavily than national honour. He also pleaded the cause of the young cotton operatives, who were often disgracefully exploited by their employers. Keller insisted that the nation's future should not be imperilled by the ruthlessness and greed of a minority of citizens. The young must be protected by suitable legislation.

Not only in politics did he take a vigorous stand. In newspaper articles he deplored the tendency of Swiss people to look towards France for cultural inspiration. This meant imposing an alien cultural pattern on the fundamentally Germanic form of Swiss life. In his repudiation of French influences Keller resembles Lessing and the Thomas Mann of the *Betrachtungen eines Unpolitischen*.

In middle age Keller took a wider and more responsible view of events in his country. As the guardian of civil liberties, he represents the politically conscious but often inarticulate Swiss citizen. Although aware of the political differences which divided Germany from Switzerland, he saw that culturally his country could not stand alone.

The men who appointed Keller *Staatsschreiber* (Cantonal Secretary) did not give him the post on the off-chance that he might not fill it too badly. While he was not known to the majority of his fellow-citizens as a man likely to make a success of high administrative office, the selection committee were fairly sure of their ground. If they had not thought that they would get value for money they would never have chosen him. It would run counter to the instincts of any self-respecting Swiss to do so. Keller clearly had a true concern for the welfare of all his fellow-citizens, and an unfeigned interest in ensuring that no section of the community should be allowed to feather its nest at the expense of its weaker brethren.

When Keller was again considering the idea of seeking a professorship of literature at the Polytechnic, the office of First Cantonal Secretary fell vacant in Zurich. Several members of the Cantonal Government decided that Keller should be given this responsible and well-paid office. To anyone who knew him only in his public character of idle poet and winebibber this opinion must have seemed misguided, yet a little reflection might have convinced the doubters that the creator of the schoolmaster in *Der grüne Heinrich*, of Frau Regel Amrain with her punctilious conception of civic duty, and last but not least of the Seven Upright Men themselves had exacting notions of service to the community.

Keller's application for the Secretaryship must be one of the briefest that have ever been made for such an office:

> The undersigned most respectfully begs to apply to be considered for the position of a First Cantonal Secretary advertised on the 28th August.

By 14th September Keller had been elected to the post by five votes to three. The first press comments were of a critical or even outraged nature. The *Neue Zürcher Zeitung* cautiously assumed the tone which English readers have come to expect of *The Times*. While admitting that Keller's appointment was a "surprise for many friends of the government" and surmising that he had been chosen not because of his opposition to the government's policies but in spite of it, the *NZZ* suggested one of the reasons which had led the government to make this surprising choice:

> It has long vexed some of his fellow-countrymen that a spendid talent like Keller has not been able to make his way in his own native country, and very probably this feeling has exercised a great influence on the election.

Other newspapers openly deplored the result of the election, like the conservative *Freitagszeitung*, which called it "a piece of folly" and prophesied dire consequences. The *Bund*, on the other hand, pointed out that there were distinguished precedents for the course of action which the Zurich Government had taken. No doubt the *Bund* was thinking of Goethe's services to Weimar.

Keller was to take up his new duties at 8 a.m. on Monday, 23rd September 1861. He had spent the preceding evening at a champagne party given by the Zurich socialists for Ferdinand Lassalle. Keller had taken a strong dislike to Lassalle and had not troubled to conceal it. Lassalle was giving a demonstration of his hypnotic powers when Keller jumped up in a towering rage, shouted, "That's the last straw, you band of ruffians, you crowd of crooks!" grabbed a chair and advanced brandishing this clumsy weapon on Lassalle. He was protestingly removed to the fresh air before any damage was done.

At ten o'clock the following morning Keller had still not appeared in his office. He was sharply rebuked for this lapse, but after this unpromising start he became an exemplary official, always punctual and prompt in attending to his duty.

The *Staatsschreiber's* office entailed much self-discipline and renunciation for Keller. He found himself at other people's disposal for six days a week from early morning till evening. The regular working hours, the tasks which could not be postponed made him overcome the bad habits which had developed after his expulsion from school and which undoubtedly took a considerable toll of his productive energies. The experience of the cantonal administration served as a window opening on to the world. Keller's mind was enlarged and his sympathies broadened by fifteen years of this valuable bondage. Besides, a little worldly success did him good; no amount of inner conviction of his own worth could make up for the fact that as a discontented radical poet he was not a person of great consequence in the esteem of his contemporaries. For his mother and sister the discovery that he was sufficiently well thought of to have been entrusted with a good and well-paid public position must have been a surprise and a relief.

CHAPTER SIX

THE CANTONAL SECRETARY

KELLER'S new position was far from being a sinecure. He had to draw up railway concessions and revise drafts of new laws. He had charge of the cantonal administrative offices, and was also chief financial officer of the Canton. He kept the minutes of the *Regierungsrat* (Cantonal Government), and conducted correspondence with the Federal Government (*Bundesrat*), as well as with other Cantonal Governments. He edited the annual reports of the various branches of the Cantonal Administration and signed passports, identity cards and trading licences. By single-minded devotion to his task Keller was able to perform or at least supervise directly all these functions of government. Naturally, his private life suffered; the first leave that Keller allowed himself apart from odd days at Christmas and Easter was taken in 1872, after eleven years in office.

If the Canton made heavy demands on the *Staatsschreiber* it rewarded him correspondingly. He received 6,000 francs a year, as well as a free house, heating and light. In 1861 this was a very good income. He was soon able to repay various debts of long standing.

After a few weeks the *Freitagszeitung*, which had so scathingly criticised his appointment, retracted generously:

> According to all that we hear he is now in full control of his post, and if he continues like this, he might well become one of the ablest *Staatsschreiber* that Zurich has ever had . . .

Keller did not merely make a better Secretary than some people had feared—he was a very good one by any standards, and soon earned praise from the Federal Chancellor Schieß, who was in a position to know.

In 1862 Keller was made Actuary of a Railway Commission. In 1863 he sat on a committee concerned with Polish refugees, and he also sometimes wrote the *Bettagsmandate* for the official day of prayer in the Canton. He had no time for authorship; even his private correspondence dwindled to vanishing point. It would have been strange if Pegasus had borne his yoke without chafing a little at times. Though he had often spoken about the obligations of the individual towards the state, it was no light matter to serve it every day for fifteen years. Even if he occasionally pined for artistic liberty he never neglected his duty.

Every year on the national day of prayer the Cantonal Government circulated *Bettagsmandate*, which were read from every pulpit. They reviewed the events of the past year, stressed the citizen's obligations towards his country, and gave moral guidance for the coming year. More often than not the Government delegated the writing of these homilies to the Cantonal Secretary.

Keller's first *Bettagsmandat*, written in 1862, proved unacceptable to the Government, perhaps because many ministers of religion in the Canton had declared that they would not read an address written by a declared atheist. But Keller had not said his last word on religion in 1849. The end of discrimination against Jews in Canton Zurich will be pleasing, he says, "to the God of love and reconciliation". Though he avoids any explicit declaration of religious faith, the whole address reveals a genuine reverence for creation and a desire to promulgate standards of conduct which would be acceptable to the "Lord of all nations". God can distinguish between the consequences of genuine effort and undeserved good fortune. It would be a mistake to take the settled state of Switzerland under the new constitution for granted; the great Architect of history might at any moment destroy this little model of His, if it had ceased to fit in with His master plan.

Keller hopes that the Zwinglian Church will free itself "from the arbitrariness of human illusion and strife" and will "advance in that fresh and charitable approach to the affairs of the world, which will once again give it universal power over men's souls and preserve it from threatening fragmentation". This sentence implies that the Church had lost its hold on the younger generation because of the contentious and parochial attitudes of some ministers. The last sentence of all may have finally decided the Zurich Government against using the *Mandat*:

May the citizen who is not a churchman, enjoying his freedom of conscience, not pass this day in restless distraction either, but in quiet composure show his respect for his native land.

While Keller nowhere commits himself to any religious dogma, one gains from the *Bettagsmandate* the impression that he believes in a God who is both judge and provider and who is not always prejudiced in favour of the Swiss. His view of human affairs is healthily unparochial.

Although the *Mandat* for 1862 was rejected, Keller was again invited to write one for 1863. This address (like the three that followed) reveals unmistakably the change which had taken place in Keller's religious opinions since Feuerbach:

Fellow citizens! Once again the national day of prayer approaches, on which all the Confederates come before God, their only Lord, to test their consciences before Him, the All-knowing One, to hear the commands of the Infinite and to thank Him for His unchanging goodness.

Keller never was a man for humbug, so he certainly meant these words; he did not put on a semblance of piety for the occasion. The *Mandate* as well as various other pointers in his later writings suggest that Keller had by middle life adopted a positive, if still critical attitude to religion. The God of the *Bettagsmandate* is the providing, sustaining God, the Judge of all mankind who is not deceived by human pretensions or by men's blindness towards their own weaknesses. He is very like the God of Frau Lee in *Der grüne Heinrich* and of Keller's mother. Faced with the necessity of declaring whether or not he upheld the ancient beliefs of the German Swiss, Keller wrote the *Bettagsmandate* which amount to an implicit renunciation of Feuerbach.

Keller now began to adopt somewhat less radical political attitudes than he had held as a younger man. He resisted pressure to have the constitution revised in the direction of "total democracy" rather than "representative democracy". In newspaper articles he pointed out that the 1831 constitution had a long and respectable history and had been frequently amended and brought up to date. A new constitution would not be an organic growth and would scarcely serve the people better than the one they already possessed.

On 5th February 1864, Keller's mother died suddenly before he came home for the evening. He was distressed that he had not been able to take a proper farewell of her. For four whole weeks after her death, he confessed sadly, he did not go near a public house.

The loss of his mother grieved him deeply. Their affection for one another had survived all his neglect of her and her failure to appreciate properly his artistic aspirations. In his bereaved and lonely state Keller made a last attempt to escape from the bachelor's existence.

In 1865 he met Luise Scheidegger at a friend's house. Though only twenty-two she had a sensitive and well-trained mind. A tendency to melancholia could only have been exaggerated by the early loss of both parents. Keller saw in her the promise of intellectual companionship and, perhaps, too, a more sympathetic purveyor of the creature comforts than his spartan sister. She refused at first to marry him, but relented early in 1866, and they became engaged. Then she began to hear attacks on his character in the newspapers and in private gossip. These so distressed her that during the summer of 1866 she drowned herself.

Although the reports of Keller's behaviour which had made Luise take her life were grossly exaggerated, they contained enough truth to make him very uneasy. Luise would probably in any case have been unequal to the ordinary stresses of living, and the stories of Keller's drunkenness only touched off disaster. Yet he was tortured by the reflection that he should at all have merited the slur on his good name which had caused such a tragic happening. He wrote these verses three weeks after Luise's death :

> Du solltest ruhen, und ich störe dich,
> Ich störe deine Ruhe, süße Tote,
> Ich wecke dich im kühlen Morgenrote,
> und wecke dich, wenn Schlaf die Welt beschlich.
>
> Die in der Morgenfrüh in leisen Schuhen
> Die Ruh gesucht und mir die Unruh gab,
> Nicht eine Feste ist dein zartes Grab,
> Drin du geborgen kannst und sicher ruhen !

Entschwundenes Gut, o Herz voll seltener Güte,
Steh auf und schüttle nur dein nasses Haar!
Tu auf die lieben Äuglein treu und klar,
Gebrochen in des Lenzes reinster Blüte!

Du mußt mit meinem Grame schmerzlich kosen,
Solang er wach, das ist die meiste Zeit,
Erst wenn der Tod mir selber Ruh verleiht
Magst kehren du, zu ruhen im Wesenlosen.

Keller never mentions Luise in his works or correspondence. He could not bear the idea that her memory should attract idle gossip. After his death his executors decided to burn the correspondence with Luise. Keller must have at least considered the possibility that the letters should be kept for posterity, for all his papers were in scrupulous order at his death, and the presence among them of the correspondence with Luise could not have been accidental.

To Keller's surprise, when the new radical government took over in Canton Zurich in 1869 he was not asked to resign. Most responsible people knew that in Keller they had a very good Cantonal Secretary, even if he did appear to be of the wrong political colour. As a mature man Keller was by no means a doctrinaire conservative, and the uncritical radicalism of his earlier days had been the product of inexperience. After some years of office Keller increasingly realised that sound administration depended on men rather than a system. While at one time he sincerely believed that a liberal constitution was the first condition of good government, after serving as *Staatsschreiber* he would have laid more stress on the quality of the people who operated it than on the constitution.

Every now and again Keller tells his correspondents that he regrets he has not more time for creative activity. Yet it was a sound instinct that kept him at the *Staatsschreiber's* desk for so long. He had to enlarge his general experience before he could achieve anything new in the poetic field. Also, Keller owed his improved standing in society largely to his position, and he must have enjoyed the opportunities it provided of mingling with the acknowledged leaders of his generation.

He knew that he ought not to give up the Secretaryship on impulse. That might well turn out to be a mistake, and he was getting too old for the time-consuming business of finding out what was best for him by trial and error.

Keller's fiftieth birthday was celebrated in fine style by his wellwishers, especially among the University students of Zurich. They had arranged for public celebrations about which he was not told till the last minute, when he could scarcely refuse to participate. The day's activities reached their climax with the award of an honorary doctorate by the University and a banquet in the Zurich music hall. Keller thoroughly enjoyed himself and did not go home till daybreak.

If the organisers of these birthday celebrations had intended to prod the creative artist into life again they were not immediately successful in this aim. Keller suffered some stirrings of conscience during and directly after the birthday feast. He wrote to Ludmilla Assing (June 1870) that he was looking at manuscripts begun years before. He gradually resolved to give up his official position. He had at one time hoped to salvage some time from his duties for literary work. After some years in office he knew he must resign if he were to have time for literary composition.

In the early 1870s Keller became friendly with Adolf Exner, an able young Viennese jurist from the University, and later with his sister Marie. The friendship with her was one of the consolations of Keller's middle age. He knew now that he would never find happiness in love, and his other friendships with women had always been overshadowed by some outside factor; Ludmilla was the representative of the very exclusive Varnhagen circle; with Lina Duncker an unfulfilled literary contract with her husband kept raising its ugly head. But nothing came between him and Marie Exner (later Marie von Frisch), and Keller savoured to the full the pleasure of being very good friends with her. In letters to her Keller is relaxed and communicative; in them we detect a note of gaiety which had been missing from his correspondence for years. Keller's natural exuberance, long suppressed by the demands of duty and the disappointments he had experienced, again comes bubbling to the surface.

Like most German Swiss whose horizons were not limited by the boundaries of their native country, Keller was interested in the events of 1870 and 1871, when Bismarck's Germany tried its strength against France. Keller naturally rejoiced in the discomfiture of Louis Napoleon. However, his participation in the Zurich German colony's victory celebrations was tactless. Many Swiss people trembled for the peace of Europe now that the balance of power had so clearly shifted in favour of Germany. Anti-German demonstrations took place in Zurich and other Swiss cities. Keller's presence at the German victory banquet in the Zurich *Tonhalle* was interpreted by the Germans and their sympathisers as a declaration of his allegiance. Unfortunately, his fellow-citizens whose sympathies were not with the Germans thought the same thing. Further indiscretions of this kind continued to annoy those Swiss who regarded the aggrandisement of Germany as a danger to peace and security. Keller thought of Germany as his second fatherland; he could hardly be blamed for not recognising at the birth of the modern German state that a new and disturbing element had entered European politics.

In Keller's private life, his excessive candour towards Mathilde Wesendonck about her drama *Edith* cost him her friendship. He had meant to dedicate his *Sieben Legenden* to her, but now decided not to. He also gave to another friend a charming water-colour of Lake Zurich and the Alps which he had intended for her.

The Stuttgart publisher Weibert had asked to be allowed to publish the *Sieben Legenden*. Keller proposed at first to call the work *Auf Goldgrund*. He planned to write a humorous preface, in which his real attitude to the legends of the saints should be allowed to shine through. Friedrich Theodor Vischer said *Sieben Legenden* by Gottfried Keller would be preferable, and under this title Keller sent them to Weibert just after Christmas 1871. A month or two later he sent a copy of the new work to F. T. Vischer with a letter of apology for his "miserable little book" which will probably be regarded as a piece of childishness and folly "in its isolation and sudden appearance".

In the early 1870s Keller began his correspondence with Emil Kuh, the Austrian critic, who had suggested a new edition of *Der grüne Heinrich* in which the whole story should be told in the first person, instead of partly in the first and partly in the third person. Keller liked this suggestion, and in due course sent Kuh a copy of the Legends:

I have been led into the publication of a little entremets, a ridiculous little dish of preserved plums, which I herewith most dutifully send you, to return the kindnesses you have shown me at least with a tiny payment on account. May these seven little legends not seem too remote and queer to you. If they are anything at all, they are perhaps a little protest against the tyranny of the topical in the choice of material, and a gesture for the preservation of free movement in every respect.

Keller's correspondence between 1870 and 1873 shows signs of his reawakening productivity. He was very interested in Kuh's suggestions for revising *Der grüne Heinrich.* Weibert, delighted by the success of the *Legends,* approached Keller about the possibility of publishing a selection of poems. Keller replied that he would like to compile a new edition of his poetry "in about two years". Keller's collected poems actually appeared in 1883 ! In the same letter he speaks of a volume of stories which "still does not have a master"; these must be the *Züricher Novellen.* The collected poems would contain in addition to material published in the collections of 1846 and 1854 a number of hitherto unpublished poems. Although Keller tells Weibert (letter of 31st May 1872) that the Göschen-Verlag, Weibert's firm, would be well suited to undertake the publication of the new collected poems, Weibert did not publish them.

Meanwhile, Keller had been approached by Vieweg's son, Heinrich, about the second volume of *Die Leute von Seldwyla.* Only three stories had reached him, and he would like to have the remainder. Keller replied that he wished to have back the manuscript of the stories already sent so that he could revise them. It turned out that the manuscript of *Der Schmied seines Glückes* had been lost. Keller was able to find another copy but the incident gave him a genuine grudge against the Viewegs, with whom he now severed his association. His second volume of Seldwyla stories now appeared in the Göschen-Verlag in 1873 and 1874.

The friendship with Marie Exner and her circle rescued Keller from the doldrums and released a fresh flood of creative energy. After ten years as *Staatsschreiber* he was in danger of becoming completely swallowed up by his official duties. In 1872 he visited Munich for ten days. As well as the Exners he saw an old intimate from the Munich days, the painter Bernhard Fries, and Paul Heyse. He looked in vain for the owner of the junk-shop to whom he had sold his pictures so long ago. In the picture-galleries, the works of Moritz von Schwind and Arnold Böcklin delighted him. He returned home refreshed and stimulated. Keller enjoyed his non-committal flirtation with Marie Exner, to whom he was at one and the same time something of a doting lover, affectionate uncle and father-figure all combined.

Keller spent a holiday in the Salzkammergut with the Exners in 1873. After two days in Salzburg he joined his friends by the Mondsee. In the afternoons he went out walking with them, and in the evenings he played at skittles and enjoyed a glass of wine in the little country inns. He throve on this regime after the rigours of the *Staatsschreiber's* office, and completed *Dietegen* during the mornings. In the evenings he told his friends about his childhood in old Zurich, and the austerity of living in the same house with his sister Regula, who had decided last winter that they must economise on fuel, a completely unnecessary mortification of the flesh because free fuel was one of his per-quisites of office. The memory of his holiday on the Mondsee shed a glow of wellbeing over the whole of the following winter. At Christmas 1873 Keller painted a charming water colour of the Mondsee for Marie Exner; a companion piece, *The road to Unterach*, should also have been ready for Christmas, but was not completed till three months later.

In 1874 Keller visited the Exners in their new house in Vienna. It was a special occasion, for one brother (Sigismund) was to celebrate his engagement during Keller's visit. Keller and Brahms collaborated to produce a little cantata for the event. On the way from Zurich to Vienna Keller telegraphed to Adolf Exner: "Das Faßl rollt heran". (The little barrel is rolling on its way.) He stayed four weeks, an indication of warm approval, for he seldom left home. He fell into a comfortable routine of work and pleasure, and almost finished the last of his Seldwyla stories. After three weeks in Vienna he went with his hosts to Brixlegg in the Tirol, from where he returned home via Munich. Afterwards Keller remembered with pleasure the heavily laden apricot trees in Adolf Exner's garden, where he had spent the warm summer afternoons.

That summer the *Augsburger Allgemeine Zeitung*, published a long essay by Friedrich Theodor Vischer on Keller's work. This influential critic's praise and support gave a fillip to the reception of Keller's books throughout the German-speaking world. Keller admitted that Vischer's essay, both in its praise and criticism, gave him great pleasure. Vischer seemed to have singled out for commendation precisely those aspects of his work which he had secretly longed to see appreciated.

As Keller grew older he preferred the company of younger men to that of his contemporaries. He liked to feel in touch with the young, as can be seen from his works. While Martin Salander is a gullible old Philistine, his son Arnold is a model of discretion, the embodiment of all the bourgeois virtues, with just a large enough dash of the heroic to make him something better than a complete prig.

One of Keller's young friends was Jakob Baechtold, his first biographer, who began his career as a schoolmaster. Keller exchanged views with him on literary topics. That Keller was not merely the passive recipient of instruction by the specialist is demonstrated by a whimsical Middle High German letter addressed to Baechtold : "Gotefrid der Schriber, och Cellerarius," wrote to his "Trut Wingesellen unde friunt" after an enjoyable reunion congratulating him on the birth of a daughter. Keller was glad that his "wirdeklich wirtinne sige eines magetlins genesen", and went on to praise the Burgundy he and other friends had drunk that evening: "Dizeren Win hant mir unde etlich ander och ze Zürich endachet unde zimelich genozzen." Keller's long association with Adolf Frey, the author of excellent *Erinnerungen an Gottfried Keller*, did not begin till after his retirement from the Cantonal Secretaryship.

Keller had begun to yearn for freedom again. He knew that as long as he remained Cantonal Secretary he could do no writing. Regula resisted the idea of abandoning financial security for literature, but his unwritten works lay heavily on his conscience. In the spring of 1875 the Kellers had left the official residence of the *Staatsschreiber* in old Zurich for an extremely attractive house in Enge on the so-called Bürgli, with splendid views of Lake Zurich and the distant mountains. In 1876 he finally decided to retire, having covered his retreat by arranging to send contributions to the newly established *Deutsche Rundschau*. He had promised Julius Rodenberg, the editor, his *Züricher Novellen*.

Eduard Mörike's death in 1875 touched Keller in an unexpectedly immediate way. Mörike had been a member of the Bavarian Order of Maximilian, to which Paul Heyse also belonged. When Mörike died, Heyse's proposal that Keller should succeed him was carried unanimously. However, Keller refused the honour, because Swiss civil servants were not allowed to accept decorations from foreign states. After Keller's resignation, Heyse had him elected a member of the Order of Maximilian without further consultation. Because the members of the order were all artists and scholars, Keller called it the Order of Pegasus.

Keller was certainly a fitting successor to Mörike, to whom he felt akin despite all differences of belief and temperament, and whom he understood in all his complex genius. If Mörike's *Maler Nolten* and other prose works are, with the exception of *Mozart auf der Reise nach Prag*, formally inferior to Keller's, they are redeemed from ordinariness by his uncanny psychological perception, particularly in dealing with abnormal mental states. The author of *Der grüne Heinrich*, which shows such a wonderful understanding of childhood problems and adolescent growing pains, was a worthy heir to Mörike; each had a deep intuitive grasp of human psychology. Mörike draws sympathetically sufferers from the various nervous and mental weaknesses to which he felt himslf exposed, and Keller remembers the difficulties, fears and growing pains of childhood with an exactness rare in the grown man. And each is on occasion thoroughly at home in the special field of the other.

Keller resigned in July 1876, and sent the following account of his leavetaking from the cantonal government to Adolf Exner:

I parted very tolerably from my democratic government—indeed it was good fun—I don't think I have told you yet. They arranged a farewell dinner for me at the Hotel Bellevue, at which only the members of the government and I were present, and presented me with a silver drinking cup. The proceedings began at six o'clock in the afternoon. At nine o'clock it looked like falling flat, and I had the crazy idea that I should do something for my own part and *consecrate* the cup, as it were. I went out and ordered vast quantities of wine, Bordeaux, Champagne and so forth, under the impression that I should be paying for them myself. The gentlemen knew, however, that everything was to be paid for from the cantonal treasury, and in order to make the damage at least tolerable, they began to drink furiously with me, and boozed desperately till five o'clock in the morning, so that we had to part from one another in broad daylight. Sieber was taken home in a cab, I was taken in a cab to the Bürgli, I had a headache for three days. The craziest thing is that the more we drank the more I regaled the gentlemen with home truths in this last moment, with my views about the merits of their government and the like, which made me furious with myself afterwards, for it was ungrateful of me to a degree. They put a good face on it, all the same, but I don't think they would give me the cup now. I wanted to pay for the wine I had ordered the following day, or rather on the afternoon of the same day, but sure enough, my money was refused.

It was all carefully kept dark, but the bill will remain as a silent witness in the archives.

After Keller's retirement the fear that he might die before completing his task was uppermost in his mind. It was sufficient to overcome his fear of financial instability. He had a genuine fear of betraying his mission, although he would scarcely have put it like that. Temporary withdrawal from the creative life had been an inevitable and necessary stage in his development; he had to become a better and more responsible person before he could reach full maturity as an artist. Then in accordance with a law as inexorable as that which causes the young animal to be born in due season or the bud to burst when it is ready, Keller had to clear all obstacles out of the way as soon as he was ready to start writing again. It was not merely advisable for him to resign his position in 1876, it was impossible for him to do anything else.

CHAPTER SEVEN

THE HOUSE ON THE BÜRGLI

In the mid-1870s, before Keller and Regula became old and infirm, their fine flat in the mainly rural district of Enge gave them great pleasure. Regula could still walk to town to do her shopping, and Gottfried's short legs did not find the hill too steep on the way home after his excursions in search of liquid refreshment.

The *Züricher Novellen* occupied Keller's energies in the summer of 1876. He did not go to meet Adolf Exner in Munich that year. Keller was becoming less mobile and increasingly corpulent. His love of good food and drink was never balanced by an active life. The dispatch to Rodenberg of the *Landvogt von Greifensee* early in 1877 completed the cycle, except that *Das Fähnlein* and *Ursula* were not among the stories published in serial form in the *Rundschau* between November 1876 and April 1877. Among the many readers who expressed their admiration of the new book was Conrad Ferdinand Meyer.

The relationship between Keller and Meyer was never cordial. Where purely intellectual appreciation of his work was concerned, Meyer had few more discriminating admirers. Keller respected Meyer as a brilliant and conscientious artist, but he did not love the man. The elaborate façade erected by Meyer to conceal his psychological weakness antagonised Keller, who nevertheless knew that to hate a man for the frailty which he did his best to combat was unjust. The barriers between them were even more impregnable than those which for so long divided Goethe and Schiller. Meyer was as willing as Schiller had been to endure rebuffs if only he could in the end win Keller's friendship, but Keller was capricious with the commodity.

Keller may have disliked Meyer because of the latter's favoured situation in life. Keller suffered from the disadvantages of poverty, small stature, rough speech, a fateful obsession which caused him wastefully to consume his tiny patrimony, and he had been compelled to sacrifice fifteen years of his already shortened working life to the necessity of earning his bread. Meyer had been born into a wealthy patrician family, and had enjoyed all the advantages of a thoroughly civilised background. Yet he suffered from a heritage of mental instability, and parts of his life were spent in institutions for the mentally sick. He lived in continual fear of the cloud that overshadowed his whole existence. No wonder if more than one of Meyer's heroes conceals behind a brave exterior the knowledge of his own inadequacy for the role in which life has cast him.

One person who might have seemed to have far less claim on Keller's time and affection than Meyer was Adolf Frey, who first visited him while still a student in 1877. Adolf Frey had the happy gift of keeping Keller in a good humour. He has served us well with his *Erinnerungen an Gottfried Keller*, but it seems perverse of Keller to have preferred him to Meyer.

Theodor Storm came into Keller's life in an oddly characteristic letter written in March 1877. He and his family had been reading the *Züricher Novellen*, which were then appearing in the *Deutsche Rundschau*. He hoped that even if a warm handshake were not possible, greetings from afar could at least be exchanged now and again. He closed his letter with a complaint that Keller did Johannes and Fides less than justice in his story.* At the point where the young people were free to marry, the subject was simply dismissed with a wave of the hand.

Storm was ill advised to be so frank. While Keller jokes about Storm's remarks in his reply, he says that it ill becomes gentlemen beyond a certain age to linger over descriptions of the happiness of young lovers. One can detect a shade of annoyance in Keller's letter. Storm, a judge by profession, found it difficult to shed a certain pedantic, pontifical and censorious tone. Keller likened their relationship to that of two old monks, living in widely separated monasteries, and corresponding about the problems of growing a particularly rare type of carnation. Just as with gardeners or fishermen there is always an undertone of jealousy which only serves to make them more human. Their correspondence well repays study. Each writer's personality shines through unmistakably, Storm's directness, bluntness and plain prejudices,

* *Hadlaub.*

Keller's complexity, suspended judgements and reluctance to commit himself. The two men never met, but *Regierungsrat* Petersen of Schleswig, who visited Zurich repeatedly, told each of them something of the private life of the other.

The appearance of the *Züricher Novellen* at Christmas 1877 proved conclusively that Keller's decision to relinquish the Cantonal Secretaryship had been right. Keller now received the citizenship of Zurich, a rare distinction which genuinely moved him. Until now he had been a citizen of Glattfelden, his father's native village. He turned with greater confidence to the difficult task of revising *Der grüne Heinrich*. He no longer felt that Heinrich Lee must die, but planned to make him take up a life of quiet and useful activity after abandoning the attempt to establish himself as an artist. The story was all to be told in the first person, instead of being told partly in the first person and partly in the third. Storm's comments and suggestions regarding the proposed revision of *Der grüne Heinrich* proved of considerable value to Keller.

Keller's home life with Regula left much to be desired. While by no means unintelligent, she had never had the opportunity of developing intellectual interests, and she had excessively spartan ideas of domestic economy, which made it impossible for Keller to entertain his friends in his own home. Keller was nothing if not a comfortable man, but she abhorred the most harmless self-indulgences. Now that Frau Keller was dead, Regula took her place in Keller's affection. In 1877 she already suffered from breathlessness and palpitations and began to find the distance from town and the steepness of the hill on which they lived a burden. She used to go to bed early, and when Keller came home in the evening she would let down the front door key in an old felt slipper from her bedroom window. The contrast between Storm's large and happy family circle and the relative isolation of the aging Keller immediately strikes the reader of their correspondence. In his fifties and early sixties Keller still visited friends in and near Zurich, Alfred Escher, for instance, or the François Wille household where C. F. Meyer was also an occasional guest. But in his last years he generally went no farther afield than to the *Meise*, one of the Zurich guild houses. Jakob Baechtold describes the usual Saturday evening routine:

6—GKLAW

What fine Saturday evenings we had at the Meise in those
years! We sat—preferably alone together—in the back part
of the long, old-fashioned, dark-panelled guild room near a big,
towering painted tiled stove. Keller liked to be served for as
long as possible by the same modest girl. One whom he specially liked he called the "Volkslied". He was always kind to
her, was familiar with the little events of her life, often brought
along a little surprise, for instance in mid-winter would produce a lovely flower for her from his pocket. A good supper
was served with a glass or two of wholesome, ordinary local
wine. Then Keller asked the usual question, whether we
should proceed to an "honoris causa", that was to say, a better
bottle. Generally it was a white or sparkling wine. Then came
a black coffee with cognac, of which it was often said the
following day that it had behaved like a street urchin in the
night. On specially good evenings Gottfried Keller stood us a
bottle of champagne, but only the best French. He couldn't
bear the other stuff. After midnight we broke up the party,
we went round the corner over the Limmat bridge to a little
beer-house, and we stayed there for an hour or two enjoying
edifying conversation. On Sundays we had a shortened repetition of the whole process. These were the evenings on which
the "frozen Christian" thawed out. The silent man became
communicative, would chat contentedly. And what a wonderful story-teller Gottfried Keller was, even at the table of a
public house! Absolutely incomparable at telling cosily humorous tales! He was assisted by a pronounced talent for comical
mimicry, and a slight speech impediment, the faulty pronun-
ciation of *Sch*, which sounded as though he put in an L before
it, increased the often killingly funny effect. . . . As well as
favourite books Keller also had his favourite songs, which,
when we were really merry, he would sing in a pleasing voice.
They were mostly old-fashioned ones: "Ein Lämmlein trank
vom Frischen aus einem kühlen Bach" or the song of the
Bettelvogt from the *Wunderhorn*.

The advent of an unwelcome stranger, particularly a literary
critic, could easily spoil the whole evening. Especially in wine
he was given to sudden and uncontrollable fits of anger, during
which he would bang on or upset the table, scattering glasses far

and wide and causing alarm and embarrassment. Sometimes there were similar scenes in private houses. In drink Keller would sometimes even start a fight. In the *Meise* he gave free rein to his fancy, in particular to his gift for inventing grotesque characters and situations. That side of his creative genius which he had learned to curb in his writings still found an outlet during these informal sessions with his friends. Sometimes he would recall scenes from literature, embroidering and extending the original narrative so that it gained new vitality and richness, sometimes he talked entertainingly of everyday events, sometimes his imaginative genius conjured up a whole new world of memorable persons and happenings.

Keller's correspondence with Storm prompted him to write a few new poems and to look critically at his previously published poems with a view to preparing a new collected edition. He once wrote to Storm that the stimulus of reading his friend's new works had made him work harder on his own poems and achieve more in one evening than in the preceding six months, "and that I owe just to the contact with the man by the far North Sea".

Keller, now nearly sixty, began to think often about death. In June 1878 a long and generally cheerful letter, mainly concerned with his new poems, concludes:

I must see to it that I manage to get my hay under cover, for the Other is already whetting his scythe at the edge of the meadow.

His sixtieth birthday was marked by a special celebration arranged by a small group of Zurich friends in the elegant rococo dining room of the *Meise*. Each dish of the dinner was named after a character in one of Keller's books: Turtle soup à la Kammacher, Partridge Pie à la Strapinsky, Haunch of Venison à la Frau Zendelwald, Strawberry Tarts à la Madame Litumlei. After the minimum of formalities everyone settled down to eat and drink; later in the evening they adjourned to the *Kronenhalle*.

Soon after Gottfried Semper's death in 1879 Keller had a curious dream, which Baechtold relates thus:

Covered in dust and untidily clad, his dead friend slips into the room; following him the shades of many Zurich men and women from the *Rindermarkt* (where Keller had been brought up), all of whom Keller had known in his youth but had long forgotten. To the question whether he were not dead, Semper answers: Indeed yes, but he had taken leave: for where he had been since, it was perfectly intolerable. Thereupon he had left the room again quietly, followed by the softly gliding crew, and in the doorway had called once more: "Don't go there, Keller! It's a bad place there!"

The revision of *Der grüne Heinrich* was making slow progress. At Christmas 1879 only three volumes of the four had been completed. The cold winter that year, Keller claimed, made it impossible to achieve a satisfactory temperature in his study. He had bought from Vieweg the remaining stock of the first edition, and as a symbolical act he burned all 120 copies of the first three volumes, to obliterate all traces of the follies of his youth. Keller is reported to have said: "May the hand wither that ever again causes the first version to be reprinted!" Naturally, this did not prevent the work from being republished in the original form within a few years of Keller's death. The modern reader who has come to know the original version of *Der grüne Heinrich* will be grateful to Professor Ermatinger for his initiative in risking a withered hand in the service of scholarship.

As soon as he had completed the revision of *Der grüne Heinrich* in October 1880 young scholars in the universities fell upon the new work and proceeded to demonstrate in what respects it differed from that which it was meant to supersede. Some of them even compared it unfavourably with the old version. In attempting to repudiate utterly the 1854–55 version of the book Keller was attempting the impossible. It would have been wiser to place the new version in the hands of the public without comment. Keller indignantly describes the young scholars' methods:

> Instead of judging the present book on its own merits, they compare it in their philological way with the old one, to demonstrate their method, and so they drag the dead stuff about and leave the living matter alone, for that is all they know how to do. It is roughly the same situation as if someone were to bury an old mongrel in the garden, and the neighbours were to come by night, dig him up again and lay the poor wretch on one's doorstep.

Keller particularly deplored the activities of Wilhelm Scherer and his school, but in fairness one must admit that these critics engaged in their studies of origin and development from a genuine love of literature. Keller's creative genius always underestimated the classifying, codifying, analytical mind.

Scarcely had Keller completed the revision of *Der grüne Heinrich* when he resumed work on the Galatea stories. He resolved to publish them under the title *Das Sinngedicht*. (An epigram by Friedrich Logau forms the point of departure for the whole series.) He was able to continue from where he had left off in 1855 without difficulty; his mind had been constantly occupied with the stories during his solitary walks and while he sat over his glass of wine. The stories were published in the *Deutsche Rundschau* early in 1881 after Keller had dissolved the original contract with Franz Duncker. Wilhelm Hertz of Berlin published *Das Sinngedicht* in book form later in the year. The book brought Keller not only considerable financial success, but also the almost unmingled approbation of his literary friends. Storm and Heyse felt that the revenge taken by Brandolf* on his wife's former husband and her wicked brothers was in poor taste; it is a fairy tale revenge, and Keller did not really mean that he condoned such crude methods of paying off old scores.

In the autumn of 1881 Keller undertook along with the animal painter Rudolf Koller the journey described in his attractive essay, *Ein bescheidenes Kunstreischen*. They visited Stückelberg who painted the frescoes in the new church on the *Tellplatte*; then they went to the Lucerne Town House, where there was a permanent art exhibition. Among the pictures on show was a Triton family by Arnold Böcklin which Keller greatly admired and enthusiastically described in the essay.

From 1881 onwards Keller's life was in evident decline. He was feeling his age, his friends were dying off all round him, and Regula was ailing. Although Keller was not, as Jakob Baechtold thought, fundamentally misanthropic, he certainly became rather querulous with advancing years.

In 1882 he received an unexpected tribute from Nietzsche, then teaching at Basle, in the shape of a copy of the *Fröhliche Wissenschaft*, accompanied by a characteristic letter: "Truly, there is no one I would rather avoid hurting than you, the

* In *Die arme Baronin*.

Rejoicer of my Heart!" Keller must have replied politely, for Nietzsche continued to send him copies of his works as they appeared, but to other people Keller expressed far from flattering opinions of Nietzsche.

In October 1882 the Kellers moved to a house called the *Thaleck* in the *Zeltweg*. Before moving Keller fell off a ladder in his library and injured the back of his head; he was badly shaken by this accident, and was still telling his correspondents about it at the end of the year. Hottingen was now a busy part of the town with many shops and unceasing street noises. Almost as soon as they had moved the Kellers regretted their choice of flat, although Regula found it easier to do the shopping. No doubt the main reason for Keller's flagging productivity and loss of hope for the future was old age, but his physical surroundings did nothing to enable him to make the most of himself.

CHAPTER EIGHT

OLD AGE

BEFORE leaving the Bürgli, Keller had already begun *Martin Salander*. Soon after the removal he completed his new edition of *Collected Poems*. Most of these had been printed long before, but there was a fair harvest of more recent work, and the earliest material had been ruthlessly sifted and pruned. Keller preferred to undertake this work himself rather than leave it to "Nachlaß-marder", literary scavengers routing among the papers of dead poets. The poems were ready by the summer of 1883. Julius Rodenberg wanted the manuscript of *Martin Salander* for the October issue of *Die deutsche Rundschau*. Keller said he could not finish the book so soon, and that printing should not begin till it was completed. Regrettably, he did not adhere to this decision. He was perfectly aware of the disadvantages of premature publication of the book, and as late as September 1883, when Rodenberg visited him in Zurich, Keller told him he could not yet have any manuscript.

When the new edition of the poems appeared in November 1883 it provoked varying reactions. Theodor Storm sounded lukewarm in his praise, and Keller felt rather hurt. He knew that he would not in the main be remembered as a lyric poet; he must also have known that within his narrower limits Storm could achieve surer success in this field. Yet Storm's almost off-hand statement that five or six poems had really moved him seemed to Keller to do less than justice to the remainder of the collection.

Keller had now reached that stage of weariness in which everything turned to dust and ashes before his eyes. He had taken a bad house, his sister was in failing health, his rheumatism was becoming more acute, his old friends were dying, his poems had not evoked a sufficiently appreciative comment from the man whose opinion mattered most to him, Feuerbach's doctrine was cold comfort for the impending journey into the unknown, people irritated him, even drink offered little consolation, his creative powers were steadily diminishing, he had neither wife nor child, the political trends of the day worried him, he felt altogether that he was nearly finished.

Adolf Frey returned from studies in Germany to find Keller an old man "more bowed in posture, with his neck fallen in, his countenance more often clouded, his tongue sharper".

At the beginning of his retirement Keller wrote many letters, and in these the quality of his mind was most abundantly revealed; the letters to his friends demonstrate both how clever and how kind he was, his verbal dexterity and his roguish sense of humour can unexpectedy illumine a whole page. But within a year or two of moving to the *Thaleck* Keller had almost ceased to write letters. Even Marie von Frisch, who continued to remember him every Christmas, no longer heard from him so often, and once when she had sent him a little present he ungraciously wrote that she did not need to feel bound to send tribute to him, as if he were "an old Levite" or "a priest of Baal".

Nietzsche called on Keller one day but did not find him at home, and a few days later Keller visited Nietzsche and his sister at their hotel. The two men talked of this and that, without ever advancing beyond polite commonplaces. Frau Förster-Nietzsche reports thus on the meeting:

> ... when at last Gottfried Keller spoke to me, too, and I said something that pleased and amused him, he smiled, which altered his face in an indescribably charming way. I have never seen a face that assumed such a completely different expression when it smiled. Generally Keller's face had something rather peevish, indifferent about it, so that one could hardly understand how a writer of such entertaining stories could look like that. But as soon as he smiled, his eyes were alight with mischief, and his whole face took on an expression of clever waggishness.

Keller did not know what to make of Nietzsche; he could sense that this was a man of extraordinary talent who yet had something queer and offputting about him. Keller and Nietzsche never met in anything more than a superficial sense; they made polite conversation, each sensed that the other had something to give him if they became sufficiently intimate, and yet somehow this never happened.

Meanwhile, Keller and Jakob Baechtold had quarrelled over Baechtold's editing of Heinrich Leuthold's unpublished papers. Not only had he denigrated Leuthold's memory, he had without consulting Keller used Keller's name in support of his opinions about Leuthold. After a stormy scene in a Zurich café one Saturday night Keller wrote to Baechtold to say that he would no longer meet him on Saturday evenings. Baechtold's attempts at reconciliation were angrily spurned, yet Keller never formally revoked the decision to entrust Baechtold with his unpublished papers after his death. Thus Baechtold became Keller's first biographer and the first editor of his correspondence. In fairness one must concede that in general Baechtold discharged this responsibility well, although in one passage in the biography he states that Keller was fundamentally lacking in goodwill towards his fellow men.

Arnold Böcklin was one of Keller's intimates during his last few years. After Böcklin, with characteristic determination, had overcome Keller's reluctance to meet a stranger, the two men became fast friends, and Keller frequently forgathered with Böcklin and his artistic circle on Tuesday evenings. Böcklin urged Keller to take more exercise in the interests of health, but without much success. In February 1886, Böcklin and some friends arranged an entertainment in Keller's honour. It took the form of a fancy dress party at which members of the *Künstlergesellschaft* in appropriate costume enacted scenes from the *Züricher Novellen*. Johannes Hadlaub and his Fides, the venerable Salomon Geßner, Herr Jacques on his Italian honeymoon and the Bailiff of Greifensee were all represented. When they had played their part, they sat down among the other guests and had supper; while the dessert was being served, the Seven Upright Men, with young Hediger at their head, came on to a lively march tune.

Keller had meantime agreed to let Julius Rodenberg have part of the manuscript of *Martin Salander*. As soon as the first part had appeared in the *Deutsche Rundschau* he was under pressure to supply the continuation. Although he did his best, he twice failed to provide his contributions on time. It had been arranged that the last chapters should appear by September 1886, since a new volume of the *Rundschau* began in October. In desperation Keller wrote a provisional ending for the work, just to get it off his hands. Subsequently, this ending was replaced by the two final chapters we know when the book edition appeared in December. Keller knew that his book was but a pale reflection of what he had once been capable of.

Perhaps Keller disliked *Salander* so intensely because it misrepresents his own true feelings about the new world that was growing up about him. He had not meant to offer a bitter and disheartening picture of modern Switzerland. The second part of the novel, which was never written, would have shown things improving with the coming to maturity of Arnold Salander's generation. Arnold embodies traditional Swiss virtues, some of which had been forgotten by his father's contemporaries in the excitement of the "Gründerzeit". The book as it stands represents a gullible and susceptible middle-aged man making a not very successful career in a corrupt and demoralised society. No wonder Keller's readers thought he had grown sour as well as old, that his fundamental kindliness and warmth had left him, that he no longer saw the world suffused in golden sunlight, but in the dark chill of a winter's evening. In points of detail he remained the old Keller, but the general impression was tragically different. With characteristic brutal honesty Theodor Storm wrote: "I couldn't make head or tail of the thing!" This only confirmed what Keller knew within himself. "There is no beauty in it. It has too little poetry in it," he complained to Adolf Frey, who tried to persuade him that *Salander* was better than he thought. Keller was not in sympathy with the ideas of the new Naturalist writers, but this book might almost have been written by one of them. Storm's frank condemnation of *Salander* dealt the death blow to their friendship.

The etching which serves as frontispiece is by the painter Karl Stauffer-Bern, who was painting Keller's portrait in oils, and took a number of photographs to work from. During a pause in the sittings, while Keller slumped wearily on a little chair, he hastily drew the sketch for his etching, the only whole figure portrait we possess of Keller in old age. Arnold Böcklin drew and painted Keller, not as he was, but as he ought to be, with every device of drawing, colour and lighting effects, background and decoration calculated to show Keller as a great man and seer of visions.

Stauffer's portrait, though actually a year or two earlier than Böcklin's, shows a poor, broken down old man, with one eye half closed, not even capable of sitting in a dignified and erect posture. Keller admitted that the work was well done, but made Stauffer promise to destroy the plate, for he objected to having been caught off his guard. Stauffer did as he was asked, but only after several copies had been printed.

Although Keller took a cure in Baden during the autumn of 1886 he suffered badly from rheumatism during the following winter, and was unable to meet Johannes Brahms, who asked him in the spring to spend an evening at the *Kronenhalle*, which lay only a very short distance from his own home.

By 1887 Keller was in really poor health, although he still had occasional good days when he rose above his miseries. When one looks at Stauffer's photographs and portraits and contrasts the obvious physical degeneration that had already taken place with the clarity and charity of mind which still inform such late works as his poem for Böcklin's sixtieth birthday or his prose essay on F. Th. Vischer's work, one is astonished that he still had it in him now and then to resume the mantle of his former self.

From 1886 onwards Keller was lovingly tending Regula during her last illness. He did much of the nursing himself and went out with touching solicitude in search of delicacies which might tempt Regula to eat. However, nothing could be done for her except to give her morphia and reduce her sufferings as much as possible. After nearly two years' illness she died on 6th October 1888. A day or two after her death Keller learned of the death of Marie Melos, whom he had once loved. "Alt werden heißt viele über-leben," (To grow old means to survive many), as Goethe said. Only Keller and a few friends attended Regula's funeral; there was no religious service. As the coffin was lowered into the grave, Gottfried took a long look at it, sighed and said : "Well, that's that!"

Regula's death proved the final blow. His rheumatism grew worse and worse till he could scarcely walk. He called himself a "corrupt old beast" and longed for release from the torments of this life. The uppermost thought in his mind began to be his own death. He scarcely left the *Thaleck*, where he was looked after by a maidservant, any more. Yet even in this desolate state he remained mindful of the needs of others, and sent more than one gift of money to his old friend Johann Salomon Hegi, who had been kind to him when they were students together in Munich and who had now fallen on evil days.

Wilhelm Hertz decided that year to publish a new edition of Keller's *Collected Works* in ten volumes. Böcklin offered to prepare a new drawing of his head which could fittingly stand at the beginning of this edition. Böcklin's drawing was excellent, a striking profile, simple and memorable, a kind of ideal abstraction of the essential Keller, with all earthly dross removed and the evidence of his physical decline glossed over or omitted. The portrait sufficiently resembled its subject to be unmistakable and yet partook in some degree of the heroic. Böcklin knew perfectly well that the noble brow was often knit with unreasonable fury, that the mouth had a peevish twist, especially now that Keller was a chronic sufferer from rheumatism. But he did not think that Keller should be remembered by these features. Any old man might be like that, but Keller was magnificent and unique. In the drawing Böcklin highlights Keller's positive qualities. The curve of the brow and crown of the head is bold and arresting, the eye is alive with intelligence and penetration, the mouth is sensitive, the chin decided and the beard orderly and even rather stylised. It is a face full of character, a Keller corresponding more closely to the impression that one might form from reading his best work than to that gained from looking at his physical decrepitude.

In 1889 the parish of Neumünster requested Keller to compile a short autobiography for the parish chronicle. In this last published work Keller gives a brief account in the third person of the main events of his life. He still envisages the possibility of further creative work; he might one day write stories on the themes which he had once intended to use for dramas, so that they might at least be preserved as "shades of memory".

While Keller had rather enjoyed the public celebrations of his fiftieth and sixtieth birthdays, he decided that with the best will in the world he could not face a repetition of these celebrations on his seventieth birthday. He would go up to the mountains till the excitement was all over. On 5th July 1889 he went to Seelisberg, where he received a kind and tactful letter from C. F. Meyer:

Allow me to offer you early congratulations on your seventieth birthday, in view of my impending departure for the mountains. I do it with a thankful heart. During my rather long indisposition I had the leisure to read slowly through all your works again, and they did me a great deal of good, more than any others, by virtue of their inner serenity. I think, too, that your firm belief in the goodness of existence is the supreme significance of your writings. One could wish nothing better for you than that you should continue in your ways! Since you love the earth, the earth will also cling to you for as long as possible. As for me, I do not have the same assurance in life by a long way; and yet I will use the time remaining to me to the best of my powers. Since I have always esteemed, respected and liked you to the best of my ability, you will realise that I, too, am certain that you will preserve your good opinion of me and your goodwill towards me despite my shortcomings. And so God preserve you, Master Gottfried.

His last birthday brought an abundance of presents and letters, flowers and telegrams. A document arrived from the Swiss Federal Council recording their gratitude to the nation's great poet. They thanked him specifically for providing the national anthem, *O mein Vaterland*, and in more general terms for his other works. Henceforward foreigners would again look to Switzerland for an example as they had done before in the days of Albrecht von Haller.

While Keller languished in Seelisberg, in Zurich all the cultural agencies of Switzerland vied with one another in doing him honour. Jakob Baechtold delivered an oration in the University; although he was still not on speaking terms with Keller, he still claimed to speak with authoritative understanding of the poet.

While still in Seelisberg, Keller spoke of publicly expressing his gratitude to all his well-wishers, but he felt too unwell to do anything about saying a collective "thank you". Before he left Zurich for Baden in the autumn, two friends, Fleiner and Kißling, brought him a belated present from a group of intimates, a gold medal bearing his portrait after a drawing by Böcklin. Keller looked long at the medal, then burst into tears and exclaimed : "I can tell you, gentlemen, this is the sign that the game is up! I feel that I won't last much longer."

Adolf Frey describes Keller's journey to Baden on 13th September 1889 :

It was a fine, rather misty autumn day; the poet pointed out the beauties of the countryside to his companion when the sun broke through the delicate veils of mist and shone on the peaceful forests. He began to feel happy. The country people, whom one saw working everywhere in the fields, rejoiced his heart. In Niederweningen they made a stop, they made their way through the scraping hens, while flights of doves shimmered in the air. He thought he would like to go into a country inn again and take a rest. A little fair haired boy brought him the first bunch of grapes cut from the espalier on the house wall, of which he ate half and gave the other half back to the little giver. A kitten climbed up the old gentleman's leg, and he played with it. Meanwhile a dragoon returning from the manoeuvres had come in, and on being greeted, talked quietly and modestly about the military exercises and how it had all gone, and then took his leave to exchange his soldier's for his peasant's dress. Keller praised the modesty and solid worth of the soldier and of the people as a whole.

Although Böcklin was also in Baden, Keller often did not even appear for meals. On his return to Zurich in November, he was plainly dying.

At the beginning of 1890, he summoned Böcklin and Schneider, a professor of law, to his bedside and made his will. The principal beneficiary was the university fund of Canton Zurich, but his medal, his books and various personal effects went to the City of Zurich Library, the *Zentralbibliothek*. Half of the actual money left at his death was to go to the Federal Winkelried Foundation for Wounded Swiss Servicemen or to the widows and orphans of the fallen. "Since in my lifetime I never had the opportunity of performing my duty towards my fatherland as a soldier, I hope, and it gives me pleasure, to be able to do it a service in this way." His surviving relatives went to law in an endeavour to prove that Keller had been of unsound mind when he made the will, but there was no evidence to support this contention, and the will was allowed to stand.

Keller's last months are almost devoid of biographical material. A letter addressed to Sigmund Schott contains a few words of thanks for an article on *Der grüne Heinrich* which Schott planned to send to the *Augsburger Allgemeine Zeitung*. The letter ends: "I will not be able to put off for very long the use of a specially ordered carriage."

One of his last visitors was Conrad Ferdinand Meyer, who recorded the visit in his *Erinnerungen an Gottfried Keller*:

> I found him in bed, completely clear in his mind. He received me in a very friendly way, and spoke a great deal, but barely audibly. It was a spinning and weaving of the fantasy, of which it is not easy to communicate an impression. . . . In this fantasy he spoke, too, of a second part of his *Salander* and of a great flood, which was to conclude it. All this time he kept turning the card, by which I had announced myself, until I gently removed it from between his fingers. "I only thought," he said, "one could write a verse in the nice, white space." "Which verse?" I asked. "Well, for example," he said, "Ich dulde, ich schulde," with which he probably meant death, which we all owe to Nature. Hours passed in this way, and it became time to go away. "We will hope for a cure in the summer," I said. "Yes, yes," he laughed, "and take a country house on the Zürichberg." It was pathetic. I didn't believe in his recovery, and I'm sure he didn't either. The tears came to my eyes, and I quickly took my departure.

Frey, who called a few days later, found Keller cheerful and perfectly clear in his mind. In the course of conversation Keller said:

> Often when I lie awake at nights I seem to myself like a man already buried, over whom a high building rises, and he hears the words resounding: Ich schulde, ich dulde! I said that, too, to Conrad Ferdinand Meyer, when he was with me, whereupon he expressed the view that I had certainly done nothing wrong. But in the life of every man there are things of which he has to render an account to himself.

When not oppressed by the sense of guilt, Keller would talk at length about different subjects. Frey says he spoke with humour and detachment about his own symptoms, about literature, about topical affairs. He did not want reassurance: "When I wanted to encourage him and give him confidence, he looked

silently away over the top of the quilt, as though to say : 'Just
you talk, I know what hour the clock has struck.' "

During that last spring Hans Weber, a Federal Judge from
Lausanne, and Storm's friend Petersen visited him. Weber was
struck by the force and clarity of his fantasies. It was as if the
frontiers between this world, that of imagination and that beyond
the grave had disappeared, and as though the dying man's mind
moved easily between them all. Petersen records that Keller wept
bitterly at the thought that this would be their last time together.
Between the dream-like fantasies he would talk about everyday
things lucidly and sensibly :

Another morning he told me how two knights clad entirely
in solid, worked gold armour stood over there in front of the
little cupboard between the two windows, quite motionless,
and looked straight at him. The apparition had seemed uncanny to him because of the staring, and yet had delighted
him because of the magnificent armour. He described in detail
how the helmets had thrown the upper part of their faces into
deep shadow, and how the light had gleamed on the fine gold.
Again and again he returned to the subject of this gleaming
apparition, and could not find words to describe sufficiently
the gleaming armour. Then he finished with a laugh : "If
Pauline (the housekeeper) had seen the fellows, she would have
dragged them straight off to the pawnbroker's." One afternoon
I found the sick man sitting in an armchair beside his bed by
the window. As the sun began to set, he was silent, and his
gaze rested vaguely on the roofs shining in the sun and the tree
tops in which birds were singing. . . . After a long silence he
began to talk softly as in a dream, his gaze directed as it were
on the Infinite. He was walking in the evening sun in blessed
fields, in a strange, light-filled infinity. I listened with bated
breath in solemn mood, and felt myself drawn into the realm
of this ecstatic fancy. Then the housekeeper came into the
room and told him to get back into bed. With a lost look the
sick man turned his head, and only with hesitation did his spirit
begin to adjust itself again to reality. Then came the day of
my departure. I said in the morning that I must be away, but
the patient only looked at me with a peculiar expression and
did not reply. I returned shyly to the subject several times, but

he didn't seem to hear anything of it. And so the conversation dragged on somewhat painfully, till I got up resolutely, looked at my watch, and exclaimed: "It must be, I can stay no longer." Now I consoled him as best I could, hoped we would soon meet again when his health was restored, but he shook his head sadly, and complained about his toughness in going on living, which was keeping him from enjoying the good rest he needed. I took both his hands, looked once again, for the last time, straight into his eyes, kissed his high, pale brow, squeezed both hands once again and turned round quickly to go away. When I turned yet again close by the door, I saw a weeping countenance with sad, cheerless, almost horrified eyes, which seemed to ask if I could bring myself to leave him alone on his deathbed.

On the afternoon of 15th July 1890, Gottfried Keller died. In another four days he would have been seventy-one.

The story of Gottfried Keller's life is by no means heroic, nor does it offer much to the lover of sensation. He did not climb mountains, or storm cities or win beautiful women or gain great wealth or see visions, at least till the very end of his life. But he was a great man. More than most German writers of his generation he lived according to the dictates of a lively artistic conscience. All of his work was done with real conviction, which is what makes it good and sound and durable. He became a painter because he genuinely thought he was meant to be one, and he changed his mind only when the evidence was quite overwhelming that he was mistaken. For years he laboured under the delusion that he could become a dramatist, mastered the theory of that art, wrote some extremely intelligent dramatic criticism, and eventually reached the inescapable conclusion that he was destined for other things. His autodidacticism made it hard for him to find his true way, but it also made the edifice of his life and work solid and well tested. Now and again it led him astray, in ways which are not immediately apparent to the casual reader of his works; thus the budding poet was too easily led to imitate Heine and other poets of lesser ability, who would not have commended themselves to a more carefully schooled taste. But by the end of his long life he had learned to correct many, if not all, of the faults of character and artistic shortcomings of his youth.

The Christian reader of his works may find it rather depressing that he should so long have sworn by Feuerbach, but the conviction grows, as one reads Keller's later work, especially *Das Sinngedicht*, that Keller at last learned insights into the nature of life and the dependence of human beings on laws established by their Creator, which exceeded any formal statement of belief he felt himself able to make. If we are to believe those who saw him in his last months, he spent this time in a strange borderland of consciousness between this world and another world of golden visions, purer knowledge and peace, which he longed to enter despite the haunting fear that past shortcomings might make him unworthy of it. The ravings of a dying man, may well be the comment of many a reader at this point. But I think not. The same men who have placed on record what Keller told them of these visionary apparitions are careful to say that till within a few days of his death he was capable of talking intelligently, critically and even humorously on ordinary topics. They say, however, that for much of the time he was withdrawn and abstracted, as though greater matters were engaging his attention. It is no doubt idle to speculate on what Keller experienced as he lay dying in the house *Zum Thaleck*, but I like to think that in those long and often lonely days Keller was being led nearer to the light of reality than he had ever been during his lifetime, that the tranquillity of expression of which Frey spoke after his last visit to the dying Keller mirrored more than the exhaustion of one who had given up the struggle. His life's story is a record of honest effort and hard-won conquest of self, and if not spectacular it is at least the story of a man who lived vigorously, generously and fully. The burning intellectual questions of his day successively engaged his attention, and where he does not answer them definitively he does at least formulate them clearly and put forward constructive suggestions towards their solution. The great men of his age were proud to number him among their friends, and his life, as well as his works, deserves to be remembered and as far as possible understood.

PART II

KELLER'S WORKS

The young Keller lying down.

Pencil drawing by J. S. Hegi, Munich, 1840

Keller in middle age.

Oil painting by Franz Buchser, 1872

CHAPTER ONE

THE LYRIC POET

POETRY, if we may believe Lascelles Abercrombie, is the "translation of experience into language", a statement which can easily be shown to be true of Keller. The whole man, and his whole life, are mirrored in his poetry. Not only the healthy and positive aspects of his personality and his more enjoyable and edifying experiences—young love, his ever open eye for beauty, his generous vision of a better Switzerland, his concern for truth, his keen awareness of the transience of life, his fundamental good will and interest in the cause of humanity, but also his diffidence, his petulance, his days of doubt and disillusionment concerning his poetic calling, his prejudices and his rancour come across to the reader of his verses. Storm, who in general perhaps underestimated Keller as a lyric poet, rightly observed of his poetry :

> With this book one wanders through your life; one sees how you have everywhere participated and yet have everywhere remained the same undivided and in a certain sense lonely man.

The book in question was Keller's *Gesammelte Gedichte* (*Collected Poems*) of 1883. Keller realised that this collection contained bad as well as good work, but he had considered that it would be insincere and misleading to publish only a selection of his best poems in old age. Accordingly, this 1883 collection, though not comprehensive, very fully represents Keller's verse of all periods. Some early poems have been edited and even considerably modified, but in most cases the original remains recognisable from the point of view of content, language, image and metre.

Keller published poetry long before he published prose, and a high proportion of his early work is included in the first section of the *Collected Poems*, the *Buch der Natur*. He writes of his love of nature in all its aspects, his predilection for night—which is partially at least inherited from his romantic predecessors—his familiarity with peasant lore and customs in Canton Zurich. Through all the poetry shines an intense sympathy with every created thing, whether person, animal, plant or object. It may be a drunken beggar victimised by children or a moth attracted by the candle flame, or the child who has died at a tender age; Keller to some extent identifies himself with them all, they mean something to him. Although he does not deal with the minutiae of nature so often as Annette von Droste-Hülshoff, for instance, he is strongly aware of the times of day and seasons of the year and the various fulfilments and problems which they bring. Not surprisingly for a poet who lived most of his life in Canton Zurich, where the weather can change violently and unexpectedly, many poems are concerned with the weather, and thunderstorms in particular seem to have made a lively impression on him.

In the earliest poems, written before Keller abandoned his Christian faith, there are occasional religious echoes; a number of poems suggest pantheistic leanings, then for a time Keller turns sharply away from the Christian faith, although in general he seems to distinguish between true religion which must be private and personal, and what he regards as the institutionalised pretence of the church. In several early poems (e.g. *Nachtfahrer, Apostatenmarsch*) he attacks Christian priests, whom he regards as greedy predators. As an older man Keller might not have felt so strongly on this subject, but he considered it proper to include several such poems for the record in his *Gesammelte Gedichte*.

Occasionally the poet is beset by irrational fears or by feelings of rebellion against the whole natural order and by the thought that the whole of his existence is futile. Yet these moods are regularly banished by the coming of daytime or a change in the weather. Like Goethe, Keller was very sensitive to weather, light and darkness and atmospheric conditions. The *Abendlied an die Natur* resumes his whole faith in the fundamental beneficence of the natural order, his almost physical awareness that Nature, the Universal Mother, will protect and guide him.

In a late poem, *Abend auf Golgatha*, Keller, the life-long agnostic, is suddenly overcome by the pathos of imagining Christ on the cross, with a moth settling for a moment on His gleaming white shoulder. The language of this particular poem, "Redeemer", "Lord", "Cross", "Creator", "the woman whom He created for His own mother", must make us at least wonder whether Keller was as loyal a pupil of Feuerbach in 1881 as he had been in 1848. Perhaps he was mainly concerned with the pictorial quality of the scene, but such concern scarcely explains his use of words so pregnant with theological implications. It seems conceivable that by this time Keller had made the reassessment of his religious position which as long ago as 1849 he had said he might feel obliged to make.

The various poems about night show how night enlarges the poet's heart and renders him sensitive to outside impressions. When his natural piety is thus aroused Keller can feel for other people and also respond to every gentle stimulus, whether of imaginative compassion, of religion or of external nature. Not all these poems are of uniform excellence, but a poem like *Unter Sternen* strikes us at once as a work expressing the poet's joyful and triumphant feeling of oneness with all creation in this for him sacred moment. *Nachtfalter* scarcely deserved inclusion on aesthetic grounds; however, it records a violently anti-clerical phase in Keller's inner development. *Trost der Kreatur* testifies to the poet's awareness of the variety and beauty of the world of nature as well as to his imaginative sympathy. Sometimes among these poems of times and seasons the poetic level is not sustained. For instance, the enchanting first stanza of *Morgen* is followed by a political second stanza in rather disappointing taste. Perhaps because this sort of thing happens fairly frequently, the occasional perfect poem appears all the more valuable.

The *Abendlied an die Natur* contains Keller's poetic confession of faith. The beautiful green world, the enchantment of daylight, the brilliance of flowers and sunshine, even the eternal repose of death are all aspects of Nature's kindly provision for man. Nature has in the past healed him from the tormenting passions of love and hatred, and to nature he will again turn at the last when his course is run. Although the *Abendlied an die Natur* is not formally remarkable, the obvious strength and sincerity of the poet's feeling combine to make it one of his best known and best loved poems.

Many poems bear witness to the ephemerality of life and the swiftness of time's passing. Certainly the most familiar and well-loved such poem is *Abendlied*. When Keller reflects that death approaches, this means for a man like him, who has always laid stress on *seeing* things, that his eyes will be darkened for ever. However, the end is not yet, and he bids his eyes absorb all they can of the golden beauty of the world. This poem, with its arresting opening, its caressing diminutives, its forceful statement of impending darkness, and the haunting image of the soul removing heavy shoes and lying down to rest in a coffin, has caught many a reader's imagination, no doubt because it so perfectly expresses the almost universal desire to enjoy life while one may, since its splendour and abundance do not last for ever.

While it would be idle to pretend that Keller is among the most graceful or eloquent of German poets, poems like *Am fließenden Wasser* show that he is on occasion capable of a sureness and lightness of touch which reveal him as one of Goethe's most natural successors among nineteenth-century poets. The second short poem of the three tells of an unexpected moment of insight; the poet has a presentiment, a revelation of the mysteries of nature, a brief awareness of the why and wherefore, the fullness and certainty of existence. It is a vision like those of Goethe or Wordsworth, and it vanishes almost before it has come. We seldom think of Keller as a poet of this kind, and only a tiny proportion of his poetry is in this vein. However, every now and again we come upon such confirmation that Keller was sometimes a seer of visions.

Winternacht dates from 1851 or earlier. The poet is standing on the frozen surface of a lake in the midst of a snow-covered landscape. No sound, no movement, Nature paralysed and seemingly dead. From the depths of the lake rises a tree, whose top freezes in the ice that covers the lake. The nixie climbs up its branches, peers through the green ice:

> I stood there on the thin glass that separated the black depths from me; close beneath my feet I saw her white beauty limb by limb. With muffled cries of distress she groped here and there on the hard covering. I shall never forget her hard countenance. Always, always, it will remain in my mind.

Nature, generally so genial and comforting, here presents herself in a completely different garb to the poet. Cold, indifferent, seemingly even hostile, she makes no response at all to him. When that monstrous tree seems to rise towards the frozen surface, he feels unnerved, as though the power that holds all Nature in thrall were threatening him. Now the dark, elemental, seemingly negative power assumes living shape; as the nixie climbs up the branches of the ghostly tree, the poet's heart stands still with fear. Suddenly he becomes aware that the apparition is not altogether evil and terrifying. He realises as he recovers from his panic that the nixie is a prisoner below the ice, frantically groping for an outlet. The alarming figure has become beautiful and pathetic; it holds no more terrors for him. How do we interpret this arresting image? Perhaps the nixie should be taken as a symbol of the hidden and imprisoned forces of Nature, preparing below the ice for the renewal of spring. This explanation does not seem to me too simple, and to see in the poem evidence of "erschütternder, bedräuender Erfahrungen"* is to read more into the poem than Keller intended. Possibly the chill and cheerless winter is meant also as a symbol of poetic stagnation, which might well induce a feeling of horror and panic in Keller. The poem is generally agreed to be one of Keller's most hauntingly beautiful.

The love poems of *Erstes Lieben* were mostly inspired by Keller's attachment to Henriette Keller when he was scarcely more than a schoolboy. *Jugendgedenken* introduces them gracefully and reflectively. Despite Keller's later scathing dismissal of his early love poetry in his autobiography, the poems have an unmistakable ring of youthful idealism and sincerity. The innocence and freshness of the first poems and the pathos of the later ones telling of Henriette's early death do not fail to make their impact. The heartbroken tone of some images remains in the memory:

> O Erde, du gedrängtes Meer
> Unzähliger Gräberwogen,
> Wie viele Schifflein kummerschwer
> Hast du hinuntergezogen. . . .

It may seem almost like a desecration for the elderly Keller, revising his early work for the *Gesammelte Gedichte* of 1883, to have included *Die Entschwundene*, inspired in all likelihood by his last love, Luise Scheidegger, among the poems which record his first love. However, the reader would not notice the poem as out of place; indeed, from all internal evidence, it might well

* H. Böschenstein, *Gottfried Keller*, Berne, 1948, p. 147.

have originated from the same experience as the other poems of *Erstes Lieben*. This is one of the cases where the purely aesthetic judgement of appropriateness must be at variance with general human considerations of tact and the fitness of things. In the deeper sense that the universal appeal of poetry must stem from a representation of the particular, personal incident, which renders that incident generally accessible and universally comprehensible, we must disregard origins altogether and consider only the end product. The early love poems and *Die Entschwundene* stem from sufficiently similar experiences of the poet to belong together as art. What is of interest to the reader is not whose death or deaths affected the poet in these poems, but how he as an artist has reacted to the loss of a loved one.

In the remaining sections of the book the proportion of ballast to good poetry becomes higher. While the verse reflects Keller's life and personality accurately, with his political fervour, his early hatred of the Jesuits, his pleasure in the joys of the table, his generous admiration for Schiller, the special appeal of childhood for him, his self-identification with the common man at times of national rejoicing, and his sense of being at home in the world, it would be wrong to think of him as a major poet but for the *Buch der Nature*. The cycle of poems entitled *Lebendig begraben* is in poor taste, an unsavoury exercise in the macabre, which cannot possibly have appealed to many readers. The whole conception of the cycle reflects a primitive, childish fear of the poet, and several lines reach a level of tastelessness and sheer ugliness which can seldom have been surpassed. The drunken sacristan and his wife, with "Ihr Katzmiaulen und sein Mondsgebelle", walking over the unfortunate victim's grave, are an example of this kind of unsophisticated crudity. Certainly in Heine and other romantic poets Keller might have found precedents for this disastrous exercise, but one cannot really plead anything in mitigation of this poem.

Feuer-Idylle, the following cycle, represents a distinct improvement. It is interesting as an early example of a work in which the epic writer is beginning to shine through. Despite the rather schoolboyish humour of the third and fourth stanzas and the moralising tone later on, the story of the conflagration is well told, and individual *motifs*, such as the burning of the apple-tree or the statuette at the fountain, are most effectively introduced.

Der Apotheker von Chamounix, a witty parody of the style of Heine's *Romanzero*, has even today a certain appeal. The edge of the satire is not blunted by Keller's evident sympathy for the little creatures of the field in his description of the marmots at play.

Other poems were inspired by the Rhine, which especially reminded Keller that he owed part of his education and cultural background to Germany. This comes across very clearly in the fifth stanza of *Gegenüber*. Other poems bear witness to Keller's keen interest in the affairs of his canton and of Switzerland as a whole. The most famous of these is certainly *An das Vaterland*, which has become the Swiss national anthem. The *Prolog zur Schillerfeier* in Bern, written for the 1859 Schiller Centenary, is a good example of Keller's occasional poems, but the level of these is by no means uniformly high, as can be seen in the doggerel verses *An Frau Ida Freiligrath* (1846), written as an entry in her autograph album. A poem like *Das Schwurgericht*, telling of an inexplicable act of violence by an older boy against a young child, is not very successful, because of the essentially prosaic nature of its inspiration, no doubt.

Keller's poetry includes work in a considerable variety of metres and rhythms. Generally speaking he succeeds best where he is not too ambitious. His sonnets show distinct signs of laboured composition. He did not take naturally to this rigorous and demanding form. Particularly in his earlier work, which of course also includes some of his best poetry, there are awkward and jarring lines, contrived rhymes and lapses from good taste. Later in life, however, he learned to handle even complicated metres with considerable skill and finesse. Even admirers of Keller's verse would admit that on the whole despite many good images and some effective choice of vocabulary he does not use rhythms and metres with much originality or distinction. His strength as a lyric poet lies in the genuineness of his feeling and the complete integrity of his thought.

The *Collected Poems* include some very good poetry. Keller's verse reflects his whole personality, his gentleness, kindness and love of beauty, as well as his irascibility, roughness, intolerance and bigotry. His poetry reveals some prejudices and misconceptions, but there remains when one discounts the trivial and the ephemeral an impressive small collection of good poems. Keller had moments of being admittted nearer than most men to the sources of light and truth, and his nature was always capable of truly generous impulses. No German poet before him or since has taken such delight in colour. He loves bright light and strong shadow, brilliant greens and reds with yellow or golden sunlight. He always remains a painter in his evocation of sharply defined scenes. Not for him the vague, transcendental aspirations of some romantic poets; his verse is firmly based on experience. The romanticism which looks backwards to a past idyllic age contrasted with a miserable and sordid present does not appeal to him. Poetry, far from being antagonistic to human progress, should accompany, even herald it; it must never be used as a form of escapism. Contradictions abound in Keller's life and poetry, but he was a genuine poet. Despite all the obstacles created by his own nature and external circumstances Keller consistently strove to be faithful to his artistic ideals. Outwardly he was a rough diamond, but his poems show that he loved little children and the humblest animals for their own sake and that he respected and revered all the works of creation, despite his mistrust of religious dogma. His creative imagination was constantly at work upon the raw material of experience, transforming and illuminating it for his readers' benefit. His poems represent part of the artistic deposit of a life most fully lived; their creator was a whole, noble and vigorous personality.

CHAPTER TWO

DER GRÜNE HEINRICH

I

Genesis

IN a diary entry of 8th July 1843 Keller claims that, while he has not written down any record of his experiences in Munich, his financial anxieties and the bright Bohemian world of the young artists remain clear in his memory:

> ... if one day I were to step out of my own skin, and, as a second self, were to seek out my own original self in the chamber of his heart and contemplate him, if I were to write the story of my youth, then, although up till now I have never kept a diary, and earlier, six years ago now, only occasionally, but very seldom, jotted down single, separate events of the outer and inner world, yet I would succeed quite well in the attempt.

The possibility of salvaging something from those lost years had at least crossed his mind, although he had not then decided to make them the basis of a novel. He merely wished to preserve in lasting form some traces of the experiences which had helped to mould his character. Life had already provided him with countless *motifs* which would have poetic value if only he could remember them; he did not like to think of all this material, some of which might possess a more than personal significance, being wasted.

The autobiography of 1876 gives somewhat fuller information about the kind of book he had in mind:

> All sorts of distress I had endured, and the anxiety which I had caused my mother, without my having a good goal in prospect, occupied my thoughts and my conscience, till my brooding developed into the resolve to write a sad little novel

about the tragic breaking short of a young artist's career, which destroyed both mother and son. This was as far as I know the first artistic plan which I consciously adopted, and I was about twenty-three years old. Before my mind's eye hovered the image of an elegiac and lyrical book with bright episodes and a cypress-dark ending, in which everybody would be buried.

For a year or two the project was pushed into the background by political excitements and by Keller's discovery that he possessed some lyrical talent. After completing the *Gedichte* he returned to his novel and even wrote down a part of it. Although he maintained that the work would soon be finished, Keller often said that a work was complete, or all but complete, when he merely had the plan ready in his head. This was almost certainly the case with *Der grüne Heinrich* before he went to Heidelberg in the autumn of 1848. In the following winter Feuerbach's philosophy engaged all his attention, and afterwards he found it necessary to revise what he had written in the light of this important intellectual experience. As well as religious re-adjustments Keller now wished to make some general changes of emphasis. Heinrich's humanity now becomes central and the fact of his being an artist almost incidental. Despite his original intention of keeping the chapters on Heinrich's early life within strict bounds, this part of the work began to assume large dimensions. When his publisher asked for a summary of the contents, Keller replied :

> The moral of my book is that he who cannot manage to keep his personal and family affairs in a proper state is also incapable of occupying an effective position in society...
> My hero is a talented and lively young man, who goes out into the world, full of enthusiasm for everything that is good and beautiful, to lay the foundations of his destiny, his future fortunes. He regards everything with an open, clear eye, and being a charming, vivacious young man, falls in with all kinds of people, makes friendships which help to round off his character and gives grounds for great hopes. But when the time comes near, when he has to adjust himself to a firm, disciplined course of action, practical activity and self-control, he is completely lacking. He does not advance beyond fine words, indulges in a fantastically vegetative, passive, inept and unsettled

existence. In this way he brings himself and his relatives to a state of extreme misery, while less gifted but more practical natures among his acquaintance, who were inferior to him, succeed and leave him standing. He gets into the most extravagantly miserable situation, cut off from his own people and quite deserted. Then suddenly his destiny takes a more favourable turn; he finds good fortune and a circle of noble people, recovers, confirms his principles and begins a new and purer way of life, at the end of which a fair goal beckons him on. And so he pulls himself together, hastens with golden hopes homewards, to seek out his old mother, from whom he has heard nothing for a long time, just as she has heard nothing from him. Before the gates of his native town he comes upon her funeral procession, joins the mourners in the churchyard, and listens to how the parson attributes the death of the poor and deserted woman to her prodigal son who still tarries abroad.

Since he is fundamentally an honourable and noble character, it is impossible for him now to take up a happy and influential position in society on the ruins of the family life he has destroyed. The tie, which unites him backwards with humanity, seems to have been bloodily and criminally cut, and for that reason he cannot catch hold of the loose half of it that leads forwards, and this brings about his death, too. This is made the more tragic, because a sound, good love affair is broken off, which had dawned for him after earlier, rather sickly entanglements. A subsidiary trait in his character is a certain enlightened, rational religiosity, a nebulous enthusiasm, which amounts to this, that in unjustified trust in a God, on whom he only half believes, he expects God spectacularly to solve all his difficulties and good fortune to descend on him from heaven. In this regard the moral of the book is: God helps those who help themselves! and that it is more healthy to hope for nothing and to do the best one possibly can than to become lost in religious enthusiasm and do nothing.

Since, as I said before, the book is a product of experience, except for the unhappy catastrophe at the end, I hope that I can flatter myself that it will be no shallow and tendentious work. I do not think there is a page in it which has not been directly lived and felt.

Keller insisted that Vieweg should begin printing the book immediately, since he imagined he could complete it very quickly. Volume I was printed by the autumn of 1851; volume II followed after a year and a half; by November 1853 volume III was ready, but Keller now planned a fourth volume. Vieweg refused to hold the book back any longer, and published the first three volumes in the autumn of 1853. Keller did not deliver the last instalment of manuscript till the spring of 1855, by which time Vieweg had abandoned hope of ever seeing it. By mid-May 1855 the final volume reached the booksellers.

The 1876 *Autobiography* tells a little more about Keller's work on the novel after leaving Zurich for Heidelberg in 1848:

> On these journeys I again took up the novel I had earlier begun; its title, *Der grüne Heinrich*, was already in existence. I still intended writing only one volume of moderate length; but as I progressed, I had the idea of inserting the early history of the hero or rather non-hero as an autobiography, leaning heavily on personal experience and my own feelings. In process of doing this I got so involved in story-telling that the book ran to four volumes and became quite formless. The reason for this was that I took a quite irresistible pleasure at my more advanced time of life in inventing a life's morning that I had not lived through, or, to be more precise, in allowing the scanty seeds and bare beginnings to achieve full poetic growth to my private delight. Yet the actual childhood, even the anecdotal part, is as good as true, only here and there, in a last attack of the imitative impulse, tinged with a touch of Rousseau's confessional acerbity, although not too sharply.... On the other hand, Heinrich's more mature youth is for the greater part extensively supplemented by the play of imagination, and in particular, the two women are inventions, and contrasts, such as oppose one another in awakening adult life.

At last, however, the book had to come to an end. The publisher, who had complained about the unexpected expansion and my slow progress with it, ended by taking an interest in the queer hero, and begged, as a representative of his customers, for Heinrich's life. But here I stuck pedantically to my original plan, without, however, achieving a unified and harmonious form. The execution I had decided on before was carried out, partly with a view to making a thorough settlement of accounts, partly from a melancholy whim. I also regarded the matter lightly, inasmuch as I thought people would regard the so-called novel as a book, in which there were all kinds of readable things, just as they put up with dramas intended to be read. And so *Der grüne Heinrich* was duly buried.

While writing the later part of the novel Keller found that much of the earlier part fell short of the standards he now recognised. A letter to Varnhagen speaks of "the really tragic fate of having to send a doubtful work out into the world when one has already within one's mind a more perfect image of the work as it ought to be". From the beginning some critics thought that the whole narrative should have been in the first person rather than partly in the first and partly in the third person, but Keller was too preoccupied with other work to consider revision of *Der grüne Heinrich* at this stage; in any case, many copies of the original edition remained unsold.

Emil Kuh provided the final incentive to revise *Der grüne Heinrich* in a newspaper article (*Neue Freie Presse*, Vienna, 7th January 1871). By this time Keller agreed with his critics that the whole story required to be told in the first person. At Theodor Storm's suggestion the revised work starts off with Heinrich's childhood; in the original version Heinrich's departure from home and arrival at the *Kunststadt* came first. Keller had admitted in the preface to the three volumes published in 1853 that the story of Heinrich's youth was too long to represent a mere episode in the book but had hoped that the unity of content connecting the autobiography with what preceded and followed it would compensate for the formal disunity of the book.

Most of the original readers considered that Heinrich's death was arbitrary and insufficiently motivated. There was no reason why he should not live on, even though he had a bad conscience about neglecting his mother. The happy inspiration of letting Judith come back into Heinrich's life may have been suggested by Keller's own late friendship with Marie Melos, whom he had loved in his youth. The awkward framework which marred the 1854–55 version was dropped completely, and the whole story is now told by Heinrich Lee in the first person.

Keller did not begin the revision till 1878, and he made rapid progress with the first part of the book. The later part, however, took longer. The task was completed in September 1880, and the *Neue Ausgabe* appeared in full that autumn. Keller considered changing the title to *Heinrich Lee*, but in the end decided to stick to the old title. The two further editions published in Keller's lifetime contain no changes of substance.

II

The Plot

The title of this section is really a misnomer, for the book has no plot, being merely the life story, told in the first person, of Heinrich Lee. Heinrich is supposed to be telling of his own earlier life from his standpoint as a middle-aged civil servant living in contemplative solitude in a Swiss mountain village.

Book I introduces Heinrich's father, a clever, enterprising and resourceful young master builder who has returned from extensive travels in Germany to set up in business in the cantonal capital. He dies young, leaving his widow with little more than the house in which she and Heinrich live. Frau Lee is after the hero himself the principal character of Book I. Although fundamentally a rather austere person she loves her son so much that she somewhat spoils him. Heinrich remembers his father with respect and affection :

> Although I preserve within my mind only the dimmest recollection of his outward appearance, a bright, clear picture of his inner nature has formed itself within me, and this noble image has become for me a part of the great Infinite, towards which my ultimate thoughts lead me back and beneath whose protection I believe I walk.

Heinrich tells of his first childish attempts to understand the idea of God and of his successive interpretations of his mother's dark saying : God is a spirit.

At first he dislikes school and finds that his teachers regard him with suspicion, largely because of their inability to project themselves into the situation of a very small boy. As time passes he becomes reconciled to school, and gradually his horizons widen as he gets to know the other families of the neighbourhood. He makes devastatingly accurate observations concerning the food in the neighbours' houses:

> Every housewife gives to the food she prepares, even when the recipes are exactly alike, a special taste in the preparation, which corresponds to her character ... one gets to know the housewife accurately from the few principal dishes of the bourgeoisie; I for my part, as an early connoisseur, was able to tell by instinct from just tasting a clear meat soup, how I had to behave towards the person who made it.

When Frau Lee tries to make Heinrich say grace at mealtimes he cannot bring himself to do so. His difficulties over this religious exercise remind him of the story of the witch child Meretlein. He proceeds to relate this story as an exemplary instance of the tragic results which can ensue from unintelligent handling and unsympathetic teaching of a child, particularly in religious matters. Meretlein's sad fate shows what might have befallen Heinrich if he had been less well balanced, or had his tormentors been a degree more malevolent.

After the story of Meret we hear about Frau Margret and Vater Jakoblein who kept a junk shop in the house opposite Frau Lee's. Heinrich tells of the magic which the curiously stocked shop used to represent for him and gives a lively picture of the shrewd but illiterate old woman and her greedy but ineffectual husband. Though Jakoblein had longed for his wife's death so that he could enjoy her money, he finds when she does die that he is completely lost without her; fortunately for him her money lasts just long enough to see him to his grave.

Heinrich relates how at one stage he experienced an extraordinary temptation to abuse God and call Him by foul names, such as he might have heard older boys using in the street. The temptation used to grow on him till it could no longer be resisted, and he would utter the dreadful blasphemy in great haste under his breath, telling God in the next moment that he did not mean it and that it must not be allowed to count against him. Yet, as soon as he realised that he had not been punished for the sin, he would do it again until the curious visitation left him.

Heinrich once made false accusations against some older boys. A visitor to the house having heard him use bad language, his mother asked him where he had heard such expressions. He immediately named four older boys whom he scarcely knew and who, to the best of his knowledge, had never used the words in their lives. At an inquiry held by the school authorities, Heinrich gave such a full and circumstantial account of the boys' behaviour on the occasion in question that their protestations of innocence went unheeded and they were harshly punished at school as well as at home. Heinrich said he was not ashamed of what he had done; he rejoiced when his invention received corroboration through the ready credulity of his mother and teachers. Later on, he naturally felt deep shame at the recollection of this episode; in due course he was forgiven by all the other boys concerned except one:

> With the deepest hatred he used to walk past me, and when he cast offensive glances in my direction, I could not return them, for the early injustice lay heavy upon me and neither of us could forget it.

Heinrich hated learning the catechism:

> A little book full of wooden, bloodless questions and answers, torn from the life of the biblical scriptures and suitable for exercising the dry intelligence of aged and petrified people, it had to be learned by heart during the seemingly endless years of youth, mulled over again and again and repeated in an incomprehensible dialogue.

Although at this stage Heinrich found school generally entertaining and informative, he retained painful memories of school justice, which tended to be both too severe and too humiliating for the wrongdoer as well as to have a bad effect on those children who might have committed a like offence to that of the victim but had not been found out. He specifically mentions the practice of making boys go to another room, remove their trousers and get beaten, and he objects to making girls sit in some conspicuous place with a placard round their necks. These punishments are too degrading for the victim and create an altogether unwarranted feeling of self-righteousness in those lucky enough to have escaped.

Heinrich was an inventive and resourceful child, who had to spend much time on his own, which encouraged his naturally lively imagination. As he grew older he played at "theatres" with other children. Once a professional theatrical company visited Heinrich's native town, and by all possible means he and his companions contrived to see their performances, which were given in a local hotel. One day he had the good fortune to be co-opted into playing the part of a monkey in the witch's kitchen scene of Faust Part I; he was so excited and so rapt up in the performance that he allowed himself to be locked into the theatre building; he spent the last part of the night curled up at the feet of the actress who had played the part of Gretchen. This episode represented a highlight of Heinrich's boyhood and he was already much preoccupied with the idea of appearance and reality in the actor's life. He was fascinated by the way in which the actors would interrupt their doings to play a part on the stage for a while, then return and continue, without batting an eyelid, with what they had been doing or saying before going on the stage. The theatre attracted him enormously, and his own brief excursion on the stage remained a treasured memory; every detail of that evening was indelibly implanted in his mind.

Throughout his childhood Heinrich had to combat a tendency towards lying and stealing. He never adopts a tone of moral indignation about his own early shortcomings. He relates them with fairness and detachment, and simply wonders at his own past conduct. Never for a moment does he seem to consider the possibility that he might have become a complete reprobate. He merely learned honesty from the painful and humiliating consequences of those early lapses, just as his natural revulsion against his own cruelty taught him in the end to be kind to animals.

On the other hand Heinrich early became aware of the existence of real wickedness in the world. The juvenile usurer Meierlein inveigles Heinrich into a fairly substantial debt which he records neatly in a little account book. Various schoolboy feats are made the subject of bets and dares, which Heinrich always loses and Meierlein always wins. When Heinrich cannot pay his dues, Meierlein goes to Frau Lee to complain about her son's indebtedness to him. Frau Lee sends him away empty-handed as does also a schoolmaster whose assistance Meierlein invokes. After this Meierlein hates Heinrich with a bitter, enduring hatred, so that Heinrich genuinely rejoices years later when his enemy is killed in an accident. The calculating avarice that could entice another child into debt and bear him a grudge when he could not have the debt acknowledged is felt by Keller to be a far worse fault of character than his clumsy dishonesties, which were generally caused only by his vanity.

Shortly after the Meierlein episode Heinrich was expelled from school. He compares his expulsion to the beheading of a criminal, which scarcely seems a reasonable comparison. He considered that he had been made a scapegoat and that the real culprits involved in the tormenting of an ineffectual schoolmaster had been allowed to go scotfree. He was now sent for a time to live in his uncle's house in the country. Everyone who has read *Der grüne Heinrich* attentively remembers the famous lines describing the first night which he spent in his uncle's parsonage:

> Not till late in the night did I lie down in bed beneath the open window; the water rushed past close below it, on the other side of the stream a mill clattered, a majestic thunderstorm made its way through the valley, the rain sounded like music and the wind in the forests of the nearby mountains like singing; and breathing the cool, refreshing air I fell asleep so to speak on the breast of mighty Nature.

At about this time Heinrich decided to become a landscape painter. Although he had been only moderately promising in the art class at school he now began to spend all his time drawing and painting. The agreeable rural setting of his uncle's house provided him with plenty of picturesque *motifs* for his painting.

All Heinrich's relatives in the village, his boy and girl cousins, his grandmother and aunts were proud to claim acquaintance with him. His cousin Judith, a beautiful young widow of twenty-two first appears coming from the garden bearing an abundance of fruit and flowers, like a symbol of Nature full of vigour, health and fertility. She characteristically offers Heinrich a drink of milk, which he at first refuses; then she presses him to drink it, which he does at a single draught, staring at her the while.

With his cousins Heinrich visits an elderly schoolmaster and his daughter who live on the other side of the hill. Anna is a pretty, pale girl a little younger than Heinrich himself. The schoolmaster warns Heinrich against allowing himself to be permanently embittered by his expulsion from school; he must regard this experience as a plain indication "that every deviation from the good will revenge itself more perceptibly on you than on others". Meanwhile, Anna makes a strong impression on Heinrich :

> I was happy and cheerful beside the charming girl, although I did not look at her; only it gave me a pleasant thrill, when every now and again her voice was heard.

Book Two of *Der grüne Heinrich* is dominated by two main themes, Heinrich's choice of a profession and his awakening to love. His mother's doubts and the opposition of her advisers only make him the more determined to become a painter. He refuses to be tied down to some safe trade or profession which would not fulfil the artistic and creative side of his nature.

Meanwhile Heinrich sees Anna regularly and the two children become very fond of one another. Their innocent awakening love does not seek any physical expression. Anna's gentle spirituality appeals strongly to one side of Heinrich's nature. He is even prepared to sit beside her by the hour shelling beans, and his highest happiness is to be allowed to accompany her from her home to his uncle's house, where Anna often goes to see her cousins. His love for Anna reaches a climax during the open-air performance of *Wilhelm Tell* by the village people, and yet even on this occasion his devotion to Anna is not undivided.

Side by side with this relationship goes an awakening coarser passion for the physically very desirable Judith, who finds Heinrich's company a welcome distraction. During Heinrich's frequent visits to Judith they exchange caresses and on at least one occasion Judith only just refrains from seducing him. Heinrich suffers torments of conscience on Anna's account, although no word of love has yet been spoken between Anna and himself.

The conflict in Heinrich's mind between the two women dominates his adolescence. Anna knows nothing of his secret visits to Judith and Judith knows that she will see no more of Heinrich if she tries to make him break with Anna. Indeed, Heinrich tells her that Anna satisfies quite different needs of his nature which she could never satisfy. Judith has something of the savage beauty and ruthlessness of Nature which she symbolises. Anna has delicate health and the refinement of appearance and behaviour that sometimes accompany it. After the performance of *Tell* Heinrich visits Judith, exchanges caresses, and then in a sudden access of shame decides that he is being unfair to Anna :

I felt my being divided into two parts, and would have liked to hide from Anna with Judith, and from Judith with Anna. But I swore never to go to Judith again or to break my vow, for I felt a boundless pity for Anna, who I know was sleeping so peacefully in the grey, damp depths at my feet.

Book Two also tells of the instruction leading up to his confirmation and his reluctance to accept the dogma of the church, though he found himself obliged to go through with the outward form of the ceremony if he did not wish to draw attention to himself. Heinrich lays considerable stress on his inability to derive any satisfaction from the traditional forms of Swiss Protestant religious practice, although he does not consider himself an irreligious person.

By the beginning of Book Three Heinrich enters upon a new phase of life with his apprenticeship to an engraver and Christmas card artist. He soon learns all that this man can teach him. A more promising relationship with a much superior teacher is cut short by the sudden departure of the teacher, who takes with him an advance of fees paid by Heinrich's mother.

Early in this book Heinrich learns that Anna has been unwell and has been under medical care. Her father seems very concerned about her, and Heinrich returns with them to his village, where he meets Judith. She tries to tell him how serious Anna's illness is but Heinrich is unwilling to believe her. During the remainder of his visit he continues to see Judith every day; in spite of himself he cannot help wanting to see her, although it makes him feel disloyal to Anna to do so. Both of them now realise that Anna will die soon; they read together Ariosto's *Orlando furioso* and Heinrich explains the work to her.

Anna's death, long expected, comes quite suddenly in the end. The description of the family's mourning and of her funeral forms one of the most affecting chapters of the book. It is related with a considerable wealth of detail, including Heinrich's own careful observations on his own reactions. At this point Judith might have been expected to come into her own, but she goes abroad.

After completing his military training Heinrich resolves to go to Munich to try to get a proper grounding in landscape painting. At first his guardians oppose the venture but in the end they allow him to encash his litle patrimony and Heinrich leaves home.

As well as some books and painting materials he takes with him a skull which he had picked up in a churchyard and had used for his first studies in human anatomy. In the *Kunststadt* he used the skull as a tobacco-jar long after it had ceased to be an object of scientific curiosity. Near the place where it was found stood a gravestone bearing the name Albertus Zwiehan (the surname might be translated as Doublejohn). Heinrich liked to imagine the skull had come from Zwiehan's grave, especially when he discovered from a family chronicle that Albertus had lived a tragic and interesting life and had lost his birthright because of his vacillations between two women. Heinrich feels that this story has some relevance to his own situation. However, there is the world of difference between the firm, tactful progress through life of a Heinrich Lee, who in his most wrongheaded moments is never shallow or fickle, and the mercurial infatuations of an Albertus Zwiehan.

The high hopes with which Heinrich comes to the *Kunststadt* quickly prove unfounded. Landscape painting has become unfashionable, and he cannot find a teacher; even if he could, he could not afford to pay him. Before he realises the hopelessness of his situation he has spent a large part of his inheritance, and a reluctance to confess failure compels him to struggle on against impossible odds. All his attempts to sell his paintings misfire, yet he does not draw the obvious conclusion and decide to cut his losses.

Two good friends save the situation from being completely intolerable. Erikson, though a talented and charming man, is not a great painter. A shipowner's son from the north, he has expensive tastes which the reduced state of his family fortunes would not allow him to indulge if he were not able to supplement his income from the proceeds of his paintings, agreeable, quickly produced decorative trifles.

Lys is a more complicated personality, whose paintings bear the stamp of true genius. Heinrich admires him, but mistrusts his ruthlessness and selfishness. Especially he is disturbed by Lys' attitude to women, whom he regards as the natural enemies of man, an attitude which does not debar him from enjoying their favours as long as he can avoid lasting commitments. During the Carnival celebrations at Shrovetide Heinrich quarrels violently with Lys because his friend has behaved discourteously towards a girl whom he is supposed to be escorting. Lys angrily challenges Heinrich to a duel, and they meet with their seconds the following morning, but in the cold dawn they decide not to fight, and each goes his own way.

Instead of painting from Nature Heinrich often sat at home and hatched out all kinds of improbable and grotesque fancies—gnarled and knotted trees, great, unsightly boulders, often a torrent of water, a lurid and highly coloured sky with the figure of a lone wanderer in the midst of it all. To this rather romantic pattern Heinrich's paintings, like those of his creator, generally conformed.

At the beginning of Book Four Heinrich, dissatisfied with his knowledge of human anatomy, attends some lectures on this subject. But the professor to whom he goes, as well as teaching him anatomy, destroys his belief in the freedom of the will. Meantime his money has run out altogether, and he appeals to his mother for money which she finds for him at considerable personal sacrifice. A famous paragraph describes Frau Lee's return home after sending her son her small savings:

> At home my mother found the lid of her desk still open and the drawers, now empty, pulled out; she closed them and in the passing opened the one in which for her daily needs a tiny pile of small change lay in a little bowl, announcing that now for the time being every choice had vanished between doing herself well and continuing to stint herself, and that the good woman with the best will in the world could not have given herself any more easy days. But she did not notice that, nor would she have considered it in any case. She immediately closed this little drawer too, put away writing materials and sealing wax, closed the cupboard and sat down again on her "chair of anxiety" without arm rests, to rest from her doings, as straight as a pine tree.

Having paid his debts with his mother's money and sold all his possessions including his paintings to a junk dealer Heinrich ekes out an existence for a time. Painting flagstaffs for a royal wedding gives him for the first time the thrill of earning money by his own efforts. He has a short flirtation with an amiable working-class girl, but does not take advantage of Hulda's evident readiness to admit him to the fuller enjoyment of her favours. Heinrich could never live his life on such easy terms as Hulda, who soon finds herself another beau when Heinrich loses interest in her.

Meanwhile, his landlady's sudden death obliges him to leave his lodgings, and he decides to go home. Since he is quite penniless he must go on foot. On the way he stops at a count's castle, and discovers that his host has bought all his paintings from the junk dealer to whom he had sold them. Heinrich falls in love with the Count's adopted daughter, Dortchen Schönfund. Though she evidently loves him too, he does not dare confess his love to her. The Count insists on paying Heinrich handsomely for the pictures which he has bought very cheaply from the dealer. Heinrich also receives an unexpected substantial legacy from the junk dealer who has meantime died. He does not take the opportunities Dortchen thoughtfully provides for him to declare his love, and in the end she turns from him, rather hurt. She loves him and knows that in his way he loves her, but she is too sensible to want a man who will not propose to her. Later on she marries a wealthy and noble suitor in accordance with her own maxim that if one cannot have exactly what one wants in life, one should make the most of the next best thing.

Heinrich returns to Switzerland just in time to say farewell to his mother, whom he finds on her deathbed. He now realises that it would have been better for him to earn his bread and support his mother, rather than to pursue an artistic will-o'-the-wisp for so long. Now a moderately well-to-do man he takes a position in the civil service in the country near his father's native village and settles down to a life of useful activity. His days are gladdened by the arrival of Judith, home from America, now older and wiser, still beautiful but no longer provocative and passionate. The cousins see one another regularly till Judith's death, which takes place during an epidemic. By early middle age Heinrich has endured much frustration and disappointment; he has now decided that the best life for him is one of service to the community in which he lives.

III

The Characters

Scarcely any character in German fiction reveals himself to us in such intimate detail as Heinrich Lee. Novelists often describe the antecedents of their heroes in the manner which Keller adopts in his early chapters. He sketches the milieu in which Heinrich's parents grew up and tells us the relevant facts about the parents themselves. Keller surpasses the majority of writers in the honesty and completeness of his account of Heinrich's childhood and adolescence. Few writers can have retained as good a memory for the experiences of their early years. Heinrich does not view his childhood through any idealising romantic haze; he neither remembers it as he would have liked it to be, nor does he judge its events by the standards and values of the grown man. With unfailing psychological intuition he records the actions and feelings of the young child. In a matter of fact way he tells us of his doings and thoughts as a little boy. Heinrich neither sees himself through rose-coloured spectacles, nor does he make himself out to have been worse than he really was. A child whose horizon was unusually restricted because of his father's early death, Heinrich is seen at his mother's apronstrings exploring the unfolding world, observing the difference between his mother's poor but generally friendly neighbours, emerging from the first state of early innocence to the fumbling quest for a God about whom his mother, generally an infallible source of information and comfort, can provide only the haunting and unreassuring words of the Bible: "God is a spirit." Since Frau Lee clearly considered that this answer was conclusive and satisfactory, and since Heinrich regarded it as neither, the child was left to exercise his imagination on the problem of the nature and substance of God. Heinrich's first theological speculations are marvellously well remembered; most people have had such thoughts, but few have recorded them so faithfully for posterity. He does not pretend to have been a truthful or an honest child; in fact we learn in detail about his shortcomings on both these scores. The adult Heinrich Lee views himself not with amusement or moral indignation or grown-up superiority, but with candour, interest and curiosity. The misunderstandings to which young Heinrich was exposed at school will certainly strike an answering chord in many a reader's heart. The book illustrates memorably how a sensitive child can suffer at the hands of stupid, uncharitable and uncomprehending pedagogues.

Anna, Heinrich's first love, also represents the first love of every adolescent boy. Carnal desire is almost completely lacking from Heinrich's relationship with her; he places her on a pedestal as being chaste, pure and innocent, as well as more cultivated and accomplished than he himself. Sensing his lack of refinement by comparison with Anna, he tries not to offend her by his roughness. She has a civilising influence on Heinrich, no doubt, but had he continued to be her devoted slave, he would have been in danger of sacrificing more than was wholesome of his own personality. She might, in other words, have had the kind of effect on Heinrich that Barker Fairley thinks Frau von Stein had on Goethe. Gently and unobtrusively she would have encircled him in her tentacles, quelling every vigorous initiative and reducing him to a state of complete dependence on herself. However, she dies before she can do him any harm. Heinrich escapes without scathe, ironically enough regarding her death as an unmitigated tragedy.

Among the women in *Der grüne Heinrich* Judith represents wholesome sensuality. She loves Heinrich despite his extreme youth, but refrains from seducing him at least partly because she does not think it would be fair to him at that stage. Though her appetite for his caresses diminishes, she continues to love him, and eventually a close companionship and a genuine understanding develop between the two of them. The relationship with Judith improves and deepens with the passage of time. Anna represents renunciation and restraint; one side of him would never have been catered for by her, although Heinrich never realises this consciously. Anna is too pale and delicate, too refined and spiritual to make him happy.

Judith first appears coming from the garden with fruit and flowers; she gives Heinrich milk to drink, a healthy, natural beverage. Judith's yearning sensuality could be dangerous for them both, but they avoid the precipice, and later on she becomes his most faithful and cherished friend. Heinrich and Judith in the end achieve a sublimated sexual relationship, passion elevated and transformed into something more valuable and enduring, unselfish and spiritual, but all the deeper and purer because in the past they have been physically attracted to one another. Judith alone among the four women whom Heinrich loves provides his affections with an enduring focus. Hulda, the pretty, undemanding and appealing little working-class girl in Munich, has neither the refined, ethereal quality of an Anna nor the passion

and motherly constancy of a Judith. With Dortchen Schönfund
Heinrich never achieves the freedom from inhibitions which
would make it possible for him to declare his love; perhaps he is
intimidated by the grandeur of the Count's castle, perhaps by the
thought of having such a clever young woman for a wife. Altogether the atmosphere of the Dortchen Schönfund story resembles that of the fairy tale or the dream, and it is clear that
Heinrich must before long return home to Switzerland and a
more humdrum normality. For him to have gained Dortchen in
addition to the spectacular change in his worldly fortunes would
have been more than the reader could reasonably be expected
to swallow; we have grown accustomed to the idea that Heinrich
has to struggle hard for everything he gains from life, and even
his most honest efforts are not always successful. His meteoric
rise from poverty to wealth and comfort already strains our
credulity quite sufficiently.

Heinrich's attitude towards women remains determined by
the special nature of his relationship with his mother. He can
hardly allow any other women much share in his affections. Even
his love for Judith does not reach its full depth and maturity
until after his mother's death. Heinrich's mother occupies the
centre of his life, and other women have to be content with the
leavings. When Frau Lee dies the implication is that Heinrich
has killed her by his neglect. Yet he had not forgotten her; he
merely would not admit, utterly committed as he was to an
artistic career, that he had made a mistake and that his mother
and her advisers had been right. Of course, in the deeper sense
that he needed a vocation which would absorb all his energies
and strain all his faculties to the utmost he was justified in trying
to become a painter. Although his mother and her advisers
seemed to have been proved right about his art, it was far better
for Heinrich to err in the way he did than never to have had
such aspirations at all. He carries over into his new profession as
a civil servant the spirit of service and dedication to the task in
hand which upheld him during his trying years in Munich. His
mother, whose whole background and training were those of the
Swiss petty bourgeois, would not understand this; for her a man
worth his salt must achieve economic independence at the earliest
opportunity. Yet, because she loved her son, she cheerfully sacri-

ficed the last of her savings to enable him to continue in a course of conduct in which she did not believe.

Having a mother like Frau Lee makes it difficult for a man to choose a wife. Frau Lee smiles on the association between Heinrich and the pale, delicate Anna, perhaps subconsciously realising that Anna will not live long. Heinrich never gives his mother a hint how things stand between Judith and himself. She would have regarded Judith as a dangerous, predatory female, and would have taken any steps within her power to keep her son out of her reach.

The first two books of *Der grüne Heinrich* ring true on every page. Whether or not every incident is based on real life, the work does give that impression. The young man's first view of Munich evidently records a very moving and important experience. Here and there we may feel that the author is not completely master of his material; the complicated personality of Lys, for instance, seems a little strained, as though he were not drawn from the life. The book really does break down, however, and becomes wildly improbable in the account of Heinrich's prolonged residence at the Count's castle.

This episode consists of a strange and fantastic jumble of elements drawn directly from life and others which simply reflect the author's unfulfilled wishes. The Count, a less dogmatic Feuerbach, does not insist that Heinrich should share his view of the world. When the Chaplain brings along Angelus Silesius' *Der cherubinische Wandersmann* and hands it to Heinrich, we are reminded that Varnhagen von Ense gave Keller as a token of regard his wife's copy of the mystic poet's works. Dortchen has much in common with Lucie, the heroine of *Das Sinngedicht*; it must be conceded that Feuerbach's arid creed sits rather uneasily on the shoulders of the pretty young woman. Lucie, who has no such burden to bear, is all the more charming for being free of it. The succession of improbabilities which delay Heinrich's return home does not improve the book. Since throughout the book Heinrich is a young man of good character who strives earnestly to realise his personality to the best of his ability, he clearly deserves a measure of worldly success, but we would rather that this came to him in more orthodox and less spectacular ways. Almost the only part of this whole story that rings true is that he was too shy to profit by his opportunities with Dortchen.

The ingredients which comprise this section of *Der grüne Heinrich* might very well have gone to the making of a chapter or series of chapters just as good as the early part of the book. The experiences on which this part of the novel is based were as memorable and significant as those that underlay the earlier chapters. However, the raw material of the castle chapters was too recent and too ill assimilated for Keller to incorporate it in a book. To use Wordsworth's famous phrase Keller had not allowed sufficient time for recollection in tranquillity.

The foregoing remarks do not mean that Keller is capable of writing realistically only when he directly records his own experiences in his works. Certainly, his touch is surer when he is talking of the things that he knows at first hand. But he sometimes successfully makes the imaginative effort required to portray a milieu which he did not actually know. In *Pankraz der Schmoller*, for instance, he conveys a very fair impression of life in the British Army in India and in the French Foreign Legion, although one could scarcely imagine forms of life more completely alien to Keller. In the *Züricher Novellen*, to say nothing of the *Sieben Legenden* and *Das Sinngedicht*, Keller repeatedly portrays settings far removed in space and time from anything he knew at first hand. In every case he has made the necessary effort of intellect and imagination to create or re-create a world which he knew of only from his reading. But in the castle chapters of *Der grüne Heinrich* he forsakes the standards of probability to which we have grown accustomed in the account of Heinrich's childhood and adolescence. Unfortunately, when he revised the book, he did not much improve this part of it.

Generally the characters of *Der grüne Heinrich* can be identified with people whom Keller knew in real life. The figure of Judith offers a seeming exception to this statement. No character in Keller's works is more instinct with life, more finely drawn and lovable than this splendid creature. Certain traits were probably suggested by Marie Melos, but Freiligrath's sister-in-law, whom Keller met in the other poet's house in Zurich, would not appear to be a likely model for this ideal figure of Swiss rural womanhood. Even an artist of Keller's genius cannot produce such a figure like a conjurer out of a hat; he must have had some one in mind, or he could not have done it. Judith is superb, as true to life as figures like the hero and his mother, who are unmistakably bone of Keller's bone and flesh of his flesh. Whoever she was in life, she has attained in the book a beautiful and honourable immortality.

We cannot attempt a complete survey of the numerous minor characters of *Der grüne Heinrich*. Frau Margret and Vater Jakoblein emerge as distinct personalities, although they appear so briefly in the book, she with her caution and sure commercial sense, and he with his self-indulgence and his resentful dependence on his wife. Others whom we remember with affection are Heinrich's grandmother, with her dark, sullen, rich husband, who is prepared to tolerate Heinrich as soon as he sees that the latter has no designs on his wife's money, the schoolmaster, Heinrich's uncle and his cousins from the village. The old junk dealer, who buys up all Heinrich's pictures, has also a certain charm. The less agreeable characters are well drawn. The horribly calculating juvenile usurer Meierlein must be one of the most unpleasant children in all literature.

In *Der grüne Heinrich* Keller reveals himself as a great connoisseur of human nature. Although he is acknowledged to be a champion of truth and honesty, he candidly shows us in the hero's history that these qualities are not inborn even in the best of mortals, but have to be striven for and achieved at the expense of bitter experience. Heinrich nowhere finds in life the satisfactions he had at first sought in exactly the forms which he thought he wanted. In love he possesses neither the graceful Anna, the passionate Judith, nor the clever and beautiful Dortchen Schönfund. Each of these relationships gives him something, but the platonic association which develops with Judith after her return from America is more valuable and enduring than any of the loves of his youth. In his intended career Heinrich has to admit defeat; he does not make his name as a painter, although his attempt to become one was less of a mistake than he had thought in his more despairing moments. Heinrich early discovers that neither his mother nor the church can give him easy answers to his theological questions. Nevertheless, he does not wholeheartedly accept the view of life held by the Count and Dortchen. He realises that religious knowledge can never be obtained absolutely, but can only be apprehended with varying degrees of dimness at the expense of years of experience. When we leave Heinrich he is practising his chosen profession conscientiously, awaiting such experiences and such new insights as life may bring. Just as he has discovered that he will be happier if he refrains from lying and stealing, that a man who unnecessarily kills or mutilates his helpless fellow-creatures also damages himself, that quick fulfilment in love may not be best in the long run, and that a man ought to earn his bread and contribute towards the upkeep of his dependants, he remains receptive for further new insights. In the end Heinrich has learned the lesson of patience; the passage of time is part of the price which has to be paid before one can reach maturity.

IV

The Artist as Hero

Perhaps German literature has more plays and novels than any other European literature about the peculiar difficulties of the artist in society. Goethe provided in *Tasso* the classic example of an artist at odds with the world, isolated by his gifts from the more ordinary people who find it easy to accept the constraints imposed by society. Grillparzer wrote play after play on the same topic; art spells unhappiness, painful renunciation; the artist may be a chosen vessel, but he must pay dearly for the privilege; in particular art often debars him from happiness in love. Nearer our own day Thomas Mann has focused attention on the differences that divide the artist from the world.

Der grüne Heinrich is *not* a novel about the problems of the artist as such. Heinrich Lee spends a great deal of time and energy trying to become a painter, and slowly and painfully acquires a scrupulous artistic conscience. But being a painter is not the essential thing about him. It matters that he is a young man of a certain moral and mental calibre, for some of his experiences are of a kind that not everyone could undergo. Art is for him the form of existence through which he approaches the world, yet Keller never makes the artist out to be essentially different from the rest of humanity; the artist is not portrayed as having special, almost insurmountable problems. In considering himself immune from the ordinary obligation to earn his living, Heinrich is shown to have erred. First and foremost a young man must ensure that he is not being an excessive burden on his parents. Keller allows no special concessions for artists. Heinrich's moral regeneration begins when he forsakes the career which in defiance of common sense and natural law he had desperately been trying to follow, and begins to paint flagpoles for the royal wedding. He enjoys the novel sensation of fulfilling for the first time a basic duty towards his relatives and the rest of society. From the moment of his decision to abandon painting and return home Heinrich's worldly fortunes take a turn for the better. The foolish romantic determination to become a painter has very nearly been the undoing of Heinrich, but fortunately he mends his ways just in time. *Der grüne Heinrich* concerns a painter, but the fact of his being an artist is not of cardinal importance; Heinrich's humanity is central, not his art.

V

Nature

Nature plays a considerable role in *Der grüne Heinrich*. Keller could never remain indifferent to his surroundings, and we are constantly being enlightened about the world that Heinrich lived in. From an early age he becomes accustomed to the sight of the Alps far to the south from the upstairs windows of his mother's house. Later he and his companions play by Lake Zurich, and altogether Heinrich Lee takes for granted the rural delights which could be easily enjoyed at that time by Zurich children. The ugly incidents of his last days at school are quickly forgotten under the soothing influence of Mother Nature, and the woman with whom he falls most deeply and lastingly in love is herself almost an ideal incarnation of Nature. Keller shows constant awareness of such things as the time of day, the position of the sun in the sky, the amount of light and shade that a room offers, and the prevailing weather conditions. This serves greatly to enhance the realism of his narrative.

Some of the greatest German writers have rebelled against the whole natural order and expressed their fundamental dissatisfaction with the world as they have found it. Examples which spring readily to mind are Kleist and Hölderlin, both of whom were destroyed by their unwillingness or inability to accept and tolerate the world. Hölderlin became insane, Kleist's tormented life ended in suicide; neither was capable of living with and overcoming his frustrations. Keller did not go under like Kleist and

Hölderlin but propounded in his novel the view that whatever questions about the world and our role in it we may be unable to answer, yet we can say with assurance that the natural order is basically benevolent. Heinrich has to endure frustration and disappointment, but he never loses faith in life. When things do not go smoothly, he does not jump to the worst possible conclusions about God and the world, but continues to look for better times or at least fuller understanding. His natural piety combined with patience makes it improbable that he will ever be too discouraged by misfortune.

The reader soon becomes familiar with the countryside around Heinrich's village, particularly the way from the parsonage to the schoolmaster's house. Heinrich's frequent walk along the hilltop dividing the two valleys almost becomes a part of our own existence, as do the country occupations of his relatives and the other villagers.

Heinrich Lee loves the world and most of its inhabitants. The buffetings he endures do not shake his confidence in life, and never in his blackest moments is he filled with despair about "the human condition" or any such abstraction. His fundamental saneness and soundness he owes in no small measure to the fact that he is a child of nature who under any unusual stress or strain remains well aware of the healing powers of the universal Mother.

VI

The Two Versions

When Keller revised *Der grüne Heinrich* he made several important changes and innumerable modifications of detail. With the latter we cannot concern ourselves here, but we can indicate the major differences between the two versions.

Heinrich now remained alive at the end. The hero's death had always seemed arbitrary and unmotivated. Heinrich had had to die because Keller had not yet reached that state of maturity in his own life which would show him what to do with Heinrich. Keller had considered letting the new version open with Heinrich and Judith living close together in old age, but at Storm's suggestion, the present strictly chronological ordering of the material in the autobiographical form was adopted. Those parts of the book which were originally written in the third person were re-written in the first person so that the whole work now possessed more formal unity. Storm suggested that Judith must not be too old to be interesting on her return from America; ideally she should go to America at the age of twenty-five or so, and on her return she should not be more than thirty-five to thirty-seven. Keller had intended putting Frau Lee's funeral at the beginning of the revised version, but Storm advised him to begin with the story of Heinrich's youth. Keller found the fourth volume the most difficult to revise; he describes it as "schundvoll und häufig albern" (rubbishy and often silly), a judgement to which the majority of readers will be inclined to give qualified assent. In the original version Heinrich's arrival in Munich is described in the third person, then we are allowed to read the story of his childhood and adolescence, which he has written down in the first person, then we return to the third person for the last part of the book. Apart from the irritating mixture of first and third person narrative, the chronology of the novel is made unnecessarily confusing by this method of narration.

Keller resented the view of some critics that the second version was not superior in all respects to the first. We cannot feel much sympathy with his expressed wish that the hand should wither that would cause the original version to be reprinted. Although the second edition is manifestly superior to the first, we may be permitted lingering regrets over at least one passage which Keller chose to excise; we cannot justify the omission from the new edition of "Judith's Bath", a highly poetic passage from the third book. The whole incident takes place during Anna's last illness, a period when Heinrich felt himself particularly drawn to Judith, but restrained from the ultimate infidelity by the thought of Anna's sufferings :

Our hands sometimes moved involuntarily towards one another's shoulders or hips to embrace them, but stopped half way in the air and ended with a timid, broken-off stroking of the cheeks, so that in our folly we were like a pair of kittens, which reach out for one another with their little paws, electrically trembling and undecided whether they will play or tear one another to shreds.

At such moments we rose up; Judith put on her shoes and went out with me into the summer night; we had a desire to go out into the open air unseen and to go in search of nocturnal adventures through the forest and over the heights. Such romantic habits delighted my companion all the more since they were new to her and she had never gone out of the village at night without a definite and unusual purpose in mind. She rejoiced in this freedom for its own sake and not from an extravagant love of nature, for she lived a lonely and solitary life, although no one was better adapted to a happy married life than she. And so she made no sentimental observations about the moonlight, but she rushed quickly and mischievously through the bushes, or broke half crossly many a green twig, with which she struck me on the face, as though she wished to conjure everything away with it, which lay between me and her, the years, my love for another and our unequal situations. She then became quite different from what she had just been in the sitting-room, really naughty, played all kinds of tricks on me, got lost in the thick undergrowth, so that I suddenly caught hold of her, or in jumping over a ditch lifted her skirt so high that I became completely confused. Once I told her about the adventure which I had had as a little boy with that actress, and confided in her quite openly what an impression the first sight of a woman's naked breast had made on me, so that I still see it before me in the white moonlight and at the same time think of the long vanished woman almost with longing, while her features and her name have become lost completely to my memory. We were walking straight alongside the forest brook, over which the moon caused a mysterious net of light and darkness to tremble; Judith suddenly disappeared from my side and slipped along the bushes, while I, somewhat taken aback, continued on my way. I might have been walking for five minutes during which I did not hear a sound apart from the gentle sighing of the trees and the splashing of the water. It seemed to me as if Judith had dissolved and silently vanished into Nature, in which her elements rustled around me, teasing in ghostly fashion. And so unexpectedly I came to the neighbourhood of the *Heidenstube* and saw now the towering grey rock wall in the bright light of the full moon, which hung over the trees; the water and the stones at my feet also shone in the moonlight. On the stones lay clothes, uppermost a white shift, which, when I picked it up, was still

quite warm, like a freshly removed earthly covering. I did
not hear a sound, however, I felt it was quite uncanny, since
the silence of the night seemed to be imbued with a daemonic
purpose. I was just about to call Judith by name, when I heard
strange, half sighing, half singing sounds, which at last resolved
themselves plainly into an old song, which I had heard a
hundred times and which nevertheless now made a magical
impression on me. Its theme was the depth of the water, something about love and nothing else; but at last it was permeated
with an almost visible, seductive smile and accompanied by a
silvery sound, as though someone were splashing in the water
and striking it in gentle waves against her thighs. As I stood
listening, I discerned opposite me a vague, white figure, which
was moving in the shadow behind the rock, hanging from
drooping branches and letting its body move about in the
water, or suddenly rising up high and remaining motionless
for a while, like a ghost. A bank of stones not far below the
surface of the water led across to that place in a fairly wide
arc, and when my thoughts had wandered for a moment, I
unexpectedly saw the naked Judith who had got to the middle
of this path and was coming towards me. She was in the water
to just below the breast; she was approaching in an arc, and
I turned as if by magnetism to follow her movements. Now she
stepped out of the shadow that fell obliquely across the stream
and suddenly appeared in the moonlight; at the same time she
was on the point of reaching the bank and rose ever higher
out of the water, and now this splashed back from her gleaming
hips and knees. Now she put a dripping wet foot on the dry
stones, looked at me, and I looked at her; she was only three
paces from me, and stood still for a moment; I saw every limb
clearly, but enlarged and beautified to legendary proportions,
like an old marble statue more than life size. On her shoulders,
on her breasts and on her hips the water gleamed, but her
eyes, which looked straight at me, shone more brightly still.
Now she raised her arms and moved towards me, but I,
trembling hot and cold at once, and suffused with a curious
respect, went backwards one pace like a crab for every pace
that she took forwards, without ever taking my eyes off her.
And so I came back among the trees, till I became caught in
the blackberry bushes and stood still again. I was now hidden

and in the dark, while she hovered and shimmered in the light in front of me; I pressed my head against a cool tree trunk and looked straight at the apparition. Now she began to feel uncomfortable herself; she was standing close by her garments, and began to dress like lightning. I saw, however, that it was only now that she began to be embarrassed, and forgetting my own confusion, I involuntarily came out and tremblingly helped her to fasten her dress over her breast and handed her the big white neckerchief. Hereupon I put my arms round her neck and kissed her on the mouth, as it were not to allow an idle moment to intrude; she must have felt this; for she was now red all over down to her still wet breast; she hastily stuffed her fine stockings into her pocket and slipped into her shoes with bare feet, whereupon she once again embraced me and kissed me violently, then hurried through the trees diagonally up the slope and disappeared, while I walked homewards alongside the water. Curiously enough, I felt the guilt of this adventure rest on me alone, although I had behaved passively throughout, while I already sensed how indelibly the nocturnal apparition, the gleaming form was impressed for ever on my senses and took possession of my brain and my blood like a white hot fire.

It is hard to imagine what considerations can have caused Keller to drop this powerful passage. Admittedly he was scornful of cheap erotic effects by the time he came to undertake his revision, but very few readers would willingly surrender these pages, which by their suggestiveness and restraint contribute something of real value to the book. Keller in old age considered that "it was the crudest and most trivial art in the world to make a female character in a work of literature pull her shift off over her head". (Letter to Kuh, 10th September 1871.)

Storm spoke with rare accents of approval about Judith's bath. "Die Scene ist schön", he writes, "als machten die alten Götter die Rund." However, Keller's mind was made up.

In nearly all respects the 1880 version represents an improvement. The gifted but undisciplined young genius has given place to the mature artist, who has learned the value of sustained effort over details of style, the narrative has become more homogeneous, the too harsh condemnation of the hero in the first version,

followed by his unmotivated death, has been tempered and soft-
ened down, and Heinrich lives on, in mellow and contented renunciation, able to tell the tale of his youth with clear judgement
and unembittered accents. This is the greatest single gain in the
revised version; Keller now sees the events of his early life in
proper perspective. Having thus gained distance, he can avoid
the too censorious judgements of the first version. *Der grüne
Heinrich* is so closely based on Keller's experience that it depends
more than most works of prose fiction on the author's balanced
view of his own life. The raw material of the book was too raw
in the early 1850s; Keller was too directly emotionally involved
in the problems of the book at this time, but this was no longer
so in 1880.

VII

Place in the "Bildungsroman" Tradition

Der grüne Heinrich belongs to that peculiarly German genre,
the *Bildungsroman*, the novel relating the progress of a single
character towards wisdom and the good life from an original
state of simplicity and innocence. It has often been said that the
first ancestor of this literary form in Germany was Wolfram's
Middle High German epic, *Parzival*, the hero of which was
brought up far away from normal human society; to pursue
Parzival through all the adventures which he must undergo
before he is both better informed and morally more mature is a
sizable undertaking, which Wolfram performs with German
thoroughness, though his poem has many moments of genuine
pathos and some flashes of wit. Wolfram, Keller's first important
literary ancestor, gives his hero unusual disadvantages to overcome. It is doubtful if Parzival's failure to show ready sympathy
towards Amfortas, King of the Graal, strikes the average reader
nowadays as an offence deserving of severe punishment. Although
the ideal of conduct which *Parzival* expounds has not altogether
lost its relevance, a considerable imaginative effort is required
today to discern this relevance. Parzival strikes us as rather a
special case, even within his own remote period. Most people
are brought up within the framework of society, not outside it
like Parzival. However, the most important insight which Parzival
gains closely resembles Heinrich's realisation towards the end of

Keller's book that none of us can live completely into himself; Parzival sees that he should have had sympathy for Amfortas in his sickness and misery, and Heinrich understands that his artistic dabbling in Munich while he disregarded his first duty towards his mother did him no credit, and that in future he should be less selfish. Both Parzival and Heinrich learn the lesson that they must love their neighbour. Both, in different ways, make themselves unhappy by their own selfishness, and recovery begins only when they recognise their guilt and mend their ways.

Grimmelshausen's Simplicius and Goethe's Wilhelm Meister undergo a rather similar development. Like Parzival, Simplicius is brought up far from the world, and the first occasion on which he meets some soldiers on horseback fills him with wonder. Goethe spurns this device of making his hero extraordinarily ignorant of normal human institutions; Wilhelm Meister has only the ordinary ignorance and callowness of the young man, but this is sufficient to enable Goethe to make his point. Early in the *Lehrjahre* Wilhelm philanders with the pretty actress, Philine, and takes a rather foolish, dilettante interest in the stage, in fact indulges in the expensive amusements of the upper class youth. From this idle and unprofitable existence he is wrested by the intervention of the *Gesellschaft vom Turm*, who have their eye on him as a good man who is wasting his talents. Once initiated into the society Wilhelm is told that there is work for him to do. He is then sent to learn the profession of medicine, abandons his aspirations to become an actor, and embarks on a career of modest and useful activity. Since Keller's Heinrich undergoes the same kind of development as Wolfram's and Goethe's heroes without the hocus-pocus of the Knights of the Graal or the *Gesellschaft vom Turm* (it should be remembered that Goethe was a Freemason), his book is more natural and straightforward. In a sense Keller makes his task easier by telling substantially his own life story in *Der grüne Heinrich*; the creative imagination plays a greater part in Goethe's work as it does in *Parzival*.

Thomas Mann's *Zauberberg* provides a notable modern example of this kind of novel. Hans Castorp has finished his engineering studies and goes to Davos to take a short holiday visiting a cousin who has been sent there with tuberculosis. Hans Castorp stays there for seven years, although he is not really ill, leading the life of a completely self-centred dilettante and aesthete, becoming more and more attached to the life of the sick society of Europe in the sanatorium. The outbreak of war in 1914 summons him back to life with a jolt; in other words Hans Castorp begins as a completely self-centred youth, and ends as a man involved in the conflicts and problems of his generation. Hans Castorp is far more of a special case than Heinrich Lee, who though unmistakably a nineteenth century Swiss bourgeois has very few experiences which cannot be understood and appreciated by any reader of good will. *Der grüne Heinrich* belongs to that age, not remote in time, but very different in spirit from the present, before all of life became problematical. Heinrich tackles and solves his difficulties, and is never in serious danger of losing faith in life. When things go wrong, he does not assume that the world is out of joint but, more sanely, that he has made a mistake, or possibly that the benevolent Providence in which he trusts has some purpose afoot with him which he does not fully understand.

In many ways Heinrich Lee feels exposed to the same uncertainties, the same fundamental doubts about life as Kafka's heroes, but his attitude to life differs from theirs in that he continues despite all to believe in life and seems confident that his frank, simple but intelligent approach to its problems will prove right in the end. Perhaps Keller's is the last of the great *Bildungsromane* in which the author's intention is to show that the confusions and uncertainties of life really can be resolved by a man of good character and perseverance. Even Hans Castorp's insight that he must identify himself with his own nation's fortunes does not help him to live out his life; it merely shows him that he ought to go and be killed like the other young Germans of his generation. In Kafka's works the last confident assumptions about life have been cast aside and man must make the most of life in a hostile world. With Keller there is no sense of alienation or estrangement; he loves the world and makes Heinrich feel at home in it.

VIII

Final Assessment

We have now considered *Der grüne Heinrich* from enough points of view to attempt a balanced assessment of it as a work of literature.

Intellectually, *Der grüne Heinrich* is a most satisfying book. Many of the most important questions of human life are touched upon in it. At a very early age the hero speculates on the nature and purpose of life, then, having discovered that no easy solution to this question can be found, he settles down to face the practical problem of how to come to terms with life and with his fellow men. Justice, truth, honesty, love all have their part to play in Heinrich's life, and we cannot help being impressed by his calm and positive acceptance of life, his tact and his natural piety. We sense that Keller has a deep, intuitive understanding of the laws of life, and that even where his hero takes a false turning, a good Providence is watching over him to bring him back to the right path, that he instinctively knows this and is grateful :

> Ein guter Mensch, in seinem dunklen Drange,
> Ist sich des rechten Weges wohl bewußt.

Goethe's words are also true of the author of *Der grüne Heinrich* who makes his hero advance through life with such modesty, confidence and assurance. Perhaps more than anything else about this book we cherish the feeling that it is the work of a wise and good man; it has many beautiful scenes, many memorable episodes, many profound comments on human affairs, but what matters most of all and wherein it really excels is in the high seriousness, not unrelieved by humour, with which Heinrich faces the whole business of living. The Count tells Heinrich that he is "ein wesentlicher Mensch", which is an exceedingly difficult phrase to translate, but exactly conveys the reason why *Der grüne Heinrich* is such an important book. It is the complete and honest record of the life of "ein wesentlicher Mensch", "a real man" of good will, intelligence and discrimination.

Artistically, however, *Der grüne Heinrich* still possesses certain weaknesses. Despite the extensive revision it remains rather shapeless and unwieldy. Occasionally we still find *longueurs*, here and there we detect that the author's perspective has changed during the revision, and the novel suffers from the basic defect of not having a properly constructed plot. Interesting and original as many of the reflective sections are, they sometimes interrupt the narrative too much, and in the end we are obliged to admit that Keller has in a sense put too much of himself into the book in a too unselective manner. The stories of Meretlein and Albertus

Zweihan have a certain relevance to Heinrich Lee's situation at given points of his career, but each of these internal narratives has developed beyond the limits of what is properly permissible within the economy of the novel. The rather tenuous parallels which exist between Heinrich's situation and those of Meretlein and Albertus do not justify these considerable interruptions of his main narrative. In the later part of the book Keller freely introduces and drops new characters and the reader may well feel that some of these do not belong organically to the whole. The earlier part of the book, up to Heinrich's departure for Munich, records real and almost universal experiences; in the *Kunststadt* itself we are less sure that Heinrich is living in the world we know, and we sense that on the journey home Heinrich is living in the clouds of imaginative wish-fulfilment.

However, it would be churlish not to recognise the enormous merits of the book. We have already seen that in philosophical depth and power of characterisation Keller has here achieved a great deal. Everywhere in the book rural Switzerland comes splendidly alive. It is evidently the work of an author who has looked with a keen and observant eye at the Swiss countryside and country people. Winter and summer, sunshine and rain, seedtime and harvest are all faithfully and memorably recorded. Anyone who has visited the countryside in the northern part of Canton Zurich knows that a true impression of that region emerges from these pages. The stages of Heinrich's growth and spiritual maturing are well conveyed too, and his considered views on various human problems are unsparingly offered. Occasionally, as in the descriptions of Frau Margret's shop or of the making of Anna's coffin, we realise how very close and intimate Heinrich's observation of other people's occupations must have been.

On balance, one is obliged to say that *Der grüne Heinrich* is a considerable work of literature. By the standards of literary competence which are generally acknowledged nowadays it has many serious shortcomings. Although Keller corrected the cruder faults of the original version, and although a great deal of genius went into its making, it remains an untidy, sprawling, diffuse book, insufficiently concentrated and of very unequal merit in its various parts. Yet the book above all reflects its maker and is the work in which he gives most of himself and his reactions to the world. Perhaps its most striking merit is its serenity, its acceptance of the confusing phenomena of life without bitterness or heartbreak. Heinrich is often cast down but never in despair. He often makes mistakes but he always redeems the situation in the end. He is always aware of the beauty in the world, ever responsive to a generous thought or action on the part of others.

Heinrich's love affairs illustrate well the process of maturing which is what the book is really about and why it does not conform to any traditional European pattern for the novel. At first Anna's gentle, sweet, rather negative, genteel spirituality seems to be all that he seeks. However, almost at once he becomes aware of Judith's magnetic femininity and even while he thinks that Anna is the person who matters most he is drawn irresistibly to Judith in whom he rather guiltily thinks he finds only physical attraction. Yet we are aware all along that Judith, despite her elemental power and often stressed closeness to nature, has a certain constancy and motherliness which makes her cling to Heinrich and go on loving him though he consistently underestimates her and even makes it clear to her for long that it is Anna whom he really loves. Heinrich wrongly regards Judith as capable only of satisfying his baser appetites. Only later on, after the episodes with Hulda and Dortchen Schönfund, after his return from Germany and the abandonment of his romantic dream of artistic fulfilment, does Heinrich begin to appreciate Judith at her true value. It emerges clearly then that although they are both much older and the turmoil of passion has subsided they still love one another and every meeting between them is still a special occasion. Perhaps this development is tantamount to an admission on Heinrich's part that he had been wrong to spurn Judith's love in the first instance, always to relegate her to second place after Anna; perhaps he is saying that a lasting physical attraction must of necessity mean a more abiding, richer relationship.

The style of the book varies a good deal from one chapter to another, although it is much more unified in the 1880 version than in the first version. Almost the whole work in its final form consists of first person narrative, the exceptions being such interpolations as the stories of *Meretlein* and Albertus Zwiehan. The work is conceived on a generous scale, and the detail of the subject matter is matched by a corresponding spaciousness of presentation and an unhurried manner of writing. This can be readily verified by opening the book at almost any page at random; where Keller has thought of an incidental *motif* that might conceivably be interesting he does not hesitate to follow it up. Everywhere he sees people and events in their natural setting, and he never considers a brief indication of the place, time of day and the weather to be wasted effort. He is always prepared to digress for a while to consider the more general implications of a particular set of circumstances. This latter feature can be one of his most endearing and one of his most infuriating characteristics. It certainly adds considerably to the length of the book, not always to its advantage. Paragraphs of a whole page or more in length are no rarity, and altogether to read *Der grüne Heinrich* with enjoyment demands mental adjustments which not every reader is prepared to make.

On almost every page one is aware of the master of German prose, whose enormous natural talent constantly shines through, even when masked by a certain lack of training. Keller really suffered all his days from the consequences of his expulsion from school. Although in many ways he more than made up for the lost ground, the last years at school represented a serious loss which could never be completely made good. If we are honest with ourselves, we have to confess that we admire *Der grüne Heinrich* for its excellent character-portraits and for individual stylistic excellences, single brilliant chapters, occasional good images, the feeling that here is an author with something to say and the gift of frequently but not always being able to say it memorably. This sounds like the raw material for a great novel, but unless properly and economically used and manipulated, it need not result in a great novel. *Der grüne Heinrich* is an important book in many respects, but undoubtedly misses being a great novel.

CHAPTER THREE

DIE LEUTE VON SELDWYLA

THE first volume of Seldwyla stories appeared soon after Keller's return from Berlin, the second nearly twenty years later. They are first mentioned in a letter to Hermann Hettner (September 1851):

> Ich habe . . . einige Erzählungen und Novellen ausgeheckt, welche farbenreich und sinnlich, und reinlich und bedächtig geschrieben, in einem Bändchen vereinigt, den schlechten Eindruck verwischen sollen, den mein formloser und unge-hauerlicher Roman auf den grossen Haufen machen wird.*

In 1853 Keller tells the same correspondent that *Ein Bändchen Novellen ist ganz spielend entstanden,*† which meant simply that he had conceived them in his mind, not that they were written down in anything like a complete form. By 1856, however, the first volume really was ready. In addition to the stories of the first volume, Keller sent Vieweg the manuscript of *Der Schmied seines Glückes* and *Die mißbrauchten Liebesbriefe,* which Vieweg pre-ferred to hold over for a second volume.

Dietegen was also begun in the 1850s, but Keller worked at it off and on for many years, and the final version differs greatly from the extremely far-fetched and improbable first version.

Keller's assumption of office as *Staatsschreiber* prevented him from completing the Seldwyla stories, although he was busy with *Das verlorene Lachen, Kleider machen Leute* and *Dietegen* at about the time he took up his post. In 1866 he wrote to Hettner that the second volume was "almost completely ready". Five years later he settled to the task of finishing the second book. He dis-

---

* I have also dug out some stories and *Novellen*, which, colourfully and sensually, neatly and thoughtfully written down and gathered to-gether in one small volume, are to wipe out the bad impression which my monstrous novel will make on the multitude.

† A little volume of Novellen has sprung up as easily as anything.

solved his contract with Vieweg, and arranged for Weibert to publish the stories. The first three *Novellen* appeared in 1873, *Dietegen* and *Das verlorene Lachen* in 1874.

Die Leute von Seldwyla had a generally favourable reception, although Theodor Fontane disliked the stories, particularly *Romeo und Julia auf dem Dorfe*, which he said was thoroughly inconsistent in style, having elements of the fairy tale followed by precise and realistic passages in the modern manner and a good deal of romantic sentimentality.

Pankraz der Schmoller

Pankraz is a *Bildungsroman* in miniature. It tells of the hero's struggle to find himself by overcoming a fault of character which threatened to undermine his whole existence. Despite his superior gifts, Pankraz cannot make anything of his life until he has learned not to sulk, and it takes him half a lifetime before he has completely eradicated this weakness. It seems on the surface that he leaves home merely because his sister has teased him by taking some of his food; the deeper reason for his drastic action lies in his dissatisfaction with his own lazy and boring existence. Although he seems to fend for himself very successfully out in the world his achievement is more apparent than real. The old weakness remains, and when Lydia teases and humiliates him, he reacts in the old way by running away in a pique from his difficulties. His whole brilliant career in the army and subsequently in the French Foreign Legion conceals the fact that he cannot face up to the stresses of life like a man; he runs away to France because Lydia does not give him the undivided affection to which he inwardly feels entitled. The encounter with the lion in the desert and his narrow escape from death proves to be an unexpectedly salutary experience; in those critical hours he comes to know himself and his obligations towards others better than ever before. He now has the opportunity of showing whether he really is prepared to live in charity with the rest of the world. Keller tries very hard to persuade us that his conversion is genuine. In this connection we must certainly regard the family's departure from Seldwyla as a symbolic action; Pankraz is leaving the scene of his ineffectual and mis-spent youth for new surroundings.

Pankraz fails to become as lovably credible as Heinrich Lee.

An able and intelligent youth would hardly allow his resentment of his own uselessness and his sister's consequent teasing to become the mainspring of all his conduct for many years. And the reader may well wonder whether his fumbling and indecisive behaviour with Lydia is attributable to the same fault of character which has caused difficulties in his relations with his mother and sister. It might be further questioned whether a man's character could be radically transformed by an encounter with an African lion, which as related seems a rather improbable circumstance. Yet we can perhaps agree that a deep-seated fault in an otherwise good character can only be got rid of by shock treatment. In *Pankraz* Keller, depressed by his lack of success in love, literature and life, compensates himself for the self-immolation which he practised in the original *Der grüne Heinrich*.

The story of Pankraz begins as a third person narrative. The poverty and narrowness of the little family's life are well conveyed, and such touches as the seasonal emptying of the butterbowl suggest to us how hard life is for them. The characters of the children and their mother are quite clearly defined too, and Keller makes it clear that although Pankraz has no opportunity for self-fulfilment in Seldwyla, he has the makings of an independent and creative mind, with his little book of drawings, calculations and scribblings. Estherchen is pretty, gay and unproblematical, loyal but playful and inclined to tease her brother. This section of the story ends with the disappearance of Pankraz on the day when Estherchen takes some of his food; the fifteen years of his absence from home are passed over in a sentence or two at this stage.

Then comes the lively narrative of the successful Pankraz's return, with the atmosphere of an unusual day in the life of the small town most effectively communicated. That afternoon at about coffee-time the organ-grinder appears, then a hawker with an exotic bird, a man with a camel, a dancing bear and a number of monkeys. The arrival of the little menagerie serves as a kind of hors d'œuvre before the main dish, which is the triumphant return of Pankraz himself as a colonel in the French Foreign Legion.

The last and longest section of the work consists of Pankraz's account of his life during the years of his absence. Most of this part is concerned with Pankraz's love for the beautiful but heartless Lydia in British India. The story is told in the first person by a Pankraz who has become comfortable, relaxed, well-disposed and successful. The bitter, frustrated boy is now a fulfilled and substantial man. Everywhere the transition is apparent, not least in his behaviour towards his mother and sister who are now shown the civilised courtesies which they would have been denied before Pankraz left home. The story is rounded off by the narrator, who tells us significantly that Pankraz and his family now leave Seldwyla.

Most of *Pankraz* is set in countries which Keller had not visited, and here his literary skill emerges. He does not run the risk of treating the exotic settings exhaustively, but by a few well-chosen details conveys the appropriate atmosphere whether of army life in India, the provincial Governor's household or the French Foreign Legion. Though he cannot draw on first hand experience, he ensures that his local colour is authentic. The main emphasis in Pankraz is on the characters, which are very well portrayed. However, the India section represents a considerable achievement for a man who did not know India at first hand.

Other touches betray the master story-teller, as when the mother and sister fall asleep during Pankraz's long narrative, showing how difficult it is even for those who love one another dearly to imagine one another's experience. The two women are so overcome by excitement and unaccustomed rich food that they cannot keep awake. Pankraz retains just enough of his old nature to refuse to tell them the story a second time.

Pankraz conquers the fault of character which threatens to undermine his life's happiness. He also achieves considerable material prosperity. Yet he never finds happiness in love, he only overcomes the need for it. For him love in the shape of Lydia breaks violently into his life as a distracting, unsettling force, which throws him for a time seriously off balance. However, since disappointment in love acts as a spur to other activities, Pankraz owes his success in life to Lydia's rejection of him.

Lydia is cruelly drawn. She regards Pankraz as a desirable conquest but cares too much about her position to allow him any real hope of marrying her. Though clever and cultivated, she lacks the generosity of nature which would make her join her fortunes to his. She rejoices in the attentions of many suitors but has probably overplayed her hand in allowing Pankraz to escape her. Paradoxically she, who thought herself too good for Pankraz, ensures his worldly success and fosters the development of his personality; through her Pankraz enlarges his mind, acquires some degree of social poise, and gains rapid promotion in the army. In the end, though with an effort, Pankraz discards her and realises himself.

Romeo und Julia auf dem Dorfe

Many readers would regard this as Keller's most powerful and affecting story. The comparison with Shakespeare does not seem wholly unreasonable when the work is more closely examined. Of all Keller's works this is the most absolute and uncompromising in its challenging assertion that life should be lived in full intensity and purity for a few fleeting moments rather than be allowed to trail on in a debased and empty form for years. Keller really says here that when one believes that one thing matters above all else, then that thing should be placed at the centre of life and given full emphasis, at whatever cost. He would regard Sali and Vrenchen, those pathetic little victims, as we might think, as conquerors of circumstance, who by their innocent and unhesitating defiance of the inhibiting and degrading circumstances of life fulfil their destiny in a splendid and worthy manner.

Romeo und Julia auf dem Dorfe provides a remarkable demonstration of the force of human passion. First of all greed for possessions leads the two fathers Manz and Marti—both of whom really know who owns the disputed piece of land—to destroy one another's happiness and wellbeing for the sake of something to which they are not entitled. The book shows how necessary it is to love one's neighbour by illustrating the consequences of not doing so.

In striking contrast to the parents' behaviour we witness the children's love for one another. This love, well rooted in long acquaintance, in community of background and in the wholesome respect which their families originally felt for one another, survives the normal hazards of growing up, and refuses to become involved in the fathers' quarrel. It preserves Sali intact from the moral degradation into which Manz has fallen; it maintains Vrenchen's self-respect through all her trials. It is a preserving and productive force, which cannot work out a proper destiny for the two young people because of the very absolute demands which Sali and Vrenchen make on life. Swiss peasants both of them, tied to their native soil, they cannot simply go away from the scene of the family feud and start afresh. Yet neither can they leave one another and begin life anew separately. Instead they resolve to consummate their union at once as love and desire dictate, before life with its ugly compromises makes their love less than perfect. So they enjoy one another for a night and fall from the hay boat into the cold, deadly water.

There are some unforgettable moments in the story. The opening scene, in which we meet Manz and Marti, each ploughing his own field, is one of these. Before the fathers surrendered to their greed for possessions they were secure in the modest prosperity resulting from hard work and frugal living. Sali and Vrenchen played together, and Manz and Marti wished one another well. None of the ingredients of tragedy seemed to be present here till the conversation touched upon the disputed field. Marti had been deliberately disingenuous in not telling the Seldwyla authorities what he knew well, that the Black Fiddler, a local ne'er-do-well, was certainly the rightful heir of the deceased owner of the field. Though both Manz and Marti seemed eminently honourable men, their desire for the field was allowed to suppress all other considerations.

In the children the values which the fathers once observed but have betrayed by their greed live on, so that even after the giddy excitement of the dance they despise the casual embraces of the down-and-outs with whom they have been associating. The children are not contaminated by the moral fault which destroyed their parents' honourable and laborious existence, but their lives are inextricably involved in the downfall of their respective houses. Without sentimentality or sensationalism Keller describes the logic of events which persuades the young people that a shared death is preferable to the long drawn out misery of separation.

Only a master of prose and a great connoisseur of human nature could have related with such tact and good taste how passion wells up in Sali and Vrenchen and makes it impossible for them to separate. Half crazed with desire the lovers reach the point where the pulse of the world is one with their heart-beats, the sweet mysticism of eros:

"Wie schön ist es da ringsherum! Hörst du nicht etwas tönen, wie ein schöner Gesang oder ein Geläute?"

"Es ist das Wasser, das rauscht! Sonst ist alles still."

"Nein, es ist noch etwas anderes, hier, dort hinaus, überall tönt's!"

"Ich glaube, wir hören unser eigenes Blut in unseren Ohren rauschen!"

Sie horchten ein Weilchen auf diese eingebildeten oder wirklichen Töne, welche von der grossen Stille herrührten oder welche sie mit den magischen Wirkungen des Mondlichtes verwechselten, welches nah und fern über die weißen Herbstnebel wallte, welche tief auf den Gründen lagen.

Speaking of his source for *Romeo und Julia*, a newspaper report, Keller writes, "man nehme an, die jungen Leute haben das Schiff entwendet, um darauf ihre verzweifelte und gottverlassene Hochzeit zu halten, abermals ein Zeichen von der um sich greifenden Entsittlichung und Verwilderung der Leidenschaften". But as Keller has shown us, Sali and Vrenchen are both good and wholesome young people with sound, healthy instincts despite the unhappiness of their home lives. They are not unprincipled young vagrants. Since for them life without love would be unthinkable, they have chosen the only possible course.

The lasting impression which remains with the reader is of Keller's skilful use of colour. The sunshine in the first pages shines on the brown earth and the white caps of the ploughing peasants; the children arrive with the little, green-painted cart, with their fathers' food wrapped in white napkins, and they all sit down to enjoy it, with the silver smoke rising from Seldwyla in the distance, for the housewives there are cooking lunch. Sali counts Vrenchen's pearly white teeth. In due course the black fiddler casts a gloomy shadow over the children's lives. The closing stages of the father's quarrel when they actually lay violent hands on one another are accompanied by rather primitive stage effects of lowering clouds and rumbling thunder. The clothes in which the two children dress for their last happy day together are carefully described, and we even learn that Vrenchen has a posy of rosemary, roses and asters. Keller does not shun less agreeable detail on occasion; we learn that from an early stage of their quarrel Manz and Marti would spit on the ground on seeing one another. This primitive manifestation of dislike would not be surprising in a naturalist work, but in Keller's early work it seems a little startling.

Keller's variation on the Romeo and Juliet story is most powerfully and movingly narrated. Surely no other pages in German Literature excel the pathos of the description of the children's last day together, culminating in the stages of their ascent on to the hayboat which becomes their funeral barge. It has been objected by certain critics, notably Fontane, that *Romeo und Julia auf dem Dorfe* contains an incongruous mixture of styles. It is certainly true that the work reflects differing moods and situations and that each change of mood, each new situation finds appropriate and memorable expression. If Keller seems occasionally to romanticise childhood and young love, he is only regarding them as many people, probably the majority of us, tend to regard them. Similarly, if the collapse of the two peasants' family fortunes is depressingly, even sordidly portrayed, Keller's view of their situation differs from that of most sensible people only in being very ably and fully communicated. His judgement of the events narrated evidently differs from that of the newspaper reporter who gave him the idea; but it differs mainly because the creative imagination can penetrate nearer to the truth than most of us. The truth has many aspects, and *Romeo und Julia* recaptures several of these aspects convincingly within its few pages.

Frau Regel Amrain und ihr Jüngster

Like *Pankraz* and *Der grüne Heinrich*, *Frau Regel Amrain* is an imaginative recreation of the relationship between Keller and his mother. Frau Regel, though not a widow, has been deserted by her husband and sees her role in life as the upbringing according to exacting standards of her three young sons. Fritz, the youngest, who, at a critical moment saves his mother from yielding to the amorous advances of her overseer in the family business, becomes the favourite and trusted son. As a reward he receives the full benefit of his mother's moral education.

With most of Frau Regel's moral attitudes the reader will

probably find himself in agreement. Most people would at any rate pay lip service to the idea that a child should be adequately but not luxuriously fed and clothed and discouraged from regarding the creature comforts as an end in themselves. Intelligent training in the handling of money is also indisputably part of a sound upbringing and education. Fritz is taught not to regard the possession of money as the supreme good, yet not on the other hand to fall into the opposite fault of regarding financial independence as unimportant. Frau Regel also deals very competently with the inevitable juvenile lapses into dishonesty, so that at an early age Fritz has realised that lying and stealing are foolish and unrewarding activities. Considerable stress is also laid upon decent and generous behaviour towards other people. Later on, when Frau Regel's restraining hand is laid upon Fritz's clumsy first overtures to the opposite sex, we must agree with her objectives even if we question the tact of her methods.

When all this has been said, one wonders whether Frau Regel's other interventions in her son's affairs would command such universal approval. The incident at the wedding, to which Fritz goes for a joke clad in his mother's best finery, leaves us feeling more than a little uncomfortable. We understand Regula's pique at her son's behaviour, but her tearing up of her own best dress, which has been defiled by being worn in unworthy company, strikes us as an extreme reaction to a comparatively insignificant provocation. Fritz is very taken aback by her extreme annoyance, and although Keller rather labours the point about the women at the wedding being unsuitable company, we cannot really feel that he succeeds in justifying his heroine. He makes her seem a severe and strong-minded woman but we can scarcely applaud her behaviour, even if Fritz's prank was calculated to exasperate her beyond measure.

The story of Fritz's adventures with the liberal volunteers who went to assist the liberals of other cantons to overthrow their reactionary governments by force is quite entertaining. Nevertheless, when Fritz is taken prisoner and Frau Regel refuses to pay his ransom since she realises that in a week or two an amnesty will be declared, we marvel at her severity in dealing with her own flesh and blood. From the point of view of the community as a whole she did act correctly, of course, but she does seem inhumanly farseeing in this episode. In his anxiety to show Regel

Amrain's freedom from excessive emotionalism Keller has depicted a woman who sometimes denies good and natural feeling.

The climax of Regel Amrain's career comes in her political intervention, which has to take place through the agency of her son, since Swiss women do not enjoy the vote. Her pursuit of Fritz to his work at the quarry with his town clothes and her insistence that he should stop work and go to vote seem to reflect adversely on the relationship between her and her now adult son. Of course Fritz should have gone to vote, but he should have gone of his own free will, not because his mother insisted. An all-male democracy whose survival depends on the determination at appropriate moments of female relatives to make their men-folk do their national or civic duty is not in good health. However, Keller effectively makes the point that every citizen ought to exercise his right to vote and must practise increasing vigilance to safeguard his own and others' rightful liberties.

The handling by mother and son of the delinquent father on his return from America leaves nothing to be desired. Having unexpectedly made a fortune, the elder Amrain has come back intending to resume control of the quarry. However, his youngest son tells him firmly but politely that, although he is welcome to stay in the house, his debts have long since been paid and he can no longer be allowed any interest in the quarry. Old Amrain submits with a good grace to the will of his wife and son.

Frau Regel Amrain scarcely commands the unqualified approval of all readers. We are willing enough to see little Fritz's early years moulded and determined by his mother's strong will and love of rectitude. Later on, however, we feel uneasy about the extent of her direct influence over him. Keller had a hankering after managing women, and he gives full play to it in this work.

Keller, at this stage still the willing pupil of Feuerbach, concerns himself exclusively with the secular upbringing of his hero. Ermatinger contrasts *Regel Amrain* favourably with *Wilhelm Meister* in this regard, but surely we are justified in wondering what are the underlying assumptions about the nature of human life in any work purporting to deal with education. *Frau Regel Amrain* provides commonsense guidance on several common everyday problems. But are we to believe that a lively and intelligent youth like Fritz never speculated about religious matters?

We cannot accept either that Frau Regel's brand of mild humanism administered by a will of iron answers every fundamental question of education. Because *Frau Regel* not only does not answer these questions but also completely refrains from posing them, it does not wholly succeed even in the more modest task that it does attempt.

The structure of the work is simple. After a brief section explaining the family's situation after being deserted by the father and a paragraph or two to show how a special relationship develops between mother and son, the work shows by means of a simple third person narrative how Frau Regel coped with the various stages of Fritz's upbringing. The method is almost too straightforward to be interesting, and one could wish that Keller were not quite so certain that everything Frau Regel undertook was a success.

Even if in general conception and narrative structure *Frau Regel* is one of Keller's less successful inventions, it possesses many good touches. In particular Keller's inimitably original and creative use of language is found everywhere. Take, for instance, the sentence near the beginning of the work describing Herr Amrain's corpulence: ". . . the food is mightily attracted by the magnetic mountain of his belly . . ." This is a truly characteristic phrase, original, vivid, bordering on the grotesque, and the work shows numerous other examples.

The story throws light on Keller's views of personal and social obligation. It demonstrates how he thinks a young man might ideally develop under the influence of a good woman. We may well consider, however, that Fritz's brothers are dismissed a little too casually, to say nothing of his wife, who never becomes a person in her own right and never seems to gain the natural ascendancy over his mother in Fritz's affection that she would be entitled to expect. Frau Regel is very evidently a bachelor's creation. As a study of an ideal relationship between parent and child it is not completely satisfying.

Die drei gerechten Kammacher

Keller says that while the existence of Seldwyla proves that a whole town populated by unjust or frivolous people can exist quite happily, three just men under the same roof would quickly get in one another's hair. In illustration of this contention he relates the story of the three comb-makers who all aspire to buy the same small comb-factory and to marry the same unlovely but not penniless old maid. The development of an impossibly tense situation between the three men and their master's rough and ready means of resolving the difficulty form the substance of the story.

One of the delights of the *Kammacher* is the rapidity with which the mood changes. When we meet the combmakers in the early part, the personality of each man emerges separately from the ironic, satirical short descriptions. As the tale advances the satirical tone becomes more marked, and Keller revels in ever more grotesque touches. By the time of the combmakers' race the story has become a riot, the two elder men panting downhill towards the town with their trolleys full of luggage behind them, both at bitter enmity with one another. Only Dietrich, the youngest, enjoys the favour and moral support of Züs Bünzlin. Jobst is so incensed by Fridolin's superior progress that regardless of fair play he throws a stick between his rival's legs and makes him stumble; a little boy jumps on to Jobst's trolley and enjoys a ride on it. From this hilarious excitement the mood changes again as we learn how Jobst so despairs at losing the race that he hangs himself; Fridolin is so upset by seeing his rival's fate that he goes completely to the dogs, but Dietrich has the worst fate of all with Züs Bünzlin for a wife.

The story demonstrates Keller's remarkable gift of characterisation. All the combmakers, though bordering on the grotesque, remain credible and each stands out as an individual, Jobst with his Saxon caution, his suspicion and avoidance of politics, his philistinism, meanness and general reluctance to become involved with life, Fridolin with his substantial hoard, his tenacity of purpose and his seeming mildness and politeness, and the successful Dietrich, who adds to the small-minded prudence of the other two an extra dash of resourcefulness, the touch of genius that makes him pay court to Züs Bünzlin to enable him to overcome the others' advantage in terms of time for saving money.

Züs Bünzlin herself is a most memorable creation, a kind of monument to what cautious bachelors of all ages and lands have thought of the designing human female. She is the absolute incarnation of a woman destined by Providence for an old maid.

By some ironical twist she manages to secure a man, whose existence she will inevitably blight. She is interested only in being
given presents and being listened to when she talks (always of
herself) in a sanctimonious, half-educated manner. Avaricious
and grudging, she has no taste in clothes, and she will not let any
of the combmakers talk about himself, a dire disadvantage in a
wife.

The story shows that a certain kind of prudence or caution
may just as readily ruin a man's life as recklessness or extrava-
gance. An exclusive preoccupation with money, ambition and
one's own rectitude may lead to disappointment and frustration.
None of the combmakers is prepared for a moment to cast his
bread upon the waters. They are essentially ungenerous in outlook and suffer for this in the long run. Those who consider only
their own interest may well find that they serve even their own
interest badly.

Keller has a dig at a traditional weakness of many Germans,
their indifference towards politics. Jobst says: "Yes, yes, the
Swiss are political people. It is certainly, I think, a fine thing to
take an interest in politics, if one is keen on that. I for my part
know nothing about it; where I come from it has never been the
custom."

From the stylistic point of view the *Kammacher* is a very characteristic piece of work. In describing Züs Bünzlin's possessions,
the contents of her drawer, or the Chinese temple made for her
by her adoring bookbinder, Keller provides the long, detailed
and ironical verbal pictures of small objects which are one of his
specialities. The mounting excitement of the combmakers' undignified race is extremely well narrated, too. Keller is clearly
quite carried away by his own exuberant imagination as he
describes how Jobst and Fridolin career downhill, and on arrival
in Seldwyla are so firmly locked in an angry embrace that they
do not notice they have passed their destination but go rushing
on and out through the gate at the far end of the town. Again we
might single out Keller's ironically incongruous use of a famous
phrase from Winckelmann: when Dietrich arrives in the comb-
maker's house Jobst and Fridolin think he will provide "a jolly
measure for them to gauge their *tranquil greatness* against". Another pleasing detail is Keller's description of the feather quilt
lying on the three combmakers before their quarrel "like a paper

on three herrings". We have already noticed the skill with which Keller effects the transition from the grotesque to the tragic when he recounts Jobst's unhappy fate. Altogether Keller gives much of himself in *Die drei gerechten Kammacher*, displaying a disciplined sense of form, acute moral perception, rich humour and that awareness of tragic overtones which is an essential constituent of the best comedy.

Spiegel das Kätzchen

Compared with the earlier tales in the collection, *Spiegel* shows clear evidence of a romantic ancestry. In fact it closely resembles a German Romantic fairy-tale. At first it might well seem a very surprising work to find in the *Seldwyla* context, but on closer examination we find that although the story takes place in a different period, and although it definitely belongs to an unreal world of the imagination, *Spiegel* is not so different in its innermost essence, its underlying attitudes from the other stories of the collection.

The romantic elements in *Spiegel* are readily recognisable. Pineiß, the town wizard of Seldwyla, the clever, industrious, heartless villain of the piece, is a fairy-tale villain with a fantastic name and a total disregard of other people's rights or interests. The talking animals are another familiar element of romantic fairy-tale. Spiegel has many human attributes, his dignity, his philosophical decorum, his turning away after achieving satiety from the pleasures of the flesh, his resourcefulness. The old owl too is an absolute paragon of owlish wisdom and helpfulness, and the ceremonious, pseudo-archaic dialogue which Spiegel and the owl utter, complete with exchange of small presents, constitutes yet another of the unexpected minor delights of the story. The old witch emerging from the chimney in the guise of a beautiful naked girl on a broomstick represents a commonplace romantic motif. Sometimes such motifs are ironically used, as when Spiegel sings like a nightingale to his sweetheart through the long, moonlit nights or when Spiegel's amorous tumblings are referred to as "Minnespiel"; there is a passage describing the delights of love for Spiegel (Stille und laute Stunden, süße Gefühle und sonniger Streit . . .) in which Keller quite deliberately imitates a lush romantic style, probably that of Jean Paul, even down to using such literary conceits as "als die Scheibe des Mondes voll geworden". Pineiß' discomfiture at the end of the story constitutes a fairy-tale revenge too.

Apart from the imitation of the romantic fairy-tale, *Spiegel* contains many good touches, as for instance when Pineiß boasts of the fine grass on his roof with its medicinal properties, or when he stresses that Spiegel for good astrological reasons should die before the next full moon, or in the detailed description of Pineiß' multifarious activities; a memorable phrase records the departure of the white cat, "kühl miauend" from the scene of her love with Spiegel. Pineiß at the wedding feast, dipping his hand in the bowl of gold on the table and revelling in the feel of the precious metal and Pineiß, broken and terrified after discovering whom he has married, are other moments which stick in one's mind.

Pineiß unscrupulously tries to take advantage of Spiegel's predicament when he is homeless and hungry. He shows himself devoid of natural human sympathy. Spiegel's healthy and natural love of food should not have been used as a weapon against him. Pineiß wrongly supposes that the best possible bargain can be driven with other people under duress. However, the tables are turned against him by Spiegel; like many another person who behaves meanly and cruelly, Pineiß finds himself the loser in the long run. Spiegel may be taken as a symbol of the ordinary human being, leading a balanced and sensible life with a certain philosophical dignity and decorum. Rather like a human refugee he is jolted out of his accustomed ways and for a time even forsakes his usual standards of behaviour, although he quickly reverts to them when Pineiß provides him with food and shelter. Pineiß, the romantic wizard, disregards the natural rights of others.

The whole story stresses the need to enter by an effort of imaginative sympathy into the situation of our neighbours and not to take advantage of their distress. Even the tale within the tale points in the same direction. The young woman in Spiegel's story who tries to exploit to excess her lover's attachment to herself pays for her cold calculation of natural law with her life's happiness. She represents another variation of the kind of ungenerous, unloving woman represented by Lydia in *Pankraz* and Züs Bünzlin in the *Kammacher*.

The appeal of Spiegel stems largely from the treatment of a modern or indeed universal moral issue within a traditional, fairy-tale framework. It is unique among Keller's works in this regard, a rare blend of novelty with tradition.

Kleider machen Leute

This story opens the second volume of *Die Leute von Seldwyla*. Although it was not written till the late 1860s or the 1870s, its origins go back a long way in Keller's life. In his boyhood Keller must have read about a young huntsman who, masquerading as the son of a Count from Baden, took in the naïve society of Winterthur and extracted considerable sums of money from a rich Polish refugee. The villagers of Wädenswil on Lake Zurich were once the victims of a similar deception, and their neighbours, the people of Richterswil, played an entertaining little Shrovetide comedy about the gullible Wädenswilers. From Wassali's *Bündnerkalender* for 1847, to which Keller himself had contributed a slight *Novelle. Die mißlungene Vergiftung*, came the story of the young tailor in the aristocratic coach.

The plot concerns a young tailor, who having lost his job in Seldwyla and taken to the road on the search for work is mistaken (by the people of Goldach) because of his pretentious attire for a rich Polish nobleman. He could not have prevented the original mistake, which was due to the credulity and folly of the inhabitants of Goldach, but he could have prevented the ensuing complications, including a love intrigue. The tailor's deception is exposed by a rival in love, and only the improbable determination of the *Amstrat's* daughter to marry Strapinsky whoever he is and whatever he may have done makes a happy ending possible.

Strapinsky's fault lies in his refusal to contradict the false impression that his affected clothes and bearing convey. Although he was not responsible for the original mistake as to his identity, it lay within his power to put an end to it at an early stage. Because he found it enjoyable to see the rest of the world deceived by his fine appearance and aristocratic bearing he allowed events to take their course until in the end he had contracted considerable financial liabilities and involved an innocent girl in a very distressing emotional entanglement. Keller by implication con-

demns Strapinsky's unwillingness to accept his own humble lot
in life and make the most of it. The humiliation of exposure—
and later very nearly death by a different kind of exposure—is
the punishment which he has to endure because of his determination to go on seeming to be what he is not. However, Keller
likes Strapinsky too well to exact the full penalty of his weakness
from him and the *Novelle* ends with the unexpected discomfiture
of his rival Böhni and the taking over of a complicated situation
by a determined and competent Nettchen who resolves the confusion to her own satisfaction and to Strapinsky's long-term advantage. Strapinsky has to learn the same lesson as so many other
characters in Keller's books: a man must not be carried away by
romantic notions of what the world owes him. He will fare far
better by doing solid work within the limits set by his native
ability.

Melchior Böhni, Strapinsky's rival, is a familiar type of person
in Keller's works. Böhni—one can almost feel Keller's contempt
in the very name—forms the very embodiment of that worthy,
solid, calculating, striving mediocrity which Keller especially disliked and which he satirised so effectively in *Die drei gerechten
Kammacher*. Though Strapinsky has the advantage of Böhni in
the end, this is not really due to any particular cunning or con-
trivance on his own part. It delights Keller to show that the
subtlest manoeuvres of people such as Böhni or Pineiß cannot
always ensure them greater success than sometimes falls to the
lot of the improvident, simple, naïve child of nature.

Just as Melchior Böhni resembles other characters in Keller's
works, Nettchen is also a familiar type, the managing, resourceful young woman who provides the initiative which her diffident
fiancé lacks. She makes a bold fight on his behalf, for we certainly cannot imagine that Strapinsky left to his own devices
would have brought the story to a happy conclusion. Like Frau
Regel Amrain she provides moral guidance and financial stability
for a young man who would not by himself be capable of attaining these desirable ends. The scene in which Nettchen takes the
half-frozen Strapinsky to the farmhouse, makes him confess his
true identity, and, having shown that she knows the worst about
him, helps him to regain his self-confidence and assurance through
his love for her, possesses genuine pathos. It is Nettchen who
in the end seizes the initiative and decides that despite all she and

Strapinsky still belong to one another: "I will not desert you!" she cries. "You are mine, and I will go along with you despite the whole world!"

Once again the story is full of good visual pictures. Strapinsky makes an engaging hero with his pallid, handsome face, his diffidence and gentleness, his readiness to be cast in the role of foreign nobleman by the silly people of Goldach who are so comically eager to take him at his face value. With his circular grey cloak trimmed with black velvet and worn over his black Sunday suit, the tailor is not deliberately setting out to deceive the world; he is merely living up to the image of himself which his mother had cherished and in which he had secretly half believed. The description of the hero's temptation in the inn "zur Waage" is unforgettable; Keller is always good at evoking the joys of the table and the bottle, but he excels himself here.

Keller's picture of the town of Goldach forms one of the minor excellences of the story. The comfortable bourgeois houses with their delightful old-fashioned names seem to stand there before our very eyes. Centuries of social history are recorded in the names of the houses, and Keller interprets a few of these names for our benefit, showing in the process a thorough grasp of Swiss history. The author of the *Züricher Novellen* merely devoted himself more completely than hitherto to a life-long interest; Keller was deeply versed in the history of Switzerland.

Kleider machen Leute is one of a group of stories—it includes also the next two in this collection—in which Keller stresses the importance of being oneself, of laying more emphasis on being than seeming, of trusting in honest effort rather than hoping for quick but undeserved advancement. Strapinsky, we may well feel, gets off rather lightly considering the deception that he practises; however, Keller thinks of him as considerably less guilty than Johann Kabis in *Der Schmied seines Glückes*, who quite deliberately attempts to renounce his own personality in favour of a false one. Strapinsky has to aim at modest success within his natural limits. He must stop pretending and over-reaching himself, then his good, if limited, talents will have a chance of developing. The same theme of recognising one's own limitations and striving to fulfil oneself within them underlies the *Züricher Novellen*, with which *Kleider machen Leute* as already indicated possesses other affinities.

Der Schmied seines Glückes

Hans Kabis' story represents a slight variation of that of Wenzel Strapinsky, but it is informed by a more bitter and satirical tone. Whereas Strapinsky finds the world pushing him into a role which he does not deserve, Kabis, after a series of subterfuges, culminating in his willingness to renounce his honourable poverty and unblemished anonymity for the sake of wealth and position to which he knows perfectly well he is not entitled, finds that in the end he must renounce all his doubtful and undeserved gains and revert to an even humbler station in life than that which he had left to make his fortune. Because Kabis is guilty of a more deliberate deception than Strapinsky, his punishment is more severe. The renunciation of his humble but respectable birth is an offence which Keller is not prepared to take lightly. *Der Schmied seines Glückes* again forcefully makes the point that a man worth his salt will cheerfully fulfil the role for which he has been cast by destiny and will not try to turn himself into what he is not. Kabis' first real happiness in life comes after he has been making nails for some time, when he has learned the value of honest and unpretentious labour.

Keller paints a very harsh portrait of Kabis, with his foolish attempts to change his plain name, his abortive endeavour to marry well, and his determination to cut a fine figure, although he is not prepared to work. An important element in this description is the long enumeration of Kabis' treasured possessions, which Keller reels off in the same way as he lists the contents of Züs Bünzlin's chest of drawers. The elaborate cigar-holder forms a particularly telling motif, and altogether we gain the impression of a foppish and shallow person, who has quite forgotten that appearances are not the only thing that matters.

Old Adam Litumlei, the feeble and impotent elderly cousin proves a natural victim of a scheming rascal such as Kabis. His naïve pretence that the family portraits in his fine town house are those of his own ancestors is a simple and harmless enough deception, it would seem, but it leads directly to the further pretence that John is his illegitimate son and hence to the whole sordid plot which proves to be the latter's undoing. Frau Litumlei emerges as an unattractive figure, lazy, greedy, lecherous and quite without principle. Her behaviour towards her lover is scarcely surprising but thoroughly discreditable.

The attentive reader will remember with special appreciation the careful description of Herr Litumlei's house in Augsburg, for Hans Kabis a veritable vision of splendour, an enchanted world of wealth and privilege to which he seeks access. The extraordinary contrast between the diminutive and insigificant Litumlei and the enormous mirror before which we first see him also remains incongruously in the memory. Another part of the story which is particularly well done is the description of John's simulated hesitation before agreeing to be a party to the old man's deception and of his elaborate preparations to ensure that he may appear to have lost his appetite over the strain of decision. However, a hundred other details could just as easily be singled out, for instance Keller's highly evocative description of the bouquet of old Rhenish wine which Litumlei produces after Kabis has agreed to pretend to be his bastard son, or the prosaic and unedifying account of Kabis' parentage which the two men hatch out between visits to public houses.

There is more than a hint of social criticism in Keller's strictures on the increasing Swiss practice of turning their girls into schoolmistresses and governesses. The Seldwylers, we are told, did not much care whether the girls received a more religious, bourgeois or aristocratic type of education. All that they wanted was that their daughters should find remunerative positions in the outside world and make regular remittances home.

Everywhere the story is written in a lively and pictorial style. The vision of armies of governesses each armed with a passport and umbrella leaving Seldwyla makes the desired point humorously and emphatically. Again, John Kabis' reaction to the news of his own child's birth in Herr Litumlei's house is to goggle with his eyes and purse his lips as though he had to kiss a hedgehog. The freshness and originality of the style, as well as the feeling Keller succeeds in awakening that Kabis' insincerities and shirking of obligations are by no means untypical of Seldwyla, fully justifies him in writing again on the same theme.

Die mißbrauchten Liebesbriefe
The misused love letters

This *Novelle* is thematically akin to the two preceding ones, in that it again exposes the harmfulness of pretence and affectation. The unjustified literary aspirations of Viktor Störteler prove to be his undoing.

The name Viktor Störteler—especially as abbreviated Viggi— suggests a prosaic and ordinary person, and indeed this is no inappropriate description of the misguided shopkeeper who at the age of forty or so begins to take an interest in literature and before long has started writing novels and short stories under the pretentious pseudonym of Kurt vom Walde. Despite his total lack of qualifications for literary success, Viggi finds people even more foolish than himself who eagerly buy the rubbish he writes. Keller's satirical account of such authors, their public and their works is clearly directed against the trashy popular pseudo-historical literature of the day such as the periodical *Teut*. However, Störteler's crowning folly consists in involving his wife in his literary activities. His steam-rollering of the reluctant Gritli into participation in his intellectual pursuits is very well conveyed, and the first letter of their contrived correspondence is a satirical masterpiece, full of hackneyed imagery and sentimental exaggeration. Amusingly enough, we observe that when Störteler wishes to communicate with Gritli about everyday matters he has to do so separately in a postscript.

The first of the two sections into which the story naturally falls describes Viktor Störteler's foolish passion for literature and its disastrous effect on his marriage. When the authorities agree to a divorce between Viggi and Gritli, the first section is at an end. The second part concerns Gritli and Wilhelm, who had played only a minor role in the first part. In the account of Wilhelm's solitary rural life after the divorce proceedings, Keller displays that love of the country and its pursuits, the intimate knowledge of nature and the faith in the restorative power of manual work in the open air which make him a worthy successor of Jeremias Gotthelf. The pace of the dénouement could with advantage have been made less leisurely.

The whole work demonstrates that justice prevails in Keller's world in the end. Viggi Störteler loses his attractive young wife and gets in her place Kätter Ambach, the absolute pattern of a vicious, pretentious, greedy and unscrupulous woman. For Keller, greed for food is one of the characteristics of the really nasty human female. The unfaithful wife in *Der Schmied seines Glückes* is seldom seen without some appetising piece of pastry in her hand, and Kätter Ambach eats Störteler out of house and home. Wilhelm atones by the loss of his job and many months of unhappiness for his share in the letter-writing episode, but he eventually receives his due reward when his character has sufficiently developed to warrant it. Gritli pays heavily too for her subterfuge in getting the schoolmaster to write her letters, but she also receives suitable compensation in the end.

The harmfulness of trying to appear to be what one is not constitutes the underlying theme of the whole story. Viktor Störteler is manifestly not cut out for the profession of literature. Keller savagely attacks the snobbish, sentimental, cheap literature of the day. The episode concerning the waiter who, after achieving some success as a purveyor of such third-rate fiction, decides that he owes it to his self-respect to revert to being an honest waiter, drives home the lesson that as far as Keller is concerned literature is a highly professional matter and cannot be produced by Tom, Dick or Harry at will. Unfortunately, Viktor Störteler never learns the lesson which the waiter has at last succeeded in learning. From Viggi himself the poison spreads to affect the other people about him. Gritli cannot live up to the stupid and unnatural standards set by her husband, and uses Wilhelm so that she in turn may seem what she is not to Viggi. Wilhelm in turn allows himself to be exploited in an unbecoming, unmanly way. His growing-up process consists in the discovery of his pride, dignity and self-sufficiency as a man. Both Gritli and he, despite their respective aberrations, have remained fundamentally good and simple people, and hence their punishment is far less severe than Störteler's, who serves in the end merely as the means by which the couple are united.

Dietegen

Dietegen has affinities with almost every kind of work Keller ever wrote. Its historical setting recalls the *Züricher Novellen*; the cheerful Seldwylers' pursuit of their stern neighbours with a long-handled black paintbrush may well remind us of similar slapstick situations in the *Kammacher*, in which an almost grotesquely satirical element can be found. Keller's insistence that each partner must contribute equally to a successful marriage foreshadows the fuller treatment of the same theme in *Das Sinnegedicht*. The detailed accounts of late fifteenth century Swiss life recall Keller's Dürer-like studies for a picture of a mediæval town. Even Dietegen's resurrection from his coffin has its parallel in other works; Keller always feared he might be buried alive. The full-blooded life in the forester's house has a familiar ring to the reader who remembers Heinrich Lee's new life in his uncle's house after his expulsion from school; and the accounts of festivities which punctuate *Dietegen* are characteristic of the poet who acted as the acknowledged official spokesman of his native city and canton at times of general rejoicing.

In Berlin Keller had read an entertaining old Swiss history book, Melchior Schuler's *Die Taten und Sitten der alten Eidgenossen erzählt für die vaterländische Jugend in Schule und Haus* (Zurich, 1839), especially the chapters dealing with the Burgundian wars and the so-called *Gesellen vom törichten Leben*, who roamed the country looting, plundering and behaving in a lawless fashion in the late fifteenth century, and the parts describing civic entertainments, witch trials and popular superstitions of those days. Keller made discriminating use of the badly ordered material of his source and also included material originally collected for a verse epic about four brothers who all fought in the battle of St Jakob an der Birs. At the battle of Grandson described in Dietegen men of varying temperament unite and suppress their individuality in defence of the common weal. Keller may also, as the text suggests, have made use of a now lost sixteenth century portrait of a woman as a further source of details for his work, but no record of this exists in any of his papers.

Keller shows himself capable in *Dietegen* of reconstructing a historical background very successfully; the world of the late fifteenth century comes alive in these pages, with its rough and ready justice, its superstitions and the constant interruption of ordinary life by the outbreak of war. The healthy and rather enjoyable routine of the forester's household comes across very well : Keller allows poetic imagination to supplement a considerable acquaintance with social history and the result is a credible account of life in a prosperous country home.

The symmetry of the beginning and end of the story forms an attractive feature; Dietegen was literally snatched from his coffin by Küngolt and at the end of the story only his willingness to marry her saved her from her condemnation as a sorceress, so the basis of their married life together is that each of them owes his life to the other; in the original version, begun in Berlin in the 1850s, Keller had probably not fully worked out the story of Dietegen's rescue by Küngolt. The effect of the work as we know it depends largely on these parallel life-saving actions at the beginning and the end.

Küngolt and Dietegen are unhistorical characters, although each owes something to an historical personage of whom Keller had read in Schuler. The young thief who recovered from death by drowning in Lucerne in 1473, and the child murderess from Solothurn whose life was spared when a young man expressed his willingness to marry her, had no connection in history, but Keller fused the two incidents in *Dietegen*.

Love is portrayed throughout the story as a powerful preservative and regenerative force. Love causes little Küngolt to open Dietegen's coffin at the beginning of the tale. Küngolt's love for Dietegen affects her mother and father and causes them to welcome the homeless boy. The two children never cease to love one another, although Dietegen goes through a phase of having to get away from Küngolt; she becomes difficult and coquettish for a while. However, when Küngolt has neither friends nor position in the world, Dietegen comes to her aid, without realising it, almost in spite of himself, he still loves her, and when he again allows his love free expression their lives cease to be problematical. As so often in Keller it is the woman who takes the initiative and sees clearly from the beginning what role the man is destined to play in her life, but because she is too demanding and in too much of a hurry she alienates Dietegen's affection for a time. Since he loves her, he realises when her situation becomes desperate that he must help her, and then he suddenly decides to join his fortunes to hers for good.

The characters of Dietegen and Küngolt come across well. He is slow, deliberate, stern and suspicious, a true man of Ruechenstein. Küngolt is warm, impulsive, quick and affectionate, and they complement one another admirably.

The inconsistent portrayal of Violande's character constitutes a serious weakness. As a young girl we are told she had schemed to prevent one marriage after another, and she had not hesitated to blacken other women's characters without any provocation. When she first moves into the forester's house she is manifestly incapable of managing the household, and she encourages Küngolt to behave badly towards Dietegen, since a marriage between the two young people might well threaten her own position. So far a consistent picture of an unpleasantly scheming woman has emerged. It is hard to believe that Violande, who has always and only considered her own interest, would go to considerable lengths to save Küngolt's life. Even her late betrothal and marriage to the forester do not sufficiently account for such a complete transformation. Keller had clearly not fully thought out Violande's role in the book. We can readily believe that she unites good and bad elements in her character, and even that the good would begin to predominate when she achieved the married state for which she had craved; but no evidence exists at all in the earlier part of the book that she had ever harboured an unselfish thought, and it seems unlikely that in middle age she would make a solitary and exhausting journey in time of war from German Switzerland to Geneva to seek assistance for a once hated rival.

The inconsistency in Violande's character mars an otherwise well told story. At first we might imagine that the Ruechensteiners are going to behave like comic opera villains, but Keller retrieves himself in time before his enthusiasm for caricature has carried him too far into the realm of the grotesque. By the end of the story the Ruechensteiners are admittedly sterner and more censorious than the Seldwylers, but they also pursue justice and rectitude more eagerly.

Das verlorene Lachen (Lost laughter)

This story treats of a marriage which almost founders because both partners give too free rein to inborn qualities, which, though good in themselves, must remain subordinated to the prime consideration of making the marriage work. Jukundus Meyenthal, the spoiled darling of a widowed mother, is popular, sociable and has a fine baritone voice. He is a soldier and progressing very satisfactorily in his chosen career. He is quite unfitted for business because of his generally cheerful and easy-going nature, his excessive frankness of disposition and his charming naïveté.

His wife Justine, the daughter of a rich and prosperous family, is serious-minded, inclined to worry, somewhat censorious and well capable of that degree of secretiveness and self-seeking which, along with a certain singleness of purpose, can assure success in business. Small wonder then that, after she has tried to bend her husband to her family's ideas of what constitutes a successful career, he proves quite unsuitable and cannot make anything of a business career.

Justine's attempt to find in religion the satisfaction which she no longer finds in her marriage ends in failure. Keller despises the unorthodox priest who will not abandon his living because he has no other source of income, and Justine finds him a broken reed, too. When the pastor of Schwanau confides his inadequacy in her she knows that he cannot help her and she must seek elsewhere the support she craves. Keller dislikes the dogmatic eclecticism practised by those of the Zwinglian clergy who had been affected by Strauß's ideas but were not prepared to accept them wholeheartedly and logically.

Through Jukundus' dabbling in politics, Keller also exposes the ugliness, insincerity and slanderous nature of this branch of human activity. Jukundus' involvement in an unwholesome campaign of personal denigration does him no credit, but at least he is soon filled with revulsion at what he is doing. The figure of the *Ölweib*, that living incarnation of slander, sticks in the mind as one of the ugliest characters whom Keller ever created.

When the reconciliation between Justine and her husband at last takes place, Jukundus tells Justine that no happiness can be gained from dogmatic belief but that they must cling fast to the good things which they possess, such as their marriage, and accept life on the terms on which it is offered without enquiring too closely into matters about which no certainty is possible. Jukundus has meantime achieved success in business, having through his misfortunes learned the value of discretion. He no longer scoffs at his wife's dear illusions about the pastor of Schwanau—she has lost them anyway—but insists that their love for one another is the nearest thing to a divine revelation that they are ever likely to enjoy.

Jukundus and Justine are properly reconciled when Justine no longer tries to usurp her husband's authority. The transformation which has taken place in their relationship is symbolically seen in the names they give to their children; Justus and Jukunde, names which correspond more properly in Keller's view to the functions of man and woman in marriage. Having rediscovered their love for one another, Jukundus and Justine are able to laugh with that particularly engaging laughter which is common to them both.

Keller's professed intention in writing *Das verlorene Lachen* was to round off his collection of *Novellen* "with a more serious cultural and social picture". Certainly important issues are raised and to some extent developed in the story. Yet Keller scarcely succeeds in his intention. Without completely subscribing to Johannes Klein's opinion that the work is a total failure and a misfit in the context of *Die Leute von Seldwyla* we may well consider that his criticism (*Geschichte der deutschen Novelle,* Wiesbaden, 1954, p. 282), although immoderately expressed, has some foundation.

In *Das verlorene Lachen* Keller strains the form of the *Novelle* beyond the acceptable limits. The story lacks a single, central theme; within its ninety or so pages we read of the social revolution in Switzerland, of the way in which the European and Swiss economy is subject to the vagaries of American trade, of the Reform movement of the 1870s in the Zwinglian Church, of the growing lack of restraint in the conduct of public affairs which resulted in campaigns waged on a discreditable personal level against leading public figures, of Keller's private religious doubts and difficulties, reflected in those of Jukundus—these are only some of the elements which combine with the matrimonial growing pains of Jukundus and Justine and tend at times to make us unable to see the wood for the trees. The *Novelle* begins promisingly, and Jukundus and Justine are skilfully introduced; also, their reconciliation is tactfully and credibly related, although it would have been better not to make it depend on a chance meeting under rather curious circumstances. However, the middle of the story indisputably sags. Had Keller expanded the work into a novel, as he considered doing, he might well have produced a more satisfying book. We recognise in *Das verlorene Lachen* Keller's tentative fumbling towards a modern Swiss novel of everyday life, such as he later attempted on a larger scale in *Martin Salander*.

The Seldwyla Series

As Keller tells us in the introduction to Part I of the Seldwyla stories, Seldwyla means a happy place from the old Swiss German *Säld*, meaning happiness, and the common place-name suffix -wyl(a), found in such names as Rapperswil or Thalwil. Though it would be wrong to identify Seldwyla with any single Swiss town, it has features common to little German Swiss and other towns the world over. The inhabitants are kind and charitable, relaxed and comfortable in their attitude to life. They are by and large rather unsuccessful, particularly those who stay at home in Seldwyla, and they share the common provincial weakness of not being able to look far beyond the ends of their own noses. Most of them tend to enjoy themselves while they are still young and can obtain credit and to settle down to a period of rather rigorous drudgery in middle life. They are politically active, especially in hard times, when there is nothing else to do but make a fuss about politics. They always want to enjoy life and generally contrive to do so.

The picture changes somewhat when we come to the introduction to Keller's second volume, written during the *Gründerzeit*. The German wave of speculation and unbridled business expansion was now sweeping across Switzerland and affecting even places like Seldwyla. Keller believed that the traditional values of his country were threatened by the impact of the new age. In *Das verlorene Lachen*, for instance, he approaches the view of the commercial and industrial expansion expressed in *Martin Salander* a decade later. The "good and cheerful" days of Seldwyla have become a thing of the past and the easygoing, undemanding life is being replaced by something a great deal more intense, but far less happy. Keller states that the second volume of *Novellen* represents a late harvest from the good old days of Seldwyla before it became too much like the rest of the world. German Switzerland, in fact, is in danger of surrendering its individuality; Jukundus Meyenthal stands as a symbol of what

Keller thinks could easily happen to all Switzerland. Jukundus should not have sold himself body and soul to the commercialism of Justine's family. He languishes and pines and does not even succeed in what he mistakenly sets out to do. When he sees the error of his ways and *returns to Seldwyla* he again begins to prosper and lays the foundation for a happy and prosperous reunion with his wife. With all its faults, Keller loves the old Seldwyla, which is not so much a place as an attitude to life. Certainly, the outstanding citizens of Seldwyla, Pankraz or Fritz Amrain, possess a sterner moral fibre than most of their fellows, just as Keller had to escape from the narrowness and philistinism of his native city, but although he did not wish to resemble the Seldwylers in every respect, he was glad that they were as they were and alarmed when they showed signs of changing their character.

The stories of *Die Leute von Seldwyla* are very loosely connected. They are not really a *cycle* at all, although they betray a strong family resemblance. There is no direct link between the very brief introductions which precede each group of five stories and the stories themselves. Although the action of all the tales takes place at least partly in or near Seldwyla, and although Seldwyla does on the whole stand for a general attitude of good-natured philistinism, smugness and not very ruthless commercialism, the stories are by no means dependent for their effect on these introductions, nor do they have any connection with one another.

By and large, the prevailing tone is that of restrained realism. Certainly, Keller's reading of romantic authors may have affected him here and there as, for instance, in the roseate view of childhood and young love found in *Romeo und Julia* or in the delightful poetic whimsy of *Spiegel*; again in *Kleider machen Leute* we have the feeling that the world of the fairy-tale with its sudden transformations, its startling rewards and the unexpected intrusion of irrational forces is never far away; in *Die drei gerechten Kammacher* we are back in the homespun world of the trade guilds with a patriarchal relationship between master and journeymen; while the extravagant and grotesque *motifs* found here may remind us of Hoffmann or other Romantic authors, the work is in general more realistic than romantic and the predominant impression is of an author who has observed things and people with a shrewd and penetrating eye. In *Dietegen* and *Das verlorene Lachen* Keller strives hard to convey the atmosphere of the remote past in the one and of the *Gründerzeit* in the other, in both cases by an abundant selection of relevant detail. He writes with great skill and power, and exactly as one might expect of an author who had fed richly on the German Romantics but had reached maturity in a new, more appraising, observing and calculating age. He realises that it would be naïve to sigh for the return of the old romantic values, but neither can he reject them completely out of hand, however much of a man of his age he may be. Two stories, the most "romantic" and the most "realistic" respectively, *Spiegel* and *Das verlorene Lachen* are not quite at home among their neighbours; indeed Keller calls *Spiegel* a fairy-tale and *Das verlorene Lachen* as we have seen is more of an insufficiently developed *novel* than a German *Novelle*.

Die Leute von Seldwyla provides ample evidence that Keller could write really well when he chose to tackle subjects within his capabilities. Despite many individually excellent traits *Der grüne Heinrich* can hardly be called an artistic whole, but within the smaller compass of the *Novelle* Keller scores one success after another. It is difficult to single out one work above another in such a distinguished collection, but a general consensus has established that *Romeo und Julia*, the *Kammacher* and *Spiegel* are all short masterpieces. Keller can sustain a high stylistic level for the duration of a *Novelle*, but somehow never learned to organise his material and construct a plot for a longer work.

CHAPTER FOUR

SIEBEN LEGENDEN

ALTHOUGH not published till 1871, the Legends originated during Keller's days in Berlin, where he read *Legends of the Saints** published in 1804 by Ludwig Theobul Kosegarten, a Protestant minister from the island of Rügen. Kosegarten hoped that his legends would be a success among German Catholics, and he dedicated them to the Emperor, without having first of all ensured that the Papists would be willing to accept this unsolicited gift. In fact, the Austrian religious censors forbade his legends. It is difficult to see why they objected to the work. Kosegarten blindly and uncritically accepts the strange and miraculous events described in his sources. He states that he has not altered the stories, except for abridging some of them, and has endeavoured to render them in a straightforward and readily comprehensible style. Some of the legends are in verse, some in prose, and all proclaim the need to mortify the flesh and reflect the same underlying conviction that this world is a vale of tears, therefore the Christian should keep his eyes firmly focused on the world to come. Kosegarten states that the profession of the Christian faith often makes life difficult. He quotes from the sayings of Jesus and the apostles in this sense; discussing the vexed question of celibacy, he quotes the Apostle Paul's authority that the unmarried state is the more conducive to holiness. (Albert Leitzmann, in his edition of the sources of Keller's *Legends*, tells us that Kosegarten was unhappily married!) Kosegarten, as a confirmed *laudator temporis acti*, gives numerous examples of the greater readiness to obey difficult commandments of Jesus and the Apostles which had obtained in primitive Christian and mediæval times. "This piety is foreign to our age", he says regretfully. He hopes his legends will lead people to return to the simple faith of long ago. His legends are quite uncritically chosen, and while some among them memorably express spiritual truths, others make it clear

* Ludwig Theobul Kosegarten, *Legenden* Berlin, 1804.

that during the Christian Middle Ages there was often a very wide cleavage between religion and morality. We are sometimes asked to applaud actions which though performed by Christian saints can scarcely be interpreted as moral. Perhaps this was the reason why the Catholic clerics refused to allow Kosegarten's legends to circulate in Austria. They would have been damaging to the Christian cause if anyone had been expected to take them seriously. In a nutshell, Kosegarten was a simple and naïve soul, whose motley collection of traditional legendary material from many sources widely separated in time and place lacked artistry and a morally discriminating point of view.

Though they seemed an unpromising source for Keller to turn to, the legends provided him with two things. Some of these traditional themes were well adapted to the treatment of topics then exercising his mind; the situations in which the heroes of the legends found themselves could be used to describe under a poetic veil Keller's situation. The heterogeneous collection of legends all advocated the maximum mortification of the flesh and wherever possible the suppression of man's natural desires in the interest of his eternal welfare. Keller disagreed sharply with the traditional Christian belief in the necessity for asceticism. He tells us in his introduction that when he read Kosegarten's legends he suspected more than once that the Christian legends were adaptations of profane stories. He was trying to recapture the spirit of the originals from behind the ecclesiastical corruptions of them which Kosegarten reproduced, and in the process of doing this he sometimes had to alter the drift of the story and make it point a very different moral from that of Kosegarten.

Apart from Kosegarten, the experience which underlies the *Sieben Legenden* is Keller's love for Betty Tendering. More than one incident from Keller's love story has been incorporated with little modification in one or other of these stories. In addition to these two central strands, the *Legenden* incorporate many minor incidents from Keller's life and air various prejudices of their author.

Eugenia

The story of Eugenia, as told by Keller, is not very different in its outward action from Kosegarten's version. His Eugenia, a young bluestocking in ancient Alexandria, tries, in the conceit

of the educated woman, to deny her femininity and causes distress
to herself and unpleasant complications for others until her true
nature asserts itself under the stress of events and makes her glad
to admit to being a woman again.

Eugenia's excessive interest in intellectual pursuits seems
dangerous to Keller, who indeed prefixed the whole legend with
a stern verse from the Book of Deuteronomy about women who
wear men's clothes and men who wear women's clothes. From
spending all her energies on philosophical disputation, Eugenia
progresses by natural stages to thinking that this activity is more
important than marriage, which must be relegated to a secondary place in her life. Having all along placed excessive emphasis
on predominantly masculine pursuits, Eugenia invades even the
most private territory of the religious male and by becoming
abbot of a monastery reaches as it were the absolute summit of
achievement for a woman of her temperament. Here she is in a
completely false position, and the comparatively trivial incident
of the lecherous widow's attack on the abbot's virtue is only one
of the unfortunate results of Eugenia's masculine ambitions.

The trend of *Eugenia* is plain. Keller has no patience with
Eugenia's bluestocking aspirations or with her Christian asceticism. A healthy and beautiful young woman should marry the
man she wants and should not be too slow to say yes once she has
made up her mind. Eugenia's misguided insistence on her superior
rights as an intellectual woman nearly costs her her life's happiness, and her brief glory as an ornament of the Alexandrian
schools and as abbot of a monastery is irrelevant, even damaging
to her proper function of becoming a wife and mother. Apart
from the danger to her own happiness and that of Aquilinus,
Eugenia turns her two Hyacinths into emasculated little prigs
and exposes the wretched widow to a temptation which proves
too strong for her. On all counts it would have been better for
Eugenia to say yes in the first place.

To make it quite clear that he disapproves of Eugenia's behaviour, Keller uses the first three paragraphs of his legend for
an open expression of his views on women who want to play
a masculine role in life. The first paragraph states as a general
proposition that women who indulge in masculine activities tend
to proceed to the total disavowal of their sex, down to wearing
men's clothes and completely concealing the fact that they are

women. Though Keller takes his example from ancient Alexandria, he does not think any better of women of his own day who behave like Eugenia. This attitude emerges plainly from fairly numerous passages in his works.

Die Jungfrau und der Teufel
The Virgin and the Devil

Keller here takes a traditional tale and, while still following the outline of its action closely, changes and ennobles its morality. In Kosegarten's legend the knight was by divine intervention redeemed from the consequences of his folly. Keller thinks this is quite wrong, and Gebizo in his version does not receive divine sanction for his irresponsibility.

Kosegarten's legend tells of a wealthy knight who delights in making ostentatious gifts and enjoys the reputation of being a public benefactor on a vast scale. Presently he finds that he has squandered his whole substance on charity and has nothing left but his good and beautiful wife. Now the devil appears and in return for his wife promises him inexhaustible wealth, so that he may continue to endow churches and monasteries and entertain generously. The knight finds in the place the devil has mentioned quantities of gold and silver. He repays his mortgages, starts to build palaces and churches, and cuts a fine figure as a generous and noble patron of the arts. On the appointed day he tells his wife to come out riding with him to an undisclosed destination and without other attendance. The poor lady is afraid, and on the way begs leave to enter a little chapel and say a prayer to the Virgin. As she prays the Virgin descends from above the altar, assumes the form and clothes of the lady, and makes the latter fall into a deep slumber. Then the Virgin joins the husband who is waiting outside. When they reach the rendezvous the devil is immediately aware of the presence of the Holy Virgin, and abusing the knight for his supposed deceit, trembles at the aspect of the Virgin. She banishes the devil to his proper place, telling him never to molest her protégée further. There is no conflict in Kosegarten's legend; the devil immediately recognises the superior heavenly power and does as he is bidden. The Virgin now turns to the knight and instructs him to return to the chapel, where he will find his lady still sleeping. He must get rid of all the riches the devil has bestowed on him and mend his ways. Having thoroughly upbraided him the Virgin leaves the Knight, who carries out her instructions. Along with his wife the knight returns home, gets rid of all the devil's treasure and lives happily ever after. In due course the couple enjoy greater happiness and riches than ever before, for which they are very properly grateful to the Virgin.

There are several small but significant differences between Keller's legend and Kosegarten. For Keller the knight's extravagant giving merely shows him to have an irresponsible disregard for the administration of his property. For Gebizo, charity is not a salutary exercise of the heart but a grandiose sport in which he participates only in order to enjoy an inflated reputation for munificence. Such charity does nothing for the recipient, but weakens his moral fibre and encourages him to sponge. In Kosegarten's legend the knight's excessive charity is regarded as a very slight fault, but Keller takes a serious view of it.

In Keller's story, after the Virgin has made known her identity to the devil, a fierce struggle develops between her and her abductor. In Kosegarten, the Virgin's victory over the fiend is taken for granted, but in Keller the pair are fairly evenly matched. The Virgin would like to drag the devil with her and chain him to a doorpost in heaven as a laughing-stock for the redeemed, but he is too strong and she is obliged to come to terms with him and extract a promise that he will no longer molest the Lady Bertrade. Then the Virgin "somewhat weary" returns to her chapel, while the fiend, also the worse for wear, withdraws to his own place. Keller's knight loses his way after delivering his wife to the devil and falls down a cliff, where he dashes out his brains on a stone. Thus Keller punishes him very severely; in Kosegarten the knight receives a stiff reprimand but is soon back in celestial favour and, as if to show that bygones are bygones, the Virgin heaps worldly wealth on the couple. Keller is a far sterner moralist than Kosegarten; Gebizo must die, for he has gravely offended against natural law and common decency.

Keller also lingers longer over the description of the devil and his accoutrements than Kosegarten. His devil seems to represent unbridled sensuality; his rose garden, invisible nightingale and erotic *tableaux vivants* combine with the dissatisfied expression of his mouth and eyes to give an inkling of the delights he has to offer. He is powerful, too; in Keller's story the Virgin has to struggle with him might and main; Keller recognises, in other words, that an unbridled appetite is a serious threat to man's happiness and security.

Keller's Bertrade is both good and beautiful; when Gebizo falls on evil days she stands by him and, fortified by genuine religious faith, remains cheerful. In the days of his prosperity she delights his guests, radiating warmth and light wherever she goes. Nevertheless Gebizo abandons her without a thought. Bertrade enjoys the special protection and blessing of heaven because she is so exactly what in Keller's view a woman ought to be. Perhaps that is why she is allowed to keep Gebizo's ill-gotten wealth, as compensation for having put up with an unsatisfactory husband for so long, and perhaps that is why in the next legend the Virgin makes the provision of a new husband for Bertrade her special concern.

Die Jungfrau als Ritter
The Virgin as Knight

This legend contains a large element of almost direct confession, for Zendelwald's behaviour towards Bertrade reflects Keller's love for Betty Tendering. Zendelwald, the only son of a widow, truly loves Bertrade, but because of his poverty and her wealth, does not dare prefer his suit. Zendelwald is recognisably a blood brother of Keller or Pankraz; while possessed of a lively imagination, he suffers from a tendency to perform great deeds and think great thoughts only in imagination. Though he has reason to believe that Bertrade thinks kindly of him, Zendelwald will not bestir himself. His mother, herself an energetic and determined person, cannot understand his reluctance, and urges him to go and try his luck in the tournament. By allowing Zendelwald to enjoy the support and help of the Virgin Mary, Keller is really allowing himself poetic compensataion for the disappointments of his own life. Just as Zendelwald dreams of great triumphs which he has not the energy and resolution to achieve in real life, Keller does the very same thing by writing the legend.

His Virgin forms an interesting character study. She is a regular matchmaker, who not only does not oppose the natural desire of Bertrade and Zendelwald to marry, but actually goes out of her way to ensure that they can do so. According to Keller,

a man's or woman's natural desire to marry was made for gratification, and a benign heavenly power would, so far from wishing
to hinder such gratification, surely do everything possible to encourage it. Keller's Virgin is a thoroughly engaging and human
personality. There is a priceless moment when, on her way to
the great contest which is to decide Bertrade's fate, she comes
across something which looks like "the tail end of a snake" peep-
ing out of the undergrowth. Realising it is the devil, she lets her
horse give a little sideways kick, whereupon the Evil One retires
hastily with a yelp of pain.

While this legend breathes the spirit of the Renaissance and of
modern humanism rather than that of mediæval Christendom,
there is nothing specifically anti-Christian about the point of
view behind it. Even Keller's conception of the Virgin as a rather
mischievous and enterprising mother figure who will go to considerable lengths to further the interests of her children does not
seem so very unorthodox.

Die Jungfrau und die Nonne
The Virgin and the Nun

The moral of this story does not differ from that of the others
in the series. Keller here vigorously upholds the values of family
life and even biological fulfilment and evidently thinks them
preferable to the unnatural austerity of life in a nunnery. This
message emerges clearly from the conclusion of the legend when
Beatrix's sons are all crowned with oak leaves as a sign of their
acceptability to the Virgin as offerings.

Die Jungfrau und die Nonne stresses the need for a woman to
fulfil herself in the role for which she is destined by nature. As a
young girl Beatrix is perfectly happy to serve the Virgin as sacristan of the nunnery. When she reaches full maturity, however, she
is filled with a longing to see the world, which quickly crystallises
into the wish to be possessed by the first personable man who
comes her way. At first Beatrix and Wonnebold are drawn together only by passion, but Beatrix soon develops a loyalty and
hankering after security which makes her return to Wonnebold
even though he is quite unworthy of her. He is so affected by
her dependence on him and her obviously genuine affection for
him that he willingly takes her to be his wife. Many years later

when Beatrix returns to the nunnery she discovers that Heaven has in fact lent its sanction to what she imagined was a wrong action on her part, though she could not help performing it. In other words, while it is perfectly in order for a woman to devote herself to other interests before and after her period of child-bearing and family rearing, the central part of her life is intended for these purposes, and only a misguided asceticism would make her want to use it for anything else.

This story is quite enchantingly told; the figure of the nun, unable to still her worldly longings, leaving her cloister on a moonlit June night, waiting by the spring till the sun rose, and as she sits by the spring beholding the splendid knight Wonnebold— this name is surely one of Keller's most pleasing inventions— could easily become a figure of fun, but somehow Keller's irony remains gentle and tactful, and we remain in sympathy with her and the knight. The frivolous game of dice that almost destroys their relationship causes the reader some anxious moments, but Beatrix's loyalty to her unfaithful protector ensures our sympathy with her. The little copse of beech trees where Beatrix tricks Wonnebold's gambling opponent out of his win-nings is most agreeably described, and indeed Nature forms a delicate backcloth to the whole action of this story. The final scene in which Wonnebold, "der eiserne Greis" approaches the altar with his eight young warriors, who look like angels in armour and cause the nuns to become confused in their music making, is unforgettable.

Der schlimm-heilige Vitalis
Bad Saint Vitalis

The theme and moral tendency of this legend resemble those of the preceding one. St Vitalis, who has devoted his whole life to the rescuing of prostitutes, whenever possible placing his con-verts in nunneries, is persuaded by Iole's feminine intrigues that renunciation and religious asceticism are not the life for him, but that a strong, energetic and single-minded person like him is ideally cut out for a husband and father.

From the beginning, this eighth century Alexandrian monk appears to behave oddly. Although he has never touched a woman he likes to give the impression that he sleeps with the prostitutes whom he frequents. He forbids the girls whom he manages to convert to reveal that he spends his time with them in prayer and moral exhortations, and as a result he has the reputation of being a moral reprobate. Approaches have been made to the Bishop with a view to having him unfrocked, but he neither abandons his work nor tries to avoid giving offence to other people. He positively enjoys his undeserved bad reputation. Perhaps this aspect of his character suggests that he is not really dedicated to the work of rescuing prostitutes after all but secretly hankers after woman's love, possibly without himself realising it. Therefore we ought not to be too surprised by Vitalis' sudden decision that he prefers domesticity to the religious life.

The earlier part of this story follows closely the account of the *Life of St Vitalis* in the *Golden Legend* (see, e.g. French edition by Teodor de Wyzewa, Paris, 1925, pp. 108–109). But the strong and beautiful red-haired harlot, for whose soul Vitalis wrestles in vain, as well as Iole herself, were invented by Keller. Keller makes St Vitalis into a renegade, from the point of view of the church, and slants the whole story so that the reader may agree that the monk has acted correctly in quitting his unnatural life for the pleasures of married life.

Iole, like Nettchen in *Kleider machen Leute*, is one of Keller's enterprising and determined young women, who, almost without immodesty, can bend to their wishes the men whom they have selected for husbands. Keller does successfully point the contrast between the brazen carnality of the whore and the legitimate feminine wiles of Iole, who still blushes at her own daring in pretending to be worse than she is. Nevertheless, one cannot sympathise quite so fully with Vitalis and Iole as with Beatrix in *Die Jungfrau und die Nonne*. Vitalis forsakes a worthwhile and socially as well as religiously desirable mission for the pursuit of his own comfort and the gratification of Iole's whim. Beatrix, a nun who has temporarily lost her vocation, feels the pull of an irresistible natural force calling her to fulfil her destiny as a woman, and the Virgin's acceptance of her offering at the end of the day shows that she has not misinterpreted the will of God. The story of Vitalis is much more uncompromising; the Virgin who seems to smile on him when he decides to return for the last time to talk Iole out of her love for him is a statue of Juno, the Roman protectress of matrimony, which has been adopted by the new religion. The statue seems to smile on him, but he cannot be certain that the smile is not merely caused by a cloud-effect and he is anyway hardly an impartial judge in his own case. Beatrix in fact changes her life's course from strength, Vitalis from weakness. Beatrix goes back to the cloister with her faith still intact after fulfilling her obligations towards her womanhood, but the uxorious Vitalis is not permitted by Iole to return to the fold.

Dorotheas Blumenkörbchen
Dorothy's Flower Basket

Perhaps Keller felt that the last story did not ring true or was at any rate far removed from his own experience. Vitalis enjoys the love and wealth of which he himself remained deprived. Altogether, *Vitalis* takes a rather rosy view of the fulfilments which life can offer, and we are puzzled by the thoroughness with which the saint changes the course of his life.

Dorotheas Blumenkörbchen redresses the balance. In case we should imagine that the story of Vitalis reflects an average situation, Keller offers for our consideration this much sterner and less comforting account of the fortunes of St Dorothy and Theophilus. Here the poetic imagination penetrates near the truth about life and love, and indeed Keller veers sympathetically towards Christianity. However, there is nothing specifically anti-Christian in the *Sieben Legenden*, except insofar as Keller freely attacks those aspects of traditional Christian doctrine and practice which he considers to be contrary to nature and good sense.

At first Dorothea displays no saintly characteristics. The daughter of cultured and intelligent parents in Pontus Euxinus who have embraced the Christian faith, she loves the Governor's secretary, Theophilus, who also loves her, but cannot find the courage to propose to her, although she gives him all the encouragement she decently can. She is also loved by the Roman Governor, Fabricius, but does not encourage him at all. A slight misunderstanding between Theophilus and herself causes an estrangement between the two lovers. Unhappily for them, Fabricius chooses this moment to renew his suit and when Dorothea will not have him he takes his revenge by persecuting her for her faith.

Theophilus, the Secretary, is a very typical hero of Keller's works. A cultured and sensitive youth, he has a difficult boyhood behind him and remains rather moody, suspicious and secretive, although he is well thought of by his superiors. And so he hangs back and refuses to make the most of his opportunities with Dorothea. The accidental breaking of her vase is by no means out of character, and Dorothea would have been a saint—which she had not yet become—if she had not been annoyed with him. His prolonged sulks after Dorothea's scolding indicate his kinship with Pankraz and others of Keller's heroes.

Dorothea somehow acquires the strength of martyrdom along with her Christian faith. It is of course unlikely that she would have taken much interest in religion if things had been right between her and Theophilus. And it is even possible to argue that it is the thought that relations with Theophilus have improved that makes martyrdom tolerable for her. For both the lovers the thought of a shared death as Christian martyrs is sweeter far than continuance in the wretched misunderstanding which had arisen between them.

The arrival of the little angel from Dorothea with the basket of flowers and fruit is beautifully narrated. The angel has all the conventional angelic attributes, golden curly hair, a star-covered garment and dazzlingly white, naked feet. As he hands the basket containing flowers and fruit to Theophilus he asks "Have you got a proper hold of it?" and vanishes.

The description of the reunion of the lovers is rather unexpected:

And so Theophilus was united with Dorothea on that very day. With the calm regard of the blessed she received him; like two doves which, separated by a storm, have found one another again and first of all fly in wide circles around their home, the united lovers winged their way hand in hand, swiftly, swiftly and without resting in the outermost rings of heaven, freed from all earthly gravity, and yet themselves. Then they separated in play and lost one another in the broad infinity, while each of them knew where the other tarried and what he was thinking, and along with him comprehended every creature and every living thing in sweet love. Then they sought one another again in growing longing that knew no pain and no impatience; they found one another and continued their pilgrimage united or rested in contemplation of themselves and beheld the near and distant places of the infinite world. But on one occasion they penetrated in most blissful oblivion too near the crystal house of the Holy Trinity and went in; there they lost consciousness and fell asleep like twins beneath their mother's heart, and they are probably still sleeping, unless they have been able to get out again meantime.

The passage just quoted with its Dante-like flavour and its beautiful imagery is a rarity in Keller's works. Perhaps Keller was only amusing himself by playing with Christian conceits in which he did not believe, but that hauntingly lovely conclusion rather suggests the opposite. The love which Dorothea and Theophilus feel for one another has been purified and simplified by renunciation and disappointment on earth; the moment early in the story which determined that they should not marry has only served to increase their love for one another. Dorothea's love has endured beyond the grave and drawn Theophilus after her, and in death they are united. The sentence about the crystal house of the Holy Trinity is not easy to explain, and in particular it is hard to say why at this moment, not before, they lose consciousness and sleep "like twins beneath the heart of their mother". But Keller does not exclude the possibility that they may have re-awakened and come to full consciousness again. He cannot believe that the power of love which has done so much for Theophilus and Dorothea can ever utterly perish.

The motto from Francis Ludwig Blosius prefixed to this story has great significance: "But to lose oneself in this way is rather to find oneself." Dorothea is being untrue to herself when she turns from Theophilus to seek comfort in religion; she cannot have him on earth on the terms on which she wants him. Equally Theophilus betrays his own deepest feelings when he allows his diffidence and pride to make him abandon Dorothea after breaking her vase. But their love cannot be destroyed by the momentary tactlessness and misunderstandings of the lovers; it must endure, surmounting even death. Life will often demand renunciation, and unfortunately human minds, even those most in sympathy with one another, can never communicate properly. The story of Dorothea and Theophilus calls in question Keller's earlier pronouncements on the finality of death; the union which the lovers achieve in heaven is better and fuller than anything they had anticipated.

As always in Keller there are some pictorially memorable moments; after the lovers' quarrel Dorothea watches "the slender figure (of Theophilus) disappear, gathering his white toga to himself and inclining his black curly head to one side, as if in far-ranging thoughts". Meanwhile, Nature remains unmoved and "the waves of the silvery sea beat slowly and gently against the marble steps of the shore". Then Dorothea picks up the pieces of her vase and goes to hide them in her room.

At one point in the story a strong hint of irony concerning Christian belief is apparent; Dorothea speaks longingly of her heavenly bridgegroom "who will take her to his gleaming breast and hand her the rose of eternal life, etc." The *etc.* has a very ironical ring in this context.

Das Tanzlegendchen

A passage in Gregorius *Dialogi* 4, 17, tells of the poor maiden, Musa, to whom the Virgin appears one night and promises that if she refrains from dancing, levity and play on earth, she will join for ever in heavenly dancing and joys. Thereupon the maiden refrains from all frivolity and does penance, and on the thirtieth day the Virgin comes to take her to heaven where she can dance for ever.

Keller describes the descent of King David towards Musa from the altar very effectively. King David is a regal personage in a purple robe, wearing a golden crown and with a black beard tinged with grey. Their dance together while the little angels above the choir stalls play delightfully on different instruments is pure enjoyment, but this is still not the heavenly dance music which the King now proceeds to demonstrate. Now and only now Musa is convinced that she should refrain from dancing for the rest of her life if this is the condition of dancing in heaven for ever.

The description of the saint's assumption is very pleasingly narrated, almost as if it were taken straight from a genuine church legend. Musa has had herself dressed in a dazzling white wedding dress for the moment of her death. She lies with hands sedately folded and smilingly awaits the glad hour. The autumnal leaves are falling, but suddenly the sighing of the wind changes to heavenly music, the trees are again clad in young greenery, flowers and fruit trees are in full bloom and the saint's face is haloed in rosy pink. The chain at her ankle snaps, the heavens are opened and King David comes on a cloud with his cherubic musicians to fetch her. For a second or so those left on earth see vistas of blessed spirits dancing in heaven; King David and Musa join the glad throng, then the heavens close and it is again autumn on earth, the wind is blowing and the trees are bare.

This particular legend seems to point in two directions. Till Musa ascends into heaven Keller follows his sources closely but embellishes them with his poetic fancy, especially in the account of King David's demonstration to Musa of the delights of heavenly music and dancing. The acount of Musa's assumption into heaven seems absolutely authentic mediæval legend, too. The whole of this first part of the story seems to advocate renunciation and abstention from the joys of the flesh in favour of later celestial rewards. The ending, however, in which the Muses turn all heaven upside down with their expressive and nostalgic song about the joys of earth points in a different direction. Keller seems to be saying that if the Muses are at best uncomfortable guests in the Christian heaven, it is no place for him, too high a price is exacted for eternal bliss.

From the point of view of the critic, the question must be asked : Why use *legends* for the purpose of opposing Christian asceticism or preaching the fulfilment of the life of the senses? And the further question arises : does the attempt come off? Has Keller produced an artistically satisfying set of stories with enough common background, sufficiently similar underlying assumptions to justify grouping them together in cyclical form?

The answer to the first question must be that it is just as legitimate to use a legend to illustrate one moral point of view as another, and that the story even gains additional piquancy if its moral tendency is the opposite from that which is to be expected. Keller was well aware of this factor, which he even specifically mentions in his introduction. He also makes the point there that underlying the ecclesiastical legends there seem to be traces of a more secular narrative art. His matchmaking Virgin, for instance, is not so utterly different from the Virgin of some Italian legends.

Most readers would agree that Keller's *Legends* are one of his best artistic successes. The neatness and daintiness of the form, the absence of extraneous material, the ironically simulated naïvety and the charming elements of nature description, the beautifully narrated miracles, all play their part in achieving this success. From this little volume a particular view of the author's personality emerges; he is evidently well-read, cultured, tolerant, ironical, he strongly resists the masochistic strain in some Christian teaching. As always in Keller's works the author is omniscient and paternalistic, even occasionally patronising towards his characters.

The *Legends* do not form a cycle in the sense that they are linked directly with one another or to a framework. However, a single common view of life informs them all; man should not spurn the natural satisfaction of his appetites, which is healthier and more pleasing to heaven than denying them. Also, the *Legends* are written in a fairly homogeneous style, which has much in common with that of the most simply and economically related of real Christian legends; it is an almost unadorned prose, but the occasional ornamentation is restrained and effective, and the special moments of fulfilment stand out because of their comparative rarity. The occasional crudenesses or lapses from taste which disfigure *Die Leute von Seldwyla* no longer appear; the artist has become more mature and more refined in the interval since his last published work appeared nearly twenty years before the *Legends*.

CHAPTER FIVE

THE ZÜRICHER NOVELLEN

KELLER had hitherto either invented his own plots or used stories of which his sources gave only the main outlines. Seldwyla, a special kind of Swiss town, is nowhere in particular and everywhere at once, and we generally behold it not exactly through rose tinted spectacles, but through the slightly distorting glasses of an intelligent but indulgent, eupeptic and ever so slightly tipsy uncle. It has some of the rather out of this world characteristics of a romantic mise en scène. In the *Züricher Novellen* Keller no longer confines himself to describing typical Swiss settings but gives detailed accounts of particular places. Anyone who knows the topography of Zurich and the surrounding district constantly recognises places and buildings as he reads the five stories. Keller has been equally careful over matters of chronology and details of social history, including the prevailing ethos of behaviour in different ages. He has taken upon himself the burdens of the historical novelist. Outwardly he has completed the transition from romanticism to realism. But, if the details of his settings are determined by history and geography, Keller has left himself some latitude as far as plot is concerned. Occasionally he makes use of the sovereign right of the historical novelist to alter dates and such details to suit his own convenience.

In 1860 Keller wrote to Auerbach about a "series of Zurich stories which should contain more positive life than the *Leute von Seldwyla*". His duties as *Staatsschreiber* made it impossible for him to write the stories for a time. In the early 1870s he spoke of this task as one of those which he hoped to complete before he abandoned narrative prose altogether. His stories appeared in the first instance in Julius Rodenberg's *Deutsche Rundschau*. Keller entrusted the book edition to the house of Göschen. The *Deutsche Rundschau* was to print only the framework and first three stories; the *Fähnlein* and *Ursula* would appear in the book edition as a separate small volume.

The history of the publication of the *Züricher Novellen* has a familiar ring. In May 1876 Keller wrote to Rodenberg apologising for his failure to finish the stories and promising that when he resigned as *Staatsschreiber* he would quickly complete his *Novellen*. In August he sent an incomplete manuscript to Rodenberg for his November issue. Early in the new year Keller failed to maintain the pace of production, but by April 1877 he had supplied the ending of the *Rahmenerzählung* (framework story).

In the summer of 1877 he revised *Das Fähnlein der sieben Aufrechten* which had been written years before for Auerbach's *Kalender*. He also resumed work on *Ursula*, which had been begun in Berlin during the 1850s. In November 1877 he finished *Ursula*, and at the end of that year, the two slender volumes of the *Züricher Novellen* appeared complete for the first time.

The framework story plays a greater part in the economy of the *Züricher Novellen* than the brief introductions to the two parts of the *Leute von Seldwyla*. The story of Herr Jacques and his godfather introduces the underlying theme of the whole series. A man must be content to know himself and accept the limitations imposed by Providence on him. Most of us are pretty ordinary, and we ought to acknowledge this in good time, and not try to seem better than we really are. Young Herr Jacques has somehow gathered from his reading that there is a shortage of original geniuses in the world and has decided to remedy the deficiency. His shrewd old godfather sees that Jacques possesses no extraordinary talent. If he can be educated to perform an everyday, unspectacular task without fuss and without pretence, that is all that can be hoped for. Despite his desire to cut a fine figure in the world, Jacques is just a run-of-the-mill young philistine, who cannot stand by a river side without calculating the cash value of the wood which he sees floating past him towards the city of Zurich. His sound commercial instinct enables him to do this very efficiently, but his poetic inspirations are tasteless, and his metamorphoses after Ovid indicate the humourless cast of his mind. He has the original idea that nymphs and young men should be turned into such homely and profitable plants as the sugar cane, the pepper, cotton and coffee bushes. However, when it comes to planning his poetic masterpiece in detail, he can get nowhere with it. Jacques suffers from unformulated and unrealisable adolescent aspirations; he does not have a flicker of the creative spark, though he will not admit this to himself. Artistic and poetic ambition represents a phase which men like him outgrow with their adolescence. When Jacques finds the old men firing mortars and is asked by his godfather to hold his pipe while he attends to his mortar, this is really a suitable occupation for the unremarkable but swollen-headed young man. A little later, Jacques confides to his godfather that he would like to do something great and original. His godfather listens sympathetically, but tells Jacques that he must rather aim at doing properly whatever task may come his way in life, even if it is nothing unheard of or spectacular. He then tells Jacques about the Manesse family, whose castle, the Manegg, they pass during their walk. They were distinguished in their best days, not for eccentricity or originality, but for the exemplary execution of duty. There is never any point in simply striving for effect; true originality comes from within. Talking of the Manesse family reminds the old man of Herr Rüdiger Manesse and of Johannes Hadlaub, his protégé, the *Minnesänger* and scribe of the Manesse manuscript of *Minnelieder*.

Hadlaub

Keller was well versed in mediæval German literature and knew the poems of Johannes Hadlaub. From the poems Keller gathered a good deal about the man, who seemed to him to offer in more ways than one parallels with his own situation at the time when he originally conceived the idea of writing a collection of *Novellen* based on the history of Zurich and the surrounding country.

Like Keller Hadlaub was of peasant origin. He came to Zurich as a young man and became proficient in the art of copying and restoring poems by almost forgotten masters. In the process of transcribing and illustrating other men's works Hadlaub discovered that he had a strong personal poetic vein, and that he was capable of writing work which compared not too unfavourably with that of his predecessors. Like Keller he was both poet and painter. From very modest beginnings Hadlaub developed until he was recognised as a considerable poet in his own right. Certain familiar *motifs* recur in this story. Herr Rüdiger Manesse, the aristocratic connoisseur of poetry who originally conceived the idea of letting Hadlaub collect all the extant mediæval poetry he could find, has his counterpart in the Count in *Der grüne Heinrich*, whose delight it was to study through Heinrich's paintings the development of a true if modest artist. Ermatinger suggests that Herr Rüdiger, in tempting and teasing Hadlaub with Fides, does precisely what the Dunckers did to Keller with Betty Tendering in Berlin. They used her, as Keller himself reproachfully said, as a bait to lure him into their household and coax him into writing for Franz Duncker. If this is so, Keller allows himself the luxury of vicariously carrying the affair to a successful conclusion, for Hadlaub does in the end win his Fides. Fides' parents, the Bishop of Constance and the Lady Abbess of Zurich, are lovers who live in the kind of voluntary renunciation which we have already seen in Heinrich Lee and Judith in the second version of *Der grüne Heinrich*. Hadlaub is an exemplary figure from other points of view. The aristocrats who act as his patrons, although generous and clever men, have no genius of their own, but merely the ability to recognise and exploit Hadlaub's talent. Hadlaub, however, raises himself through his creative ability to be the equal of the aristocrats and even to take one of their number home to be his wife. Hadlaub's father shows himself capable, by long exercise of the bourgeois virtue of thrift, of buying a fine house in the city for Johannes, so that the latter can set himself up suitably with his aristocratic wife. Fides, who has discovered the secret of her illegitimate birth, is a person of stern moral fibre. She gladly escapes with the young bourgeois from the degenerate ways of her parents. They in turn feel reproached by the attitude of their daughter and cease to be lovers at last partly because her distress about their relationship pains them. Hadlaub was a poet of the transitional period between the aristocratic culture of the Middle Ages and the bourgeois culture of modern times. Keller demonstrates that Hadlaub's success is based on a genuine superiority of talent over the aristocrats, who are merely guardians of tradition, not creative individuals in their own right. *Hadlaub* is a tribute to the Swiss bourgeois way of life, and shows how the gifted and determined individual will make his way despite all outward obstacles. No evidence in Keller's sources suggests an irregular connexion between the historical Bishop of Constance and the Abbess of Zurich, but they are mentioned in the same breath in one of Hadlaub's poems. Other incidents from Hadlaub are similarly exploited; the part of the story where Fides gives him her ivory pin box, for instance, is based on one of the poems.

Hadlaub, then, is a success story with an historical setting. As always in Keller's historical *Novellen* he shows more interest in geography, buildings, the customs and amusements of his characters than in great historical events. For example, Keller more than once points the contrast between aristocratic and bourgeois manners. He lays considerable emphasis on things like dress and hair styles, and shows himself learned in the etymology of proper names. He has evidently taken considerable trouble to find out something about how various occupations were carried on in the later Middle Ages in Switzerland.

Keller displays a true knowledge of and love of the people and age with which he is dealing. Life in the castle of Schwarz-Wasserstelz and in the town house of the Manesse family, as well as in the more modest dwelling of Hadlaub and his parents is credibly recreated. The account of the great hunting party which begins in Burg Manegg and goes on for a day's falconry to the Schnabelburg shows how thoroughly Keller, that fat, immobile little man, had steeped himself in the life of those open-air, pleasure loving aristocrats of long ago. One sometimes feels that Keller is rather too preoccupied with getting in as much local colour as possible with the result that Hadlaub rather limps and loses interest. But *Hadlaub* is a formidable performance for an almost complete newcomer to the field of the historical *Novelle*. Keller unites with a wide background of historical knowledge a high degree of sensitivity in the appreciation of Hadlaub's poems.

Der Narr auf Manegg
The Fool at Manegg

The story of Hadlaub, his poetic achievement and worldly success, was calculated to provide Herr Jacques with a pattern to follow. From very modest beginnings Hadlaub had made his way in the world, and he had always been inclined if anything to underestimate his capabilities. That was why, in Jacques' godfather's opinion, he was such a suitable model for his godson. This second story of the collection is intended as a warning example, an illustration of the dangers to which one exposes oneself by trying to be what one is not.

Derr Narr auf Manegg concerns itself with the narrow dividing line between sanity and insanity. Buz Falätscher's excessive pre-occupation with self is his undoing. Though only an ignorant, half-educated chaplain he pretends to be a great churchman like some of his illustrious forebears; though a wretched coward, useless on the battlefield, he pretends to be a fearless warrior. He tries to make his mistress believe that he is a wonderful person, and when in exasperation she tells him that he is all talk and no fulfilment he goes berserk and attacks her violently. Keller main-tains that a man must be prepared to labour at a dull and seem-ingly unrewarding task and not expect to achieve spectacular success without effort. Anyone who tries to insist that the world should accept him at too high an assessment may well ruin his life and topple over into insanity. Buz consistently tries to achieve quick recognition on too easy terms; he will not acknowledge his own limitations; that way lies madness. He fails to recognise the laws by which all human activity is regulated, and pays the price with the loss first of sanity and then of life itself. His poor little mistress and the due performance of a humble task repre-sented the best that life had to offer him; by despising this, he brought greater misery on himself.

Keller believed firmly in the need for a man to know himself properly. Buz Falätscher possessed no remarkable physical or mental attributes. He had a certain amount of superficial know-ledge which he liked to flaunt in the shape of half-understood Latin phrases and ecclesiastical jargon, he knew enough about hunting wild animals to catch them like a beast of prey, not like an accomplished huntsman. But he was determined to be thought a great man. Had Buz been content with the humdrum destiny which was properly his, he could have ensured himself a modest but honourable place in society. But this was not what he hank-ered after. He wanted to make a fine impression wherever he went; but the world was never prepared to accept him at his own valuation. The story of how he took over the deserted feudal castle of Manegg and began to behave as though he were lord of the stronghold would be funny if it were not so pathetic. When he saw the young aristocrats of the town—to whose number he imagined he belonged—fascinated by the Manesse Codex he decided to steal it and set himself up as a *Minnesänger*. But his determination that the world should take more account of his miserable poetic attempts than of any of his other doings led to the discovery that he was the thief who had removed the manuscript from the hostelry where the Zurich gentry were in the habit of meeting. We last see Buz running from room to room in the empty castle, like a cornered animal before his captors. His delusion has brought him to a sorry pass; he serves to show what can happen to a man who disregards the limits set upon him by life, one who has not learned the lesson which Heinrich Lee and Strapinsky and others in Keller's works were sooner or later prepared to learn. We may rather gain the impression that Jacques' godfather is using a steamroller to crush a gnat in telling this horrible and frightening story to cure Jacques of comparatively harmless adolescent delusions of grandeur, but if one disregards the context the story is affecting and even impressive.

A criticism which might reasonably be levelled against the *Narr auf Manegg* is that our interest is rather divided between Ital Manesse and the fool. Ital Manesse is merely a rather feckless and improvident youth who drinks too much and lets opportunity pass by him repeatedly. The fool does not simply allow this to happen; he repeatedly embarks on positive follies which in the end destroy him. When he is lying dead outside the castle at the end of the story we are told that he is released from the torment, a genuine mental disease, of wishing to seem to be what he is not. One might be forgiven for supposing that Ital Manesse was to be the main centre of interest in the story, and for a measure of irritation that this person who engages our attention for the first few pages then disappears till near the end.

Keller's principal source for *Der Narr auf Manegg* was the *Beiträge zur Geschichte der Familie Manesse*, published by Georg von Wyß in 1849. From Wyß and possibly the Swiss chronicles of the sixteenth century Keller gathered that in the end only a poor fool dwelt in Burg Manegg. It was Keller's own idea to make this figure, who had accidentally perished in a fire started as a prank by some gay young blades, responsible for the disappearance of the Manesse Codex from the family's possession.

Although well enough told *Der Narr auf Manegg* has never

caught the imagination of Keller's readers, possibly because the subject is so depressing. Sandwiched between two such fine and interesting personalities as Hadlaub and Salomon Landolt it is small wonder that Buz Falätscher has never made much impact.

Der Landvogt von Greifensee
The Bailiff of Greifensee

I

This is generally agreed to be the best of the *Züricher Novellen*, and it is also that which most directly reflects Keller's personal experience. In the art with which it is constructed, in delicacy, psychological finesse and happy lightness of touch, this *Novelle* excels the others in the collection. This fine fruit of resignation mirrors an aspect of the author's life which caused him for a considerable period much distress. The true triumph of the artist is to create from his own disappointments and ruined hopes a beautiful, serene and enjoyable work of art. Keller has done this in the *Landvogt*, and it is moving to see him in the autumn of his life survey the frustrations and blighted hopes of his youth with humour and detachment, and weave his succession of unfulfilled loves into an entertaining story. He had little sympathy with the kind of person who found the very conditions of human life intolerable; he faced his own problems courageously and in the end gained a position of vantage from which the miseries of his early manhood seemed more like necessary and inevitable growing pains on which he could look back with mingled amusement and wistful affection for the young man he had been. There is nothing like self-pity in the *Landvogt von Greifensee*; but rather a conscious pride in the bachelor form of existence and a kind of gratitude that he has been spared long enough to see that his way of life, too, has much to recommend it. Salomon Landolt actually *likes* being a bachelor, and he reflects Keller's opinions on this topic more accurately than anyone else.

II

Keller's principal source for the *Landvogt* was a biography of Salomon Landolt, the *Landvogt* of Greifensee by David Heß. This work appeared in Zurich in 1820, and Keller leans heavily on it, often taking passages verbatim from it, but stresses that he is principally concerned with a side of Landolt's life which Heß scarcely mentions, namely his relations with women. Heß had observed that Landolt was not completely unsusceptible, but that he had never considered that he could afford to marry; he had at least twice been much in love. For Keller Landolt's love life was all important, and in default of exact information about Salomon Landolt and his loves, Keller imputes to Landolt his own experiences. Fortunately, Keller and the real Landolt had a good deal in common. The old dragon of a housekeeper, the monkey Cocco and the matrimonial disputes which Landolt solves all figure in Heß's book. From Heß Keller derives information about Landolt's childhood and family, including the on-goings in General Hirzel's castle. Finally, the section of Keller's story dealing with Salomon Landolt's later life, declining years and death owes much to David Heß.

The first volume of a biography of Pestalozzi published by Josephine Zehnder-Stadlin in 1875 under the title *Pestalozzi, Idee und Macht der menschlichen Entwicklung* was an invaluable source of information about the Zurich of the late eighteenth century. The *Sittenmandate* (moral by-laws) of old Zurich expressed an attitude to life which evidently commanded wide acceptance at one time. However, not all citizens were prepared to observe the irksome restrictions on freedom to pass through the city gates on Sundays; the young and frivolous invented excuses to enable them to sally forth despite the *Sittenmandate*. On such topics Keller found Zehnder-Stadlin an absolute treasure-house, and he enlivened his story by the judicious use of such details of social history. From the same source Keller also learned about a striking Zurich character, Captain Gimmel, the father of Kapitän, one of the heroines of *Der Landvogt*.

Keller was also widely read in the Swiss Literature of the late eighteenth century. He knew and used with discrimination Johann Jakob Bodmer's *Discourse der Mahlern*; he greatly admired Salomon Geßner, the author of charming pastoral idylls and romances and a landscape painter of pleasing if modest talent; Keller also knew Geßner's biography by Johann Jakob Hottinger (Zurich, 1796). Other works of secondary literature such as Karl Morel's *Helvetische Gesellschaft* and Mörikofer's *Schweizerische Literatur des 18. Jahrhunderts* were available

to and no doubt used by him. He prepared the ground very carefully for this particular story. Keller quotes verbatim from the
preface of Wieland's early epic *Der gepryfte Abraham* and he
had certainly made a serious effort to absorb the spirit of that
age and render himself familiar with many aspects of life during
Salomon Landolt's day.

III

Landolt is drawn in large measure from the life. The historical
Landolt, the founder of the Zurich *Scharfschützenkorps*, had
been invited by Frederick the Great to lead a contingent of Swiss
mercenaries in Prussia. A man of many parts, he showed an
agreeable if undeveloped talent as a painter, dabbled in other
arts, administered his *Landvogtei* with amiable eccentricity and
lived altogether very much as the hero of Keller's story. Keller
saw in Landolt in 1878 an idealised image of himself in much
the same way as his Pankraz, also incidentally a military man,
had represented his personal ambitions and hopes in 1856.
Landolt, however, is a more rounded, mellow and balanced personality than Pankraz. Landolt personifies ideal bachelorhood
and represents the justification and near-apotheosis of a form of
existence which might well be regarded by many people as a
failure in terms of human relations. Keller shows us in him a
person who has come to terms with what had at first seemed a
harsh lot, and has even become a judge over the frailer mortals
who are condemned to the married state. We have to admire
the insight and lack of passion with which Landolt judges the
people who come to his court room. He fully understands the
difficulties encountered by others in married life. Landolt seems
almost glad that he has never married. Had he linked his life
with one of the ladies who attend his charming congress, he
would hardly have fared as badly as the unhappy husband in his
court room, but he might nevertheless have found his freedom in
some ways curtailed, his life impoverished, his talents suppressed.
Though he has had no child of his own, he has shown himself
a sympathetic, fatherly figure to a little dying boy, whose fear
of death had so distressed his parents. The *Landvogt*, treating
death as something natural and inevitable, persuades the child
to face impending dissolution with a good grace. He views the
problems of younger or less educated people with a kindly and

indulgent eye. He is a brave man and a thorough one, an exemplary official and a jolly, convivial fellow. He is at once a paragon of the manly virtues and not insensitive to aesthetic delights. He is a remarkably *whole* man—the kind of person that Keller nearly was and would have liked altogether to be. With his susceptible heart, his active, enquiring mind and his well-exercised body Salomon Landolt embodies the kind of ideal humanity to which the Renaissance humanists aspired; he has more of the German appetite for discipline than the inhabitants of the Abbaye de Thélème but he resembles them in the variety of his pursuits. One engaging quality which he shares with Keller himself is his modesty; the letter in which he tells Distelfink of his strange ancestry reminds us of Keller writing to Luise Rieter and playing down his virtues and exaggerating his faults. Indeed, if one looks closely at Keller (or Keller's Landolt) one wonders in the end whether they wrote those letters merely from modesty. Was it not that, perhaps subconsciously, both Keller and Landolt needed to be free, and in spite of themselves adopted a course of action calculated to let them retain their freedom? Their perfectly genuine modesty reflects an overriding subconscious desire for liberty. Salomon Landolt, like Keller, held public office for many years; from the *Landvogtei* of Greifensee, near Zurich, he moved to the *Landvogtei* of Eglisau, where Keller's mother had known him as an old man. Salomon Landolt's real authority and best knowledge lies like that of his creator in the field of human relationships, and oddly enough for a bachelor in his understanding of matrimonial affairs.

IV

Other elements of Keller's experience were used in the story. The women resemble the women whom he had loved, although no single one of them corresponds exactly to a single person in real life. The sum total of Landolt's experience with the other sex corresponds closely to Keller's, but the details are different. Salome has much in common with Luise Rieter; Figura Leu suggests Johanna Kapp and Luise Scheidegger, both of whom lived under the shadow of insanity. Barbara Thumeysen's deep mistrust of Landolt's artistic and intellectual preoccupations reminds us of Luise Scheidegger's fear and suspicion of Keller's mental superiority which in the end had such tragic consequences.

The very frankness and openness of Aglaja's relationship with Landolt stems from the knowledge that she loves and is loved by another. This had been Keller's situation with Johanna Kapp. All Landolt's loves except that for Figura are eventually regarded by him as more or less regrettable aberrations; at least he would regard them as regrettable if they had not providentially come to an end in time. Landolt is glad he has loved repeatedly but not sorry that he has never married. It would have been contrary to his destiny to do so. The suggestion in the *Landvogt* of a marriage with the handsome boy (who is admittedly masquerading as a young woman) perhaps indicates the direction in which Keller's thoughts were turning now. This may be the real reason why the *Landvogt* can look so serenely on the loves of his youth.

Pankraz der Schmoller offers us a version of Keller's affair with Betty Tendering, Franz Duncker's sister-in-law. This story told by Pankraz in the first person soon after the event is obviously written with a good deal of rancour. In the *Landvogt*, which he wrote years after his last attachment to a woman, Keller surveys his whole love life with the detachment of the third person narrator. He can easily be charitable about women now; looking back he can see that the worst torments of unrequited love did not afflict him for long, although they may have seemed to do so at the time. He could now see that the young women who preferred not to marry him were probably right, and he should not hold it against them as he had held it against Betty Tendering long ago. Incidentally, although there are echoes of all Keller's other loves in this story, Betty Tendering probably did not serve as a model for any of its characters. Perhaps Keller could still not think of her with charity.

Apart from the *Landvogt's* love life, which is the author's principal concern and very well related, one remembers this *Novelle* for the numerous vignettes of life in eighteenth century Switzerland, which Keller knew well both from books and from conversations with his mother and other older people of his acquaintance. Keller opens the work with a description of a military parade near Zurich, with Landolt commanding the Zurich *Scharfschützen*. This section of the book includes a pleasing account of Landolt's outward appearance, and a good quotation from David Heß's biography. Frau Marianne, the old housekeeper, provides the excuse for another enjoyable excursion on her past life and present character. Later on we might remember Landolt and Salome planting the cherry orchard and enjoying their farmworkers' lunch on the grass. The old days of the *Sittenmandate* come alive again as we read of Figura Leu dividing up according to their merits all the people who wish to leave the bounds of Zurich on a Sunday. Herr Professor Johann Jakob Bodmer no longer seems a dull figure from the history of literature when we meet him surrounded by his young friends, and Salomon Geßner, living among his books and paintings in his little forest retreat, is a civilised and hospitable person. Keller draws a sympathetic picture of old Bodmer remembering his younger days when Klopstock and Wieland visited him and he enjoyed the sensation of being at the very heart of the renewal of German literature in the 1740s and 1750s. Perhaps the impression that remains most vividly in the reader's mind is that of all the numerous small personal possessions and items of dress and furniture which Keller mentions from time to time. A great deal of close observation of old pictures and household objects must have preceded the writing of this book. It forms one of the most delightful and comprehensive literary monuments to Swiss life in the age of the *Aufklärung*.

Das Fähnlein der sieben Aufrechten
The Banner of the Seven Upright Men

In order to understand *Das Fähnlein* properly, we must think of the *Volksfest* as a typically Swiss form of self-expression, which provides much the same sort of outlet for communal emotion and the demonstration of national solidarity as a coronation or royal wedding in Great Britain. *Das Fähnlein* argues the case for the new Swiss democracy, and at the same time shows what is of lasting value in the old national virtues. The foreign reader must in approaching the work try to understand the ideals and aspirations of a different kind of democratic state from his own, but one which has shown a remarkable capacity for self-adaptation, development and survival. Perhaps because it is so closely bound up with Swiss customs and ways of thinking *Das Fähnlein* has always been especially liked by Keller's Swiss readers and less esteemed by others. However, it is a thoroughly interesting work because it represents in artistic form the considered opinions of

a most intelligent, right-thinking and articulate Swiss writer as
to what constitutes good citizenship.

The seven men who call themselves *Die sieben Aufrechten* are
modelled on those friends of Keller's father who had pledged
themselves to help to support the widow and dependants of any
of their number who might die prematurely. They are all well
drawn, and their characters are clearly differentiated, particularly
those of the tailor Hediger, that fire-eating democrat who broad-
casts his political convictions with such fervour that he alienates
his customers, and the cautious and diffident, very prudent
wealthy carpenter Frymann. It is completely in character for a
man like Hediger to object to his son's association with Frymann's
daughter out of false pride, and it is equally natural for the close-
fisted Frymann to object to the relationship. The other members
of the society, not being directly involved, can see the matter more
objectively; they realise that Karl is an able, industrious and
honest young man, and they see that Hermine is determined to
marry him, so there is really very little point in the fathers'
raising objections to the match, especially for quite insufficient
reasons. Karl's mother, sensible, kind and ambitious for her son,
naturally sees no sense in her husband's objections to the idea
of marriage with Hermine, and it is perfectly natural for her to
aid and abet the young people in their plans.

The decision of the Seven to march as a body with their own
banner to the Federal Marksmen's Contest at Aarau in 1849 is
symbolical. The revised Federal Constitution of 1848 had represented a triumph of the liberal, democratic principles in which
they all believed, and the banner and the gift which they propose
to hand over as a marksmen's prize serve to set the seal on their
work. The argument among the Seven as to the form their gift
should take illustrates how in democratic procedures self-interest
will always tend to assert itself, yet with goodwill and straight
speaking on all sides the interests of the community will in the
end be placed first. The reluctance of any of the Seven to act as
spokesman for the group even after they have agreed on their
course of action is well portrayed. The decision that Frymann as
the wealthiest of the old democrats should take this burden upon
him must also have many precedents in democratic practice!

Karl represents the younger generation, and in him Keller has
provided an almost idealised portrait of Swiss manhood. Karl

cheerfully goes off to do his military service, and he can scarcely be blamed for the little intrigue to prevent his rival Ruckstuhl from being able to appear at Frymann's lunch-table. His generous offer to act as spokesman for his elders is at first viewed with suspicion, then eagerly accepted by all of them except by his father whose objections are soon overruled. Karl now proves that he combines with the sound democratic attitudes of the older men an evident capacity for leadership and undoubted eloquence.

Karl's speech deserves brief consideration since he serves as Keller's spokesman as well as the Seven's. He refers ironically but not scornfully to the older men's fear of Jesuits and aristocrats, knowing that political and ecclesiastical reaction no longer seriously menace Switzerland—in this respect the older Keller smiles at the fears of his own youth, when he literally marched against those bogeys of the Seven. The motto on the banner, Friendship in Freedom is no hollow phrase for them, for friendship in freedom is what they believe in. They are not very religious men, and you would hardly see any of them in church, but as soon as the safety of their fatherland is in question, they begin, at first tentatively and diffidently to believe in God again. They are all firm believers in the theology that says: The Lord helps those who help themselves. Karl praises the country in the love of which they are all united, mentioning the variety of human types and landscapes which one finds in Switzerland. He concludes by asking all the other Confederates to drink to Friendship in Freedom.

Das Fähnlein reflects the sunniest period of Keller's life. Early poverty, his prolonged artistic adolescence, the strongest grounds for dissatisfaction with the body politic, all lay behind him. Like Salomon Landolt he now knew that he would never marry and was determined not to take his misfortune too seriously. Keller realises that the old political order is now receding; the constant preoccupation with the iniquities of Jesuits and aristocrats which had once exercised his mind and had been expressed in his early poems, is one of the slightly ridiculous but lovable foibles of the Seven.

In one sense the message of *Das Fähnlein* is uncompromising. The old men are worthy citizens who deserve all credit for helping to bring about the new, liberal Switzerland, but like aged colonels in English clubs, they are still fighting the battles of the last war but one. Though the victory of liberalism has been

accomplished they behave as though the Swiss still had to fight
for their rights against the forces of reaction. Now, however, the
Seven with their banner and their fear of public speaking and
their attempts to behave like tyrants in their own homes do not
really count for much any more. Karl can cope with the rather
different demands of a new age. He is intelligent, he has great
manual dexterity in his trade, he is aware of wider issues, understands the political situation, and if the need arises, can shoot
straight. He is a good soldier and has won the affection of a
beautiful, charming and rich girl. Beyond a doubt it is on him
that Keller wishes to focus our attention. Gently but firmly
Keller states his confidence in the rising generation and shows
how the parents' attempts to keep them down come to naught.
Keller relates all this with affection and restraint, but his point
is none the less effective for being soberly made. In *Martin
Salander* Keller no longer showed the same tolerance of the follies
of the older generation. Arnold Salander has all the virtues, but
his father is a poor fish, an amorous and gullible old fool; the
book breaks down largely because the hero is so patently unworthy of our serious attention. Arnold plays too small a part
in the novel, and his father's emotional and commercial flounder-
ings do not form an edifying spectacle.

Das Fähnlein is a cardinal work for the understanding of
Keller's literary individuality. Without being blind to the faults
of his fellow Swiss he loves them all and the country which has
produced such a diversity of human types. While he has a healthy
respect for the older generation he can see that their minds are
still darkened by old prejudices and that they are too rigid in
outlook when it comes to facing the problems of a later age. More
lively and flexible minds are needed, and the gift of rhetoric,
which the old men view with intense suspicion, is seen to be a
necessary qualification for the ideal modern citizen. Karl is the
kind of young man whom Keller would like to see everywhere
now that the struggle against the forces of reaction has been
won. Karl and his contemporaries can allow themselves the
luxury of open minds, thanks to the efforts of men like his father
and his friends. The young men have time for cultural pursuits
because they are not too preoccupied by the harsh daily struggle
for bread and basic political rights. Keller has a vision of a more
beautiful, leisured and gracious existence in Switzerland, but he

never forgets the debts of gratitude which he and his contemporaries owe to his father's generation. *Das Fähnlein* affirms Keller's faith in the future of Switzerland.

Das Fähnlein, like the other *Novellen* in the series, is concerned with the history of Zurich, although of course Keller here treated much more recent history than in the other four stories. Perhaps because it is less openly moralising in tone, perhaps because it is more idealistic in its view of Swiss destiny, it represents in the present writer's view a considerably higher artistic achievement than *Frau Regel Amrain*, which seems pedestrian by comparison. The range of characters introduced, the variety of Swiss life which is represented in its pages, the ever-present feeling that the author deeply believes both in the Swiss democratic ideal and in the ability of younger Swiss citizens worthily to uphold this ideal make this story a refreshing and inspiring work.

Ursula

I

This last story of the series has much in common with *Dietegen*, which deals with the same period and also records in considerable detail the habits of life and customs of country people in sixteenth century Switzerland.

The plot shows no great complexity. Hans Gyr returns in 1523 from the Wars of Religion in which he has fought for the Pope against the French. He finds the people of the Bachtelberg district near Zurich in the grip of a collective religious delusion. They have all, including his fiancée Ursula, become the disciples of a group of so-called *Winkelpropheten*, sectarian religious leaders who specialise in simulating fits, delivering pseudo-mystical sermons, pretending to have become children again and generally indulging in activities which involve the suspension of rational cerebration. Hans Gyr witnesses the image-breakers at work in the churches and returns by chance to the Bachtelberg just in time to save Ursula from the *Winkelpropheten*, two of whom have cast a lecherous eye on her. The sectarians fall foul of the law and many of them, including Ursula, are sent to prison in Zurich. Hansli succeeds in releasing Ursula, then sells his farm and returns to military service. He acquires the reputation of being a fanatically pious, puritanical N.C.O., who also tries to foist his standards on others who do not believe in them. However, even this paragon is not above the occasional lapse from virtue, as we see in the incident with the beautiful Italian girl near Lake Como. After an uneasy truce the Zurich army with Zwingli goes to fight the Catholic Cantons at Kappel. Ursula, still mentally somewhat confused, has followed the Zurich army. At the sight of Zwingli bravely riding among the Protestant soldiers Ursula's delusions have left her, and she knows that her task is to find Hans and return home with him. However, the Zurich army suffers disastrous defeat; Zwingli and most of the Zurich elders are killed, and Hans Gyr is wounded and left for dead on the battlefield. After the battle Ursula searches among the dead and wounded, finds Hans just alive, nurses him back to health and is permanently reunited with him. Together the couple return to the Bachtelberg where they take over Ursula's father's farm. There they live for the rest of their days.

II

Ursula is a victim of a widespread religious delusion. Affected by her environment she loses her mental and emotional balance. Normally the most chaste of maidens she is prepared to offer herself to Hansli before marriage. Later she confuses Hansli with the archangel Gabriel. Yet through all her deranged imaginings runs one consistent thread; she may mistake the identity of her lover but she remains loyal to him and even puts him on a par with the archangel. Her love for Hansli forms the anchor which ensures Ursula's final recovery from mental sickness. Without him Ursula would scarcely have resisted the influences of her environment; she would have lost all hope of human dignity and happiness.

Hansli Gyr does not make a very satisfactory hero. Generally speaking he is too good to be true, and his momentary lapse from virtue with Fresca does not seem to play any organic part in the story. He is another of those wise, virtuous, careful, economical young men, whom Keller delights as a rule in portraying satirically, as for instance in *Die drei gerechten Kammacher*. Keller now and again pokes fun at Hansli's worthy, puritanical ways, but without proper conviction, and except at occasional moments of real pathos we do not know whether to love or hate him. There is very little reason why we should like Hansli Gyr, whose character lacks generosity and warmth. Keller became so interested in the historical background that he gave less than adequate attention to the delineation of character. Ursula on the other hand is well drawn, and there is a real element of truth in her clinging, even in her deranged state, to her love for Hansli, since girlhood the most important factor in her life.

Zwingli emerges as a figure of truly heroic proportions. We see him at first moving naturally and easily among the Zurich soldiers, joining in their good fellowship with moderation and enjoyment. Like Hans Gyr he is an upholder of law and order who does not believe in fighting for its own sake, or for the sake of money or booty. The author of *Ein Feldhauptmann, wie er sein soll* (*A Military Captain as he should be*) believes that a Christian should be prepared to defend the independence of his native country, uphold its laws and stake his life for the sake of freedom of conscience. Keller writes appreciatively of the service which Zwingli rendered the human spirit, and says that one of the virtues of Zwingli's Reformation was that its intent could be discerned by a simple man of good will like Hans Gyr. Keller questions Zwingli's political judgement, saying that a people could just as properly refuse to accept Zwingli's doctrine as a woman may refuse an unwelcome suitor; Zwingli and his adherents failed to realise this.

The stern discipline of the Zurich army, in which no female camp followers were tolerated, is approvingly described. Every day the soldiers were summoned by the drum to prayers and sermons; no drunkenness was allowed, and cursing and swearing were frowned upon. The soldiers had to respect the property of citizens over whose land they marched, and were encouraged to treat everyone they met, even the enemy in the field, in a decent and humane manner. The English reader is reminded of Cromwell's army.

Side by side with the genuine movement of ecclesiastical reform, which was led by men of vision, pure motive, and considerable organising ability, existed less worthy sideshoots of the great intellectual and spiritual impulse. The supreme authority of the church once shaken, dangerous and unscrupulous men sought to fish in troubled waters. By appealing to primitive depths in simple souls they won the allegiance of many people even if they and their victims all became perverted in the process. By such cheap tricks as the imitation of childhood habits and games and an elaborate simulated "dying" ritual the *Winkelpropheten* pandered to the simple countryman's love of sensation. How shallow such religious experience was is shown in various ways; old Enoch Schnurrenberger places so low a value on it that he insists that his co-religionists should shell beans or core apples when they attend meetings in his house so that they may not utterly waste their time; at the end of every meeting they settle down to real amusements such as card-playing and drinking. Ursula is nearly ravished by two lecherous self-styled "prophets"; they form living embodiments of the danger of allowing Tom, Dick and Harry to set themselves up as religious authorities. The behaviour of these *Winkelpropheten* and their crude and tasteless sermons, which were principally based on a false understanding of traditional mystic lore, are well illustrated by Keller. For this aspect of *Ursula* Keller was indebted to Melchior Schuler's popular history book, *Taten und Sitten der Eidgenossen* (1838), which contains full information about the Anabaptists. The grown up children were a sect in St Gall, and "dying", with foaming at the mouth and extravagant convulsions, was a speciality of some Appenzell sectarians.

Keller also drew on J. C. Mörikofer's biography of Zwingli, which gave him useful information about the discipline of the Zurich army. From Mörikofer Keller also learned of the disposal of the abbey treasures and of the way in which sectaries appropriated and used religious vestments and church ornaments. Keller's vein for the grotesque finds an outlet in his account of the behaviour of the religious fanatics.

III

As we learn from Keller's notes *Ursula* dates in its first origins from his days in Berlin, but it was not completed until many years later. In 1878 Keller wrote to both Paul Heyse and Theodor Storm, complaining that he had not had time to finish the story properly:

> The thing is just not ready, the second part not executed with a critical eye, because the publisher was sitting on my neck on account of the usual Christmas trade. (Letter to Heyse, June 1878.)

Keller found it so hard to master the wealth of historical material that the work is deficient on the human and moral side. Ursula's mental sickness and its sudden cure may seem just credible, but even the most forbearing reader can hardly remain long in sympathy with such a prig as Hansli Gyr. *Ursula* would certainly have benefited from less hasty composition. The work is intended to testify to the cleansing, healing, revivifying power of an honest human instinct, nature asserting itself over a perverted culture. However, the reader of the *Sieben Legenden* will probably consider that Keller makes his point more effectively there.

Perhaps more than *Die Leute von Seldwyla* the *Züricher Novellen* require to be viewed as a whole and judged as a cycle. They offer a rich and varied picture of Zurich life through the ages from the fourteenth century to the mid-nineteenth century. They illustrate well the progressive strengthening of the position of the bourgeois from the age of Hadlaub when only the exceptional bourgeois individual could raise himself to be accepted more or less on sufferance on an approximately equal footing by his aristocratic contemporaries to the mid-nineteenth century when the Seven and their successors are not only honest men who have fought a good fight for liberal democratic principles but also the founder fathers of a new Swiss way of life which in young men like Karl has excellent prospects of survival. There are ups and downs in the course of their history, and sometimes sensible men like Zwingli or Hans Gyr may appear to be at the mercy of their less balanced and responsible fellow-citizens, but in the end the honest intention and integrity of purpose always prevail over the specious promises and erroneous teachings of those who like the *Winkelpropheten* reject traditional values and try to supplant sound doctrine with their own heady and arrogant fantasies.

The stories contain ample evidence of Keller's familiarity with cultural history over a period covering many generations. Not only is he acquainted with great events, important people and major artistic achievements, but he has an intimate knowledge of the everyday pursuits, customs and dress of humble people. This is everywhere apparent, but perhaps *Der Landvogt von Greifensee* is the most successful story from the point of view of combining good presentation of details of dress and domestic interiors with lively characterisation and a genuine sense of artistic inevitability. In some of the other stories, especially *Hadlaub* and *Ursula*, one has the feeling that the author is striving rather too hard over the local colour at the expense of event and character.

The first three stories are carefully integrated with the framework narrative of Herr Jacques and his godfather. The little intrigue about Herr Jacques and his unrealistically excessive adolescent ambitions may be considered rather moralising and trivial, but the *Novellen* represent Keller's most thorough-going attempt so far to construct a cycle of short stories.

The *Züricher Novellen* do not show much of the occasional romanticising strain of *Die Leute von Seldwyla*. Everywhere the author's affection for his native city is apparent, as well as his pride in constitutional advance down through the ages. One senses that he has moved away from the exclusive preoccupation with individual morality which lies at the heart of *Die Leute von Seldwyla* and that he is now thinking in terms of the community as well, however much attention he may pay to individuals in stories such as *Hadlaub* and *Der Landvogt*.

CHAPTER SIX

DAS SINNGEDICHT (THE EPIGRAM)

IN *Das Sinngedicht* Keller took up a theme dear to his heart and dwelt upon it with greater depth and concentration than ever before. The relationship between the sexes had often engaged his attention in the past, but here he explores the subject systematically and from the different points of view of man and woman. Written before it became generally fashionable to talk of a war between man and woman, the book is largely concerned with the fundamental antagonism between the sexes. Keller was well aware of this, and the reader constantly perceives "nature red in tooth and claw" behind the civilized conversations and sophisticated but always tendentious story-telling. This tale—with illustrations—of the courtship of two gifted people is told with great delicacy and finesse by an author who, having lost all illusions about the nature of love and marriage retains goodwill towards his fellow men and women.

As early as 1851 Keller noted on a piece of paper: "Variations on Logau's epigram: Wie willst du weiße Lilien usw?" On the same sheet are jottings about two of the *Sinngedicht* stories, *Regine* and *Die arme Baronin*. Four years later he asked Franz Duncker, the publisher, if he would undertake the publication of a volume of short stories with a narrative framework. The collection was to be entitled *Galatea*. The work as originally conceived was also to have contained the *Sieben Legenden*, but by 1871 Keller had decided that these formed a distinctive unit by themselves, and they were separately published. Keller's unfulfilled obligation to write *Galatea* kept casting a cloud over his otherwise cheerful and lively correspondence with Lina Duncker. As he told Adolf Exner in 1881 the first seventy pages of *Das Sinngedicht* were written in Berlin in 1855. After his return to Switzerland Keller neglected *Das Sinngedicht* and tried to wriggle out of the obligation to complete it; in 1860 Duncker refused to accept *Der Apotheker von Chamounix* in lieu of the *Galatea* stories. Even in the mid-1870s Duncker still tried to persuade Keller to finish *Galatea*, but although Keller's interest in the project had revived, he was resolved to entrust the book to another publisher. Keller knew that Duncker's business had been going downhill and preferred to ensure that the work went to a leading publisher. Therefore he repaid to Franz Duncker the advance which he had already received and was then free to dispose of the work elsewhere.

The *Novellen* first appeared in the *Deutsche Rundschau* from January to May 1881 under the title *Das Sinngedicht*. The book edition containing as an additional item the story of Lucia's youthful infatuation with her cousin Leodegar was not published till the following autumn.

II

The stories are based on Friedrich von Logau's epigram:
Wie willst du weiße Lilien zu roten Rosen machen?
Küss' eine weiße Galatee; sie wird errötend lachen.

(How will you make white lilies into red roses? Kiss a white Galatea; she will blushingly laugh.)

The seventeenth-century moralist and epigrammatist formulates neatly the moral conflict between law and freedom, sensuality and morality. The phrase "blushingly laugh" illustrates this contrast perfectly. While laughter conveys wholesome, natural pleasure in the kiss, the blush shows that the person concerned recognises certain moral restraints. Keller took Logau to mean that an ideal relationship between man and woman would be one in which instinct and restraint would co-exist and complement one another.

The young scientist Reinhart has lived for years a hermit-like life among his books and experiments. His life has been impoverished and his eyesight impaired by his excessive preoccupation with his scientific experiments. Human and moral considerations have been banished in favour of logarithms and tables. He has allowed himself in his ruthless scientific ambition to become quite one-sided. The elements of sweetness and light are missing from his life, and in due course it comes as no surprise that the woman of his choice turns out to be a Lucia or even "Lux, my light" as

her uncle at one point jokingly addresses her. Reinhart has literally been buried alive in his Faust-like experiments and studies,
and has become cut off from the world of nature and human
happiness, fullness of life and a reasonably rounded existence.
In the words of Keller's early poem *Alles oder Nichts*:

> Alles Wissen ist ein Totenschrein,
> In dem der Mensch lebendig wird begraben;
> Ein Vampyr, der das Herzblut will entsaugen.

From this restrictive and graceless existence he instinctively
turns in the end to seek the qualities in which he knows himself
to be deficient. Keller points out rather censoriously how much
Reinhart is missing by this self-imposed scientific discipline. Fortunately, Reinhart has enough commonsense to draw the appropriate conclusion when his eyes begin to hurt during his spectro-
scopic enquiries. Reinhart's situation as a man with scientific
and intellectual interests which threaten to take over and destroy
or at least impair his life is meant, I think, to indicate the danger
to which men in particular are subject of allowing professional
cares and ambitions to dominate their whole lives.

The early stages of Reinhart's quest for his ideal woman provide good examples of Keller's narrative art. The girl at the
bridge has something in common with Judith (in *Der grüne
Heinrich*); Reinhart first sees her combing her hair at the well, an
embodiment of the beauty and enchantment of Nature. The early
morning sunshine completes the picture, which, however, lacks
the fullness and complexity of Judith. The girl's unabashed
laughter when Reinhart kisses her dispels any pretensions she may
have had to be taken seriously by the earnest seeker after
womanly perfection as understood by Logau; she is too natural,
even brazen for his liking.

The vicar's daughter also proves a disappointment for precisely
opposite reasons. Her excessive modesty and frightened shrinking
from life prevent her from satisfying Logau's exacting conditions; the glass jars which protect all the family's treasures, her
keeping of a diary as a substitute for real life and her practical
inability (shown in her clumsy attempt to feed and water Reinhart's horse), also her silly determination to make a great fuss
about her thoroughly unimportant letter to Lucie, are all revealing of her ineptitude for life, and we are scarcely surprised when

she fails the test of the *Sinngedicht*. Just as the little toll-keeper represents Nature in her unadorned and rather shameless state, the vicar's daughter is an example of a person so preoccupied with appearances that she will not or cannot face the reality of life, of one for whom culture has become the means of quelling nature, of inhibiting and repressing every sound, spontaneous impulse. The acquaintance with these two very different girls impresses on Reinhart the difficulty and importance of his self-appointed task. That he is not a frivolous lady-killer is demonstrated by his brief encounter with the inn-keeper's daughter, from whom he literally almost runs away, so uneager is he to obey the epigram's injunction with an unworthy candidate.

Up till this point in the narrative Reinhart has approached his task in a spirit of rational, almost scientific inquiry. He would really have preferred to continue in this way, but now rational experimentation begins to be supplemented by other elements. His journey through the forest, accomplished in a half-dreaming state, forms a typically romantic motif; luck can come to this hero only after he has surrendered to some extent to the forces of chance and let himself drift, it cannot be attained solely by a conscious, deliberate act of the will. His first appearance at the great house, when he rides rough-shod over finely-swept paths and elegant flower-beds, possesses an evident symbolical meaning; Lucie must also yield to this crude and disturbing assault on her carefully guarded citadel. Reinhart's first glimpse of Lucie reads like the climax of a fairy-tale, and indeed the setting of the marble fountain in front of the great house with the white-clad maiden sorting red roses in the evening sunshine contributes in no small measure to this atmosphere. Not only Reinhart is in a dream-like state at this point; we read that Lucie went over to look at the intruder, "wie um zu erfahren, ob sie wache oder träume". He is by now in such confusion that he gives Lucie the paper with the epigram written on it instead of the letter from the vicar's daughter, and at this point Lucie is at an advantage over him, for she soon takes stock of the situation and regains her composure.

By this stage in the framework narrative the reader has realised the difficulties that face Reinhart in his search. The early part of the *Sinngedicht* introduces with much charm and lightness of touch the issues which will dominate the whole work. It must be admitted that the extreme care and art shown in these early pages are not consistently maintained throughout the work; one or two of the stories are comparatively trivial in content and disappointing in execution. However, the cycle as a whole is remarkable for its organic unity, to which the artfully constructed framework largely contributes.

Lucie stands in complete contrast to Reinhart. She is clearly a cultivated woman. Her preferred reading suggests pronounced tastes, a strong individuality. She manages her maids with gentle but definite authority. She reads several languages not only in their modern but also in their older, historical forms. She herself had designed the maze which caused Reinhart such confusion. The fact that she is the authoress of his confusion cannot be regarded as accidental. She likes pictures, and is seldom seen without some occupation. Unlike Reinhart who had for years almost forgotten human life Lucie lives in the world, participates in other people's joys and sorrows, does not try to run away from life. She somewhat resents Reinhart's surprise at discovering that she has so many serious interests. Reinhart finds that she has the effect upon him of making him wish to be completely honest and frank with her even if this should turn out to be damaging to him. She has charm, artistic talent, a lively interest in the people who surround her, a happy gift of running a house and garden.

Lucie's limitations consist in a certain smugness, a certain virginal aloofness, which causes her to be rather defensive and almost arrogant towards Reinhart. A marked lack of charity colours some of her judgements of other people, and she is inclined to view the other sex with the rather jaundiced eye of the female emancipator. Falling in love herself causes her to take a much more friendly view of the rest of the world, in fact we are entitled to expect that she will undergo a development rather like that of the Baroness in the story.

Lucie's story of Salome serves to show that in an ideal marriage some shared interest of the partners is essential. Salome, handsome but empty-headed, is betrothed to an equally foolish and empty-headed young man. Since their relationship lacks any basis of shared interest it proves impossible to bridge the gap between their respective backgrounds. Their violent quarrel is sparked off by their sheer boredom with themselves and with one another. They have literally nothing to say to one another. Lucie judges both young people rather severely, for it is clearly part of her own rule of life to ensure that one is never without interest or occupation. Reinhart's attempt to defend Salome sounds weak and ineffectual. One discerns a certain pedagogical harshness in Lucie's view of Salome and Drogo.

Reinhart will not admit that differences of background and upbringing are important, and relates the story of *Regine* in support of his contention that a man must simply like, and go on liking, the face of the woman he loves and plans to marry. He admits that the story ends in tragedy, but maintains that this was not because Regine married a man of superior wealth and station. Nevertheless, the reader may be permitted his doubts about this question.

Erwin Altenauer, a Boston German, enjoys the advantages of wealth and position. He has been well educated, holds a post in the diplomatic service, is gentle and well-mannered and has a great deal of charm, so that in the early stages of the story the reader cannot help wishing him well. His natural kindness towards Regine seems completely in character, as does also his sudden decision that despite her lowly station she is the woman whom he wishes to marry. Keller conveys well Erwin's sudden jealousy of the corporal whom he finds one day talking to Regine and his relief on discovering that the corporal is her brother. Erwin's delicacy about offering financial assistance to Regine's family reinforces our good opinion of him.

However, Erwin's excessive solicitude about Regine's education for wifehood gives the show away about him. Even before his departure for America on urgent family business we realise that he sets very great store by his wife's correct behaviour; the smallest lapse from the standards on which he insists would represent a blow to his pride, so before marrying Regine he has her carefully groomed for matrimony by a reliable matron. To give Erwin his due, he is proud of her progress in deportment and French speaking, but we are never fully convinced that he loves her. Our suspicions are confirmed when he returns to America and does not feel confident enough about Regine's ability to live up to the required standards to take her with him. The ensuing tragedy stems naturally enough from his excessive pride which will not allow him to trust Regine although he ought to regard her as completely worthy of him and his family. It is the lack of confidence shown in her by Erwin that makes Regine take her own life.

Keller emphasises that it is not Regine's lowly birth or ne'er-do-well relatives who spoil her marriage but Erwin Altenauer's foolish patrician pride. Regine loves him with a selfless devotion and will do anything to please him, even stay on in Germany while he goes back to America without her. She has already learned all that she needs to know and only an obsessive concern with details of social convention makes him insist on leaving her in Germany. Regine's tragedy may seem insufficiently motivated, but this is not so. Erwin faces the logical consequence of his mental reservations about Regine's fitness to be shown off in Boston. If he had loved her as much as he loved his self-esteem he would have taken her with him. Regine, alone in a strange world, needs the active support and absolute moral backing of her husband without which life is not only unpleasant but impossible for her.

Regine makes it clear that married love must include mutual esteem and consideration of one's partner's feelings. Erwin was without imagination as far as Regine's sufferings were concerned; he did not see that he was literally immolating her on the altar of his self-esteem. There was no failure on Regine's part as far as measuring up to her new station in life was concerned, only despair that her dearly loved husband would not trust her.

Die arme Baronin, also related by Reinhart, shows how Brandolf's genuine, sustained affection rescues Hedwig from the distress and bitterness which poverty and ill treatment had caused. The feeling that she is loved and cared for makes Hedwig bloom again, and Keller clearly intends us to have every confidence in her marriage with Brandolf. Brandolf's revenge on Hedwig's husband and brothers shows rather poor taste. In a completely unsuitable context Keller introduces motifs like those to be found in *Die Kammacher* or the extravagantly grotesque pictures of the religious cranks in *Ursula*. It is as though one found a mediæval gargoyle in the middle of a Doric pillar. However, despite the fairy-tale revenge there is truth at the heart of the story; one can easily believe that someone starved of affection as Hedwig had been would feel a great sense of renewal and gratitude towards her rescuer, and that her life would blossom in these favourable circumstances as never before.

It is to be regretted that Hedwig is portrayed as such a very aggressive person before her change of heart. To stab with a knife at the heels of a perfectly innocent stranger as he passes her on the stairs suggests not only a soured and disappointed but a positively malevolent and violent disposition. Keller was well capable of making his point, that Brandolf's love and kindness transform Hedwig's life without resorting to such devices.

Die Geisterseher, the Novelle related by Lucie's uncle, who has belatedly joined the young people, is a personal recollection which establishes a connexion between Reinhart and Lucie's family. The whole episode reminds us of the extraordinary coincidences which form part of the stock in trade of eighteenth century novelists. In fact, this whole story breathes the atmosphere of the Enlightenment, whose values it upholds and proclaims. Apart from its place within the framework story, *Die Geisterseher* does not contribute a great deal to the cycle. Its whole theme is somewhat pedestrian and the treatment not very distinguished. Reinhart's mother, Hildeburg, had been unable to decide between Lucia's uncle and Reinhart's father. Since both young men had many good qualities Hildeburg was in the end acutely distressed by the *embarras du choix*. She resolved the question by staging a mock haunting episode, to which both suitors were subjected. Her subconscious preference evidently determined the nature of the test. She married the man whose rational faculties remained unimpaired throughout the time of testing. The man who remains capable of acting in accordance with the spirit of rational enlightenment wins the victory over the other who believes that something mysterious and supernatural is afoot.

The two parts of *Don Correa* are really separate tales. Don Correa's first marriage with the wealthy Portuguese noblewoman, who lives in isolation on a remote estate, turns out to have been a disastrous mistake. At the time of their marriage both Don Correa and Donna Feniza Mayor are completely infatuated with one another, but this phase passes quickly as far as Don Correa is concerned. Donna Feniza deeply resents his eventual determination to assert his independence, and openly rebels at his desire to be master of the household.

Donna Feniza is portrayed as a vicious, lecherous and self-centred woman who believes only in "herself, her riches and her church". At first she wants Don Correa, but only as a plaything, an ornament of her self-esteem. It may be argued that if she had known from the beginning who he was she would perhaps have treated him differently, and certainly by his elaborate devices to conceal his identity and then reveal it in a moment of triumph on board his flagship he brings out the worst in her. The judgment on Donna Feniza and her accomplices, although harsh, can more readily be accepted than what happens to Hedwig von Lohenhausen's husband and brothers, because we can at least put it down to the barbarous customs of a remote age, and can to this extent absolve Don Correa from direct responsibility.

The next part of the story is strongly contrasted with the first part. Don Correa first meets Zambo-Maria in a position of abject slavery; she is literally being sat upon by her owner, Princess Annachinga. Don Correa decides almost on the spot to give her a Christian education and the freedom of self-determination which has hitherto been denied her. He does this simply because he has fallen in love with Zambo at first sight, and his care over her and efforts on her behalf are rewarded by her loyalty to him, which makes her escape from the nunnery in Cadiz and walk to Lisbon to rejoin him. In the first part of *Don Correa* Donna Feniza tries to limit Don Correa's personal freedom to an improper extent. He reacts by rebelling against this bondage and her refusal to accompany him on board his flagship proves the last straw. Realising that she is unfaithful as well as merely undutiful Don Correa takes violent measures against her. In the second story Don Correa gives Zambo-Maria her liberty and educates her properly. Her whole existence as a civilised, responsible human being is a result of his generous and imaginative behaviour towards her. Zambo-Maria is full of gratitude to Don Correa for having restored her to a proper human dignity. There is an unforgettable last scene on board ship while Don Correa and his bride sail towards West Africa:

"Has the sea, too, a soul, and is it also free?" asked the lady.
"No," answered Don Correa, "it merely obeys the Creator and the winds which are His breath. But now, tell me, Maria, if you had known your freedom before, would you still have given me your hand?"
"You ask too late," she replied with a not unsubtle smile, "as now I am yours and cannot be otherwise, like the sea."

But since she saw that this answer did not satisfy him or accord with his hopes she looked earnestly into his eyes as she stood tall and erect before him, and gave him with a free and sure gesture her right hand.

Keller's principal source for *Don Correa* was E. A. W. Zimmermann's *Taschenbuch der Reisen*, 1. Jahrg., Leipzig 1802, pp. 68–70. This tells how the proud negro princess faces the Portuguese governor and commands a slave girl to kneel on the floor so that she may sit on her back. Another Don Correa, the Spaniard Don Diego Alvarez Correa (d. 1557) was shipwrecked in the bay of San Salvador in 1510. He spent some years with an Indian tribe and married one of their women, whom he afterwards took with him to the French court. From this story Keller took the idea of marriage with a savage. A Portuguese sailor, Salvador Correa de sa Benavides (1594–1688) was for a time Governor General of Rio de Janeiro, and later went to Africa where he drove the Dutch from Angola, also waging war against the natives. Keller combined these historical figures, separated as they were by nationality and time, and wove them into a single tale. The first unsuccessful marriage with Donna Feniza-Mayor is no doubt introduced mainly to motivate Don Correa's second, on the face of it risky and outlandish marriage. The Jesuits' attempt to kidnap Maria reflects Keller's hatred of the Order, whom he regarded as enemies of freedom and wholesome education.

The last story from the main part of *Das Sinngedicht* also concerns an exotic love. Lucia relates *Die Berlocken* (*The Watch Chain Ornaments*) as a kind of riposte to *Don Correa*, which seems to her to allow too much authority to the male in the making of marriages. She portrays Thibaut de Vallormes as an accomplished and shameless young lady-killer. Without scruple he had played with the affections of numbers of women simply in order to persuade them to part with the elegant trifles that adorned his waistcoat. It is ironical but fitting that the first time Vallormes falls in love it is with a redskin girl who neatly tricks him out of his trinkets so that she can give them to her brave. The finale of the story, in which the grotesquely attired and painted Indian, wearing the trinkets on his nose, picks up Quoneschi from where she is sitting at de Vallormes' feet, swings

her over his shoulder and rushes from the scene, makes Lucie's
point with dramatic cogency.

Lucie tells this story in revenge against Reinhart for suggesting,
as he certainly does in *Don Correa* and *Regine*, that the man is
the superior being and that the most that a woman can look for
is to be chosen from among her sisters for a man's favour. In
Die Berlocken, at the very moment when de Vallormes thinks he
has broken the last resistance of the beautiful but unyielding
young savage, she teaches him the lesson of which he had been in
need at least since the age of seventeen. Quoneschi exercises her
fredom of choice against a man who had imagined that all female
hearts were his for the breaking. There is a savage justice about
what happens to de Vallormes' trinkets. By foul means he had
won them all; Quoneschi took them from him by fair means
because of her single-minded devotion to her brave. She does
exactly what her good and loving nature dictates for the man
of her choice, but de Vallormes has used all his arts of wheedling
and cajolery simply for the adornment of his own waistcoat.
Keller's source for *Die Berlocken* was Baron Grimm's *Corre-
spondance littéraire*, October 1778.

Die Berlocken, though a pointed and amusing story, certainly
makes nothing like so deep an impression on the reader as *Regine*
or *Die arme Baronin*. Lucie's stories, while more directly tendentious than Reinhart's, are rather trivial and lacking in emotional
intensity. Keller must have known that this was so, but it is hard
to determine whether it happened thus by accident or by design.
Reinhart is capable of destroying his own case by a would-be
illustrative anecdote which in fact invalidates it; Lucie tends to
see issues rather too clearly and simply; she never fails to make
her desired point, yet she sometimes makes it in too crude, simple
and unequivocal a fashion. In the long run one must hand the
palm to Reinhart, for even when he fails in his intentions, he
succeeds in moving us and conveying the impression of a generous and imaginative personality.

After hearing *Die Berlocken* Reinhart understands what Lucie
is getting at, feels disturbed and somewhat resentful, and
announces that he must go home. Thereafter several months
elapse, a kind of cooling-off period. Later, when his father and
mother go to visit Lucie and her uncle, he is invited to join the
party. During this visit, while the old people go on an excursion,

Lucie and Reinhart are left in the house. This is their chance
to settle the issue between them.

The settlement is introduced in a rather oblique way. Lucie
tells Reinhart that she is a Roman Catholic and explains how
she came to adopt this faith. She tells him of her youthful passion
for her cousin Leodegar, and how she has been left with a lasting
reminder of this part of her past in her Catholic faith. Lucie's
confiding in Reinhart creates a much warmer and more intimate
atmosphere. This thaws out her heart, which has been chilled
and petrified by the old experience of her vain love for Leodegar.
Now she is won back to life and has abandoned the idea of
remaining for ever faithful to an unattainable ideal. The intimacy
born of Lucie's frankness about her own past is reinforced by
the shared experience of rescuing the pretty little snake from
certain death. Now Keller works towards his grand finale with
calculated art. First of all he describes the idyllic situation of the
shoemaker's house under the walnut tree with pears and grapes
growing over it. The sun streams into the house and the young
shoemaker is busy working and singing Goethe's *Mit einem
gemalten Bande* with great feeling. Reinhart and Lucie also share
this experience, and the glance of understanding which they
exchange, in which genuine emotion aroused by the song is oddly
mingled with amusement at the cobbler's very individual render-
ing of it, helps further to seal their covenant. The tumult of the
canaries singing in rivalry with their master absolutely sweeps
Reinhart and Lucie off their feet. They kiss, and immediately
Lucie realises that they have fulfilled the condition laid down in
the epigram. In these last pages of the *Sinngedicht* Keller not
only draws all the threads of his narrative together but makes the
Sinngedicht the most beautiful, rounded and artistically complete
of all his works.

III

Among the distinguishing features of this cycle of *Novellen*
are its leisurely pace and careful construction. Basic assumptions
of *Das Sinngedicht* are aristocratic standards of conduct, a sophisticated yet generous ideal of the cultivated individual and a
reserved but free manner of life. The milieu is no longer the
petty bourgeois world of small tradesmen, shopkeepers and publi-
cans; we are here moving among leisured members of the upper

classes. Keller never discusses directly the social position of his characters, but this becomes clear from the surroundings in which we find them and from their evident freedom to spend their time as they prefer.

Corresponding to the change in milieu as compared with Keller's earlier works is the development which has taken place in his style. Our earlier observations have shown that he liked to load his pages with descriptive detail, sometimes almost to the point where there was a risk of allowing descriptive passages to assume a life of their own. This tendency could even on occasion disrupt the narrative economy of a *Novelle*. Also he liked to use occasional outré metaphors and similes, which had the effect of startling the reader into paying closer attention. Compared with the style of *Die Leute von Seldwyla* that of the present work seems spare, economical, restrained; it is lucid, formal, rather severe. Certain familiar idiosyncrasies persist; he still prefers "welcher" to "der" as a relative pronoun, and there are traces of *Kanzleisprache*. Indirect speech occurs more frequently than one might expect, but in general *Das Sinngedicht* shows a polished and uniform style.

Das Sinngedicht does not demand in any crude or superficial way woman's "emancipation", in which Keller did not believe. Nevertheless, Lucie often adopts feminist and emancipated attitudes. In this respect perhaps she reflects Keller's acquaintance with intellectual women in the Berlin salons during the 1850s. The *Sinngedicht* does embody a conception of life in which each of the sexes has a separate but equally important place. It is perhaps worth while recording that Lucie is more nearly self-sufficient without Reinhart than he is without her; her way of life is more reasonable and satisfying than his. The work reflects both Christian and Goethean thinking about the place of man and woman as partners in marriage.

When we read of the sophisticated, yet modest and enjoyable pattern of existence which Lucie has evolved for herself, we may think for a moment of life in the *Rosenhaus* in Stifter's *Nachsommer*, yet Keller does not labour the point of the leisurely, full, ordered, gracious existence. He leaves more to the reader's imagination, he is not so ruthlessly encyclopaedic as his Austrian contemporary. His economically sketched background is sufficient, and we are grateful to him for leaving us part of the task of imaginative reconstruction to do ourselves.

Keller fully realises the difficulties involved in the marriage of unequals. He thinks, however, that these may be overcome as long as the more sophisticated, freer partner—in the cases of *Don Correa* and *Regine* it is the man, but it need not be—is prepared to watch over, love and protect the less worldly-wise. A man who merely seeks sensation and novelty, like the Rousseau-tinged M. de Vallormes in *Die Berlocken*, may expect the shallow cult of the primitive to lead to discomfiture and ridicule. The redskin girl uses the Frenchman's infatuation in furtherance of her own ends.

By and large justice prevails in the world of *Das Sinngedicht*. Salome and Drogo both get exactly what they deserve in one another, and the break-up of their engagement results naturally from the vacuity and irresponsibility of both partners. Regine's fate may seem tragic out of all proportion to Erwin Altenauer's fault, yet this is not so; although Erwin imagines he loves Regine, he really loves an ideal woman of his own imagination. Regine is perfectly capable of behaving creditably in the world of her adoption, but Erwin has no regard for her feelings and he destroys her by his selfishness. Don Correa marries his Zambo-Maria in the end, but only by the skin of his teeth, for like Erwin Altenauer he lays excessive stress on a proper education for wifehood. The humiliation which overtakes the rascally husband and brothers of *Die arme Baronin* is tempered by the fact that they go to begin a new life in America, a more modest but also more wholesome existence, made possible for them by Brandolf's generosity. We are clearly intended to accept cheerfully the summary execution of Donna Feniza Mayor and her accomplices. Yet the reader must feel that Correa's deception of Feniza Mayor as to his identity is largely responsible for the development of events. In the last story Lucia retains a legacy of her infatuation for her cousin in the Catholic faith which she holds without conviction yet cannot publicly abandon without drawing unfavourable attention to herself.

The whole conception of the cycle is somewhat artificial; the idea of the epigram sending the hero out on his search, and of Reinhart and Lucie sorting out their opinions on love and marriage by means of telling tendentious stories to one another sounds more like an intellectual or artistic exercise than like life. Matching the unreality of the conception we have the ideal remoteness of the beautiful house on the hill, the gentlemanliness of Reinhart, the aristocratic self-assurance, poise and highly idiosyncratic personal culture of Lucie. The occasional romantic traits found in *Das Sinngedicht* are introduced with self-conscious skill, and are never allowed to assume excessive importance.

Nowhere in Keller's works has he taken such trouble over the cyclic construction of a group of *Novellen*. The framework story of Reinhart's and Lucie's courtship is furthered stage by stage by the various *Novellen*, each of which illustrates a different aspect of the relationship between man and woman in love and marriage. The *Novellen* help to enlighten and purify the lovers' understanding of one another and of the respective functions of man and woman in marriage. Oddly enough physical passion is nowhere mentioned; indeed it scarcely ever appears in Keller's works after the original version of *Der grüne Heinrich*. The stories explore the effects of riches and poverty, differing religious beliefs, race and a person's general view of the world on marriage.

Reinhart relates three long *Novellen*, four if we regard *Don Correa* as two stories. The ghost story really forms part of the framework or at least is more directly connected with it than the other stories. Lucia's two *Novellen* are *Salome* and *Die Berlocken*. (Her confession of her love for Leodegar forms part of the framework, which in *Das Sinngedicht* is fully integrated with the rest of the cycle as an organic whole.) The earlier *Novellen* concern people known directly to the narrators, the later ones are based on literary sources.

Throughout the work Logau's epigram recurs as a Leitmotiv. All the women other than Lucie either laugh or blush on meeting Reinhart. Keller underlines the symbolism of the roses and lilies in various ways. When Reinhart first sees Lucie she is wearing white and sorting red roses; Lucie's maids blush and laugh, Hedwig (the baroness) has to learn to smile again, Zambo learns to smile as she gains confidence and so does Regine. In the last scene of all, of course, the demands of the epigram are fulfilled for the first time during the final embrace of Reinhart and Lucie.

In Keller's general view of the world a certain mellowing is noticeable. The Christian religion is treated less harshly than in earlier works, and in *Die arme Baronin* Hedwig's love for Brandolf is directly ascribed to divine influence. (Sie war jetzt vollkommen erstarkt und beweglich, aber immer besonnen und still waltend, und die helle Lebensfreude, die in ihr blühte, von der gleichen unsichtbaren Hand gebändigt und geordnet wie die Wucht der goldenen Ähren, die jetzt in tausend Garben auf den Feldern gebunden lagen.) Regine finds consolation in her prayers, the minister and his family near the beginning of Reinhart's quest are portrayed with gentle, almost affectionate irony, and in *Don Correa* one can readily distinguish between the genuine religious faith of the hero, who insists on Christian baptism for Zambo, and the spurious religion of Feniza Mayor and the devious practices of the Jesuits. Lucie's Catholic conversion is described with tact and respect. Perhaps more revealing than any of these superficial signs is the evidence of Keller's attitude towards marriage, in which charity and mutual forbearance are seen to be elements as indispensable as passion. The lasting reciprocal respect and consideration which Keller demands of ideal partners in marriage is constantly stressed. Inclination and impulse must be tempered and supplemented by long-suffering, patience and goodwill. "Love thy neighbour" is the golden rule for success in marriage. When the characters of the *Novellen* fail in this duty trouble overtakes them, but when they perform it properly their life is full and happy and their relations with the other sex good and untroubled.

Over and above the relationship between the sexes *Das Sinngedicht* is concerned, like so many of Keller's works, with the general question of how life should be lived. It constitutes in fact Keller's ripest wisdom and most advanced thinking on this topic, more artistically and elegantly presented than in any of his other works. It is no longer concerned with the more elementary aspects of human existence, with the first, fumbling steps of the boy and young man towards acceptable standards of social behaviour which at the same time satisfy his self-respect. It rather deals with the element of free choice in human conduct, with the deliberate cultivation of attitudes and activities which make life as fully as possible what it can be and ought to be. At the very centre of Keller's view of the good life lies a healthy and balanced relationship between man and woman, but this must never be allowed to crowd out or destroy the other positive aspects of human aspiration and behaviour; a lesson which both Reinhart and Lucie must learn is that each has before marriage cultivated a strong individuality with pronounced personal tastes and opinions. From the stories it definitely emerges that Keller does not wish to see the free individual personality sacrificed upon the altar of marriage. Reinhart must respect Lucie's right to follow her own interests and indulge her personal preferences, even if these sometimes seem to him highly unusual for a woman and perhaps rather at odds with his sense of the fitness of things; and similarly the man must also be allowed the right to live a life of his own within reasonable limits; Feniza Mayor's attitude to Don Correa is portrayed as quite indefensible.

The epigram itself is on the one hand a somewhat obscure injunction concerning the right way to seek a partner in marriage; but over and above this it is also a general rule about conduct in life as a whole. Sense must be ruled by modesty and restraint, which themselves constitute an embellishment of life, but to deny it altogether would be an impoverishment and wrong. However, other extreme attitudes must not be over-indulged either; Reinhart's one-track intellectual curiosity and Lucie's virginal arrogance are alike attributes which must yield in the long run to the more productive and less selfish scale of values represented in and by an ideal marriage.

Das Sinngedicht may be said to offer Keller's conscious and generous tribute to a somewhat more elevated, formal, even aristocratic pattern of existence than that in which he had grown up. The framework story possesses considerable importance from this point of view. It is evident from the care which Keller lavishes upon the description of Lucie's house and garden that he wishes us to applaud her style of life. We appreciate the size and elegance of the house and the courtyard with its great plane trees. We are glad to hear that Lucie thinks of her guest's comfort to the extent of putting flowers in his room and offering him wine and biscuits on arrival; we enjoy learning of her predilection for paintings by talented but obscure painters, and the knowledge that her taste is schooled on works by acknowledged masters like Poussin and Claude Lorrain gives us confidence in her ability to discriminate among her contemporary artists. Into this ideal setting Keller projects his vision of the good and civilised life, in which man and woman learn to curb and control the tensions which naturally arise between them and to find fruitful and productive outlets for potentially destructive forces. Keller wrote in the finale of *Das Sinngedicht* not of life as he had known it but as he would have wished it, and we cannot fail to see in this work his most carefully planned and most fully pondered, as well as his most delicately and delightfully presented commentary on life. Because *Das Sinngedicht* shows such careful and calculated construction, because Keller handles so many traditional motifs of literary art with such superb control and discrimination, because of the variety of narrative matter which he offers for our consideration, because of his lucid yet profound symbolism, because of the tolerance and charity which underlie the whole work, it represents Keller's finest artistic achievement. *Der grüne Heinrich* obviously deals at greater length with many aspects of life, but the selection, handling and presentation of the material used in *Das Sinngedicht* has been performed with the skill, breadth of perception and psychological finesse of the mature artist. For all these reasons we must undoubtedly acclaim it as Keller's masterpiece.

CHAPTER SEVEN

MARTIN SALANDER

I

KELLER wrote on 8th April 1881 to Julius Rodenberg, editor of the *Deutsche Rundschau* :

> Now I am gradually beginning to think of a little novel in one volume, what will become of it Lord only knows. I will yield yet again to the vice of irresponsibility and begin a book the shape of which I do not yet know. But I will write it all out to the end, and copy it again afterwards myself, fairly and clearly.

Later letters to Petersen and Frey do not add anything to the above remarks. Writing to Storm in August 1881 Keller promises that his new book will be of such a kind that some of his critics (like Storm) who objected to *Das Sinngedicht* and earlier works will wish they were reading those now :

> I am now working on a one-volume novel, which will make a perfectly logical and modern impression; admittedly, in other respects it will be such strong meat that people will perhaps wish they were still reading my other little things.

He does not, however, indicate more closely why this should be such an "offputting" work. A later letter to Rodenberg reveals that he is by now "turning the novel rather more vigorously this way and that", although he has still no idea how the project will take shape. Keller noted most of the proper names from the Zurich directory, although Salander's name (the accent is on the first syllable) comes from the village of Saland in the Töss valley (Canton Zurich). As ever, he was far too optimistic about finishing the book; as early as January 1882 he wrote to Exner that he hoped to finish *Salander* that year. At Easter 1883 he gave Jakob Baechtold a fairly full summary of the action. The sons of an ambitious, worldly "mamma" were to turn out to be failures whereas the only son of a plain "mother" would have a fine career. The young man's father would return from America and lose at once every penny he had made during a long absence. He would see his son briefly from a distance and not recognise him. The middle of the novel was not yet worked out, but somehow it was to finish with a great natural catastrophe; all the characters were to be assembled on a mountain side and a flood or forest fire was to take place. He was not clear about the details, but the bad characters were to come off worse in the confusion that was to follow. At about this time Keller abandoned his original title *Exzelsior* which (as J. M. Ritchie points out in *MLR*, Vol. LII, No. 2) he almost certainly found in a translation of Longfellow's poem contained in Chapter 31 of Spielhagen's novel *Angela*. This title was probably intended to symbolise the lofty idealism of the hero, but Keller dropped it as being too pretentious. His notes confirm that he had planned a great final scene with a natural catastrophe. However, he must have considered the proposed ending too sensational or improbable. By mid-1883 Keller had forsaken his other work in favour of *Martin Salander*. In January 1884 he wrote to Rodenberg:

> This opus you must understand has undergone a period of standstill of the kind which is connected with organic evolution, and must be calmly borne. The skeleton is still there, but all the joints are cracking, and the bones are growing stronger. In such a situation one may or rather ought to make use of the old right of leaving the thing to itself for a while.

The following year Keller decided that Rodenberg might as well begin publication. This meant that he now had to go on producing whether he felt like it or not. As a result the work bears all the signs of having been hastily written. The *Deutsche Rundschau* began to print the manuscript in January 1886, and the last chapter appeared in September. The book edition which followed at Christmas contained two short extra chapters in an attempt to tone down the abruptness of the original ending.

II

The plot of *Salander* shows no great complexity. Martin Salander returns from South America to his wife and three children after seven years' absence. Just before going there he had lost all his money through having stood surety for a friend. Now, on the day of his return he loses all again by unwittingly entrusting his money to the same man, Louis Wohlwend, who is now in business as a banker under a different name. Hereupon Martin again departs for America, having taken steps to relieve the extreme poverty in which his wife and children are living. This time he leaves Marie in charge of a little shop, which she manages with great success. He returns after three years, having made enough money to establish himself comfortably in business in Münsterburg, a thinly disguised Zurich. Some years after Martin's return he and his wife are disturbed to find their two grown-up daughters being pursued by the twins Julian and Isidor Weidelich, the sons of a washerwoman. The parents are much opposed to the idea of marriage with the Weidelichs, but the daughters egg one another on in their infatuation. Salander reluctantly consents to the marriages, which soon turn out to be complete failures. The daughters, Setti and Netti, are spared a lifetime's misery, when both husbands are found guilty of embezzling large sums of money; they have taken advantage of their positions as notaries to do this. Both twins are condemned to twelve years' hard labour, and in these circumstances Salander's daughters easily obtain divorces. Salander's evil genius Louis Wohlwend now comes back to Münsterburg, having married the daughter of a rich Hungarian timber-merchant. Salander and his friends suspect that the money which has made him acceptable to his father-in-law is Salander's money, but cannot prove this. Meantime, Wohlwend is so flattering and attentive to Salander that the latter almost begins to feel kindly disposed towards him. Salander is a rich man, and it is probable that Wohlwend is simply trying to interest Salander or his son Arnold in his (Wohlwend's) beautiful but unintelligent sister-in-law Myrrha Glawicz so that she may make an advantageous marriage. Just as Martin Salander begins to take too much interest in the young woman, Arnold returns from Brazil with definite proof that Wohlwend had deliberately swindled his father. By chance Arnold happens to meet Myrrha and soon dismisses her as beautiful but hopelessly stupid. Now the Salander family celebrates a glad reunion; Arnold turns out to be a model son, and his father is particularly delighted that his friends and associates are young men of character and ability.

The foregoing summary of the action does not in itself tell us a great deal about the book. It says nothing, for instance, about Martin Salander's democratic idealism, which Keller constantly stresses. Nor does it convey the disillusionment and concern for the welfare of his country to which Keller gives expression in *Martin Salander*. The events which form the book's skeleton might have been treated in many different ways, yet Keller's selection of material here does suggest that his whole outlook on life is less warm and positive than it had been. A man striving after wealth and position twice loses his all through the bad offices of an unreliable friend; two young men, children of a vulgar and ambitious mother, win positions of public trust and political eminence and quickly prove themselves undeserving of these honours; a couple of foolish young women talk one another into marrying these youths, and soon regret it; their father has hardly recovered from the shock of seeing his daughters make a tragic, possibly irreparable matrimonial mistake when he, as a man of fifty-five, makes a fool of himself over a young woman less than half his age, and is saved from becoming embroiled with her only by his son's superior judgment and ruthless commonsense. It would have been a considerable test of any author's skill to make this an edifying, entertaining or aesthetically satisfying novel.

III

Keller had included few wholesome or heartwarming episodes in *Salander*; the truly tragic plays only a very small part, but the dreary or depressing bulks large. In all his other works we are conscious of a questing mind, every now and again overcome by the beauty and wonder of the world, delighting in the unexpected and open to sense impressions which he would allow to influence him spiritually. *Martin Salander* misses fire completely; it is a dull book about dull people leading dull lives; the best of them on the whole ask no more than that they should be able to conform to a thoroughly philistine norm of existence; Arnold Salander, who is supposed to be a paragon of all the virtues, is a rather dehydrated prig. Young Arnold behaves throughout with exemplary circumspection, he has an old head on young shoulders, he completely lacks the warmth and passion, the faculty for human failings which on the whole make his father a rather endearing old fool. The projected second volume in which Arnold was to have played the principal part was never written; perhaps Keller had realised the shortcomings of the first part and decided that enough was enough.

In his attitude to contemporary life Keller shows himself to be out of sympathy with his age. The swindling and neglect of duty of which the Weidelich twins are guilty is portrayed not as a rare phenomenon, but as an everyday occurrence. They are in a sense merely victims of a disease which affects considerable numbers of men in public positions like themselves. They are not exceptional, they are if not typical at least common. The encounter between the Swiss and the German whom Martin meets during his walk after his second return home reveals Keller in his harshest satirical vein. The German politely praises Swiss customs and institutions and abuses those of his own fatherland, the Swiss vaunts the advantages of his country in the manner common to parochial minds. Martin Salander upbraids them both publicly, which almost involves him in an undignified fight. Keller's sojourns in Germany had made him aware and ashamed of the smugness of some of his fellow-countrymen and had also shown him that in Germany men vacillated between self-assertive chauvinism and grovelling national self-abasement. Keller finds both attitudes distasteful. Coming from the pen of the man who had taken such a positive view of his country's qualities and prospects in *Das Fähnlein*, one must conclude that Keller had changed more than his fellow-countrymen.

Keller tries very hard in *Salander* to write a new kind of novel. A feature of his former style had been the comparative rarity of dialogue; where dialogue did occur it was rather strained and stiff. In this regard he differs sharply from Fontane, whose novels rely to a great extent on dialogue for advancing the narrative. Keller breaks with the past in *Martin Salander*, a great part of which consists of conversations, although he never achieves the easy skill of his Berlin contemporary in telling a story by means of the dialogue. The conversations recorded in *Martin Salander* generally sound natural enough even if their substance is more trivial than Keller would at one time have thought worth while recording. While Keller had survived into a new age, he was too old to grow up with and improve and render personal its new literary techniques, yet he was aware of them and tried hard to move with the times. He had read Flaubert and Zola, and he could not remain altogether unaffected by their work; he was also interested in Spielhagen's novels and critical theories.

Martin Salander differs from most of Keller's earlier works in the comparative absence of descriptive and moralising passages. Although much of the action takes place in Martin Salander's house we are never told what the house was like. Occasionally the old Keller shines through; thus in Chapter V during Salander's walk with his family we find the following brief description, which might well represent a scene painted in water colours by the young Keller:

> And so they had gone a considerable way,. and they went down into a litle forest glade through which flowed a beautiful, clear brook, which rolled its abundant water over coloured stones and boulders which had fallen down from the mountain. In the rounded bay a little waterfall poured over some mossy blocks of stone, straight from a young beech thicket, and Martin Salander at once recognised the charming corner from long before.

Such passages, in which *Der grüne Heinrich* abounds, are a comparative rarity in *Martin Salander*, which also offers nothing to correspond with the detailed description of Züs Bünzlin's knick-knacks or the account in *Spiegel das Kätzchen* of the contents of a little bird's stomach. The relaxed, observant interest in all the phenomena of the external world has given way to an almost doctrinaire preference for the seamier side of human conduct and motives. Keller denies his own genius to the detriment of the work; rare passages like that just quoted, or the fairy tale which Marie Salander tells her starving children in Chapter III before her husband's return, serve to show that the author never entirely succeeded in suppressing his true artistic personality. They are among the few redeeming features of a disappointing and soulless book. The attempt to gain objectivity and distance has succeeded, but the life and warmth, the mellowness and sunniness, the kindly, mischievous humour are lost. The conflict that pervades all Keller's work between romantic and realistic elements has been resolved, but at too high a cost. The book forms a tract on the decadence and corruption of the times in narrative and dialogue form, not a living work of art.

The characters are nevertheless extremely interesting. Martin Salander himself owes a good deal to his creator with his open-mindedness, his democratic idealism, his sudden rages, his didactic tendencies. In some ways he is like a more modern Rudolf Keller, a business man with acute political interests and definite ideas about the education of youth; he is the successor of *Der grüne Heinrich* in his concern for his country. His financial struggles remind us of Keller's own early difficulties, his attitude towards the young men in the last chapter is Keller's own attitude towards the very young, whom he preferred in his old age to his contemporaries. His successful career in the corrupt world of the *Gründerzeit* may be intended to show that even in such circumstances an honest and able man can still thrive and fulfil an important function as a transmitter of untarnished ideals to the young. Martin's principal weakness lies in an inclination to act too much on impulse in his relations with other people. He trusts Louis Wohlwend too readily, he is not emphatic enough about preventing his daughters' marriage with the Weidelich twins, his still susceptible heart almost compromises him with Wohlwend's attractive but empty-headed sister-in-law. Here, however, he is fairly easily swayed in the reverse direction by his clever son's immediate condemnation of Myrrha's stupidity. We are reassured by Salander's final triumph over all difficulties and hazards, but we should like to know what remains in life for a man like him, what satisfactions he can still attain when he has conquered poverty and put his family affairs in order. At the end of the book we feel that Salander has achieved a certain security, but the serenity which we would wish him is lacking.

Marie Salander is a stock figure among Keller's characters, the capable, managing woman who keeps her family above water even when left on her own for a long period by her husband. Like Frau Lee, Pankraz's mother, or Frau Amrain she is the provider for her family, the source of comfort and solace when things go wrong. She is much more realistic and perspicacious than her husband about their daughters' marriage with the Weidelichs and about the dangers of associating with Wohlwend. She relies mainly on her mother's instinct; she cannot give actual reasons why Julian and Isidor should prove disastrous husbands for her daughters nor will she make any allowances at all for Wohlwend, even when it is by no means certain that he is the deliberate author of her family's misfortunes. She is right, as it turns out, but she might not have been. She would not dream of giving the Weidelich twins or Wohlwend the benefit of any possible doubt as to their true intentions. For her these people do not exist as persons, they are merely dangers which threaten her children's or her husband's welfare. However, when disaster overtakes Frau Weidelich and she makes a pathetic scene in Frau Salander's house the latter treats her kindly. She has the determination and strength of a tigress in defending those near and dear to her, but she has little imagination. Secure in the knowledge of her husband's fundamental loyalty she laughs at his platonic love for Myrrha, which she regards as the rather funny aberration of a great child. She has not a flicker of imagination but she is patient and long-suffering in the fulfilment of her duty.

Salander's children are less well drawn than the parents. Setti and Netti have hardly any separate identity, and we learn very little about them except that at the ages of twenty-six and twenty-five they allowed themselves to be wooed and won by the Weidelich twins, who were then only twenty. Surely Keller need not have made the lives of both sisters take such a similar course; he greatly lessens the verisimilitude of the novel by doing so. That both marriages prove equally disappointing, that both young wives remain childless, that both husbands fall foul of the law and are prosecuted, that both receive identical sentences and that both wives are simultaneously released from their unhappy unions is hardly credible.

Arnold Salander disappoints us, too. He is clearly meant to be a paragon of all the virtues in which his father is deficient. Though he is more prudent and law-abiding than his father, his father's impetus and drive seem to have passed him by. He confesses his anxiety about becoming too rich, a danger which his father more or less reluctantly acknowledges. Surprisingly, the father seems very ready to accept the moral authority of his son. Arnold is no gentleman, of course, or he would not have made the offensive remark (near the end of Chapter XX) about Myrrha's breath smelling of sausage, incidentally a naturalistic detail which would scarcely have occurred in Keller's writings before *Martin Salander*. As a boy Arnold has some features in common with other heroes of Keller's stories, his shyness, his unwillingness to play with other children, the fact that others laugh at him, his secretive ways. In the end, however, he gives the impression of being rather unsure of himself, for he wishes to remain in his father's business but does not want to do too well, and yet does not wish to abandon altogether the intellectual pursuits which he is not quite prepared to place firmly at the centre of his life. He is lukewarm as business man and scholar and one cannot imagine that in the long run he will do well at either occupation. Keller assures us that he has a whole group of friends just like himself; they sound rather frightening.

Louis Wohlwend makes an effective enough villain with his "evilly squinting book" and his deep-laid plots to encompass Salander's ruin. It somehow seems improbable that a man like him would return twice over to the attack on the same victim. Since we do not hear the remainder of Salander's history we do not know definitely that he remained immune from Wohlwend's ministrations for the rest of his life, but we must assume that with definite proof of Wohlwend's past offences against him Salander will give the other man a very wide berth. There are other difficulties about Wohlwend's character. Such a man, married to an honest, straightforward woman, would hardly openly avow his intention of marrying Myrrha off to Arnold Salander. Not unnaturally Wohlwend's wife rises in her sister's defence at this point; surely Wohlwend would find it easier to carry out his plan without confiding in anyone else. There are some very good touches about him, though. When Martin Salander goes to see him for the first time in his house after the collapse of Schadenmüller and Company, the motto on Wohlwend's house wall runs: "Care for my wife and my children" (Chapter IV). Then again, in Chapter XV, when Salander goes to lunch with the Wohlwends and from pure spite Wohlwend makes his son Georg say grace at table just after Salander has already picked up his soup spoon, we begin to understand the extent of his hatred for Salander whose successful career he envies and whose wife's moral rectitude he dreads.

The washerwoman Amalie Weidelich with her ambition, her floral hats, her love of drink, her enormous energy and her social aspirations is at first an amusing and finally a tragic character. For as long as possible she makes allowances for her twins, even when it is scarcely possible for a reasonable person to doubt their guilt. The news of their trial and sentence is too much for her;

she has a stroke and dies. Despite her certainty that she is as good as anyone else and her determination that her twins shall have every chance in life, whether they are capable of profiting by it or not, there is no real harm in her, and the bitter blow that fate deals her seems undeserved.

Her husband Jakob Weidelich has a dignity and pathos of his own. A quiet market-gardener, he assents by his silence to all his wife's ambitious schemes and works hard to provide the money for their realisation. During his wife's illness he takes upon himself the additional burden of caring for an invalid, and after her death he is prepared to work to mitigate his family's disgrace, though he is an old man, and his sons have brought him nothing but disappointment.

The Weidelich twins themselves are among the less well drawn characters of the book. Julian and Isidor (the names reflect their mother's social aspirations) are insufficiently differentiated. The spoilt darlings of an indulgent mother and an unexacting father, they develop expensive tastes but not the aptitude for hard work which would enable them to maintain the standard of living to which they feel entitled. Mamma Weidelich had hoped that by marrying Salander's daughters they would be set up for life, but Salander leaves the young people to make their own way after providing his daughters amply with linen and other household effects. Idle and inefficient, the two youths soon begin to use their public positions for their private advantage. Before long their affairs are investigated, and they are brought to trial and convicted. Although their offence was of a common enough character, and although Keller does distinguish to some extent between their respective methods of helping themselves to other people's money, one feels that the parallels of situation are too exact to be wholly credible.

Martin Salander reflects Keller the official. He would not have had the information or experience to write it had he not served as *Staatsschreiber*. The book contains many references to legal procedure, displays a considerable knowledge of business practice, and in particular more than a nodding acquaintance with the intricacies of the bankruptcy courts. Occasionally this results in longueurs; too much specialised knowledge can overburden a novel, though Keller never actually allows himself to become unintelligible to the ordinary reader. Local Zurich history, especially the cases of two rascally notaries Rudolf and Koller, who had misappropriated public funds on a large scale, forms the real life basis of the Weidelichs' crimes. Like everyone else in Zurich in 1881 and 1882 Keller had followed these cases with mingled fascination and horror.

In conclusion we are obliged to say that despite many excellences of detail, despite Keller's resolute determination to write a new kind of novel in his old age, even despite the many links with his past artistic practice, the work is a failure. Although it is all solidly based on things that actually happened or on experiences that were commonplace in the Zurich of the *Gründerzeit* the work lacks that inner truth which is the hallmark of a great work of art. The humour which pervades all Keller's short stories, the tolerant understanding of human failings which is seldom absent from his earlier writings, the warmth and serenity which are generally among his most endearing characteristics, have given way to a satirical sharpness, a jaundiced eye and a fundamental disillusionment which make a degree of misanthropy inevitable.

CONCLUSION

THE reader who has studied Keller's works in the chronological order of their appearance will not fail to have noticed that a considerable development takes place between the earliest and the later works. *Der grüne Heinrich*, though full of interest and containing many memorable pages, remains unsatisfactory as an artistic achievement. It impresses as a work of wide range by a talented and sensitive writer, but it is quite apparent that on the technical side the author still had a great deal to learn. The revision which he undertook as an older man merely removed the cruder faults of the novel; it did not deal with the central issues of absence of plot and excess of autobiographical content. Keller could not select ruthlessly enough from the abundance of his own experience. The book is further removed from real life than such a carefully edited autobiography as *Dichtung und Wahrheit*, yet somehow Heinrich Lee does not generally speaking develop a sufficiently separate identity from that of his creator. In other words the question whether we are dealing with autobiography or a work of fiction cannot be satisfactorily answered. On the other hand every reader remembers with pleasure the figures of Anna and Judith, and there are many good descriptive passages. The whole book accepts the natural order so serenely that one must be glad that it exists, despite its shortcomings.

With *Die Leute von Seldwyla* one realises that the rather amateurish author of *Der grüne Heinrich* has vastly improved his professional competence. Instead of trying unsuccessfully to handle a large-scale form, he now writes with success much shorter works. The absence of a firm and continuing narrative line, a plot, had been a major weakness of *Der grüne Heinrich*, which strikes most readers as very episodic in character for a long novel. Keller manages the small-scale prose works with considerable expertise. It is certainly true that he tends to greater amplitude and even diffuseness in his *Novellen* than most of his predecessors. He does not feel bound by the limitations of the short form to omit descriptive detail; on the contrary, he frequently revels in it. The *Novellen* are mostly concerned with life among the peasants and bourgeois of German Switzerland, but this does not imply uniformity; in atmosphere, style and plot the Seldwyla stories are very varied. This is more true of the first part than of the second, but altogether *Die Leute von Seldwyla* constitute an impressive achievement.

Keller's *Legenden* along with *Das Sinngedicht* represent his greatest success from the formal point of view. To have taken all the legendary material and so successfully imitated the naïvety of the original narratives while ironically twisting their moral teaching was no mean literary feat. The legends do not seem moralising or doctrinaire despite their uniformly secular tendency. Keller has achieved a technical *tour de force*; he successfully recaptured the simple charm of the genuine legends and at the same time called much of their original teaching in question. Viewed as a whole the *Legenden* bear out Keller's certainty that the world is good, and that human nature, provided it is not perverted by false teaching, can be trusted.

Once again in the *Züricher Novellen* Keller broke new ground, especially from the point of view of the subject matter. Thematically, all these *Novellen* are close to the second part of the *Leute von Seldwyla* in their insistence on being true to oneself, shunning pretence and carrying out one's duty conscientiously. The historical background has in each case been thoroughly mastered, but the stories show that Keller has only sometimes been able to assimilate it properly. He is most successful in *Der Landvogt von Greifensee*, perhaps because he found the Landvogt's character so completely sympathetic that there was no risk in that particular case that the historical background would be allowed to crowd out the human interest. Viewed as a cycle the *Züricher Novellen* are somewhat imperfect, since only the first three stories are integrated with the framework story of Herr Jacques and his godfather. Most twentieth century readers will agree that the framework story is disappointing, even trivial, compared with the quality of the internal *Novellen*. However, everyone agrees that in *Der Landvogt* and *Das Fähnlein* he made delightful contributions to the German historical *Novelle*.

Das Sinngedicht represents the summit of Keller's artistic achievement. In this collection of short stories the framework story of Reinhart's and Lucie's courtship is completely and successfully integrated with the other *Novellen*, which are also arranged in such a way that differing points of view about marriage are successively presented. The Swiss petty bourgeoisie is no longer the milieu of the stories; some are taken from literary sources, but the others, which deal with contemporary German or Swiss life, are set among the upper classes. Possibly Keller's service as *Staatsschreiber* of Zurich brought him into touch with more people of this kind, perhaps he had simply become more interested in general ideas and less aware of the minutiae of existence; however that may be, the whole work seems to be pitched at a fairly high level of detachment from the grosser aspects of human life. There is no evidence whatsoever that Reinhart or Lucie are capable of passion but both have evidently active and disciplined minds. Corresponding to the milieu we find Keller's style less homely, less sensual, more full of symbol than ever before. The twin concepts of red roses and white lilies run through the whole work from beginning to end. What *Das Sinngedicht* may possibly lack in spontaneity and freshness it more than makes up for in well-considered and ably managed artistic effects. Taken individually the stories which it comprises are no better than the best of the *Seldwyla* stories or the *Züricher Novellen*, but the total achievement of *Das Sinngedicht* as an example of cyclic construction surpasses anything hitherto written by Keller.

Das Sinngedicht was followed by Keller's second attempt at the novel, which for different reasons proved even less successful than the first. *Der grüne Heinrich* contains all the raw material of a good and interesting book, though the author's inexperience and technical incompetence prevent the work from achieving anything approaching formal excellence. *Martin Salander* suffers from different weaknesses. Although the author had by this late stage in his career attained a high degree of professional competence, and although the book constantly reveals his willingness to take account of new developments in the German and European novel, it founders on weakness of characterisation and a general sourness of outlook, which contrast unfavourably with the excellent characterisation and vigorous optimism of almost all his earlier work.

Keller's poetry forms an interesting sideshoot of his literary activity. A small number of poems will continue to be remembered, mostly for the same qualities which attained fuller, more varied and more artistic expression in the short stories. Only occasionally did this pre-eminently epic writer achieve lyric greatness, and only a handful of poems contrives to avoid a rather pedestrian mediocrity. However, the whole man is reflected in his verse, which shows considerable variety of theme and a willingness to attempt many different rhythms and metres.

Keller's prose style cannot easily be characterised briefly, but certain salient qualities may be mentioned. Everywhere he writes a leisurely and spacious style, and he always seems to have time to follow up an interesting detail. The author's keen visual sense, his delight in close observation of people, animals and other phenomena often prompts him to describe things more exhaustively than might seem advisable within the economy of a *Novelle*. He delights in exploring small objects thoroughly, Züs Bünzlin's cardboard temple, the crop of a little dead bird, details of the interior of Herr Litumlei's house, the possessions of the Landvogt's women friends. The obvious pleasure which he takes in these descriptions communicates itself, and we enjoy them so much that we do not notice that they can only be included at the expense of slowing down the action. Sometimes a leisurely description forms an organic part of a *Novelle*; Manz and Marti ploughing in the opening pages of *Romeo und Julia* do not only form a delightful rural picture, but the whole scene represents the good neighbourly life which they lead before the peasants' acquisitive passion begins to destroy their lives.

After *Der grüne Heinrich* Keller generally employs straightforward third person narrative by an omniscient narrator. Sometimes the tone of the narrative may be paternalistic, even patronising, and there is sometimes a satirical or contemptuous inflection in his use of diminutives. He does not hesitate to pass judgment on his characters or to anticipate their reactions to a situation. At any time he may pause to exchange confidences with the reader about his characters or their situation and prospects. Very often indeed he uses adjectives implying moral judgment, and he does so without embarrassment. Sometimes there is a strongly ironical note in his descriptions. Consider for instance the following phrases from the opening paragraphs of *Der Schmied seines*

Glückes: "ein artiger Mann", "mit nur wenigen Meister-schlägen", "So hatte er dennals zarter Jüngling den ersten seiner Meisterstreiche geführt". The examples could easily be multiplied, for Keller is a master of irony.

Keller's fifteen years of service as *Staatsschreiber* left their mark on his prose style in the shape of occasional words of *Kanzleistil*, often used quite self-consciously. Such expressions as "Dergestalt", "ebenda", Fährlichkeiten", "einstweilen", "das besagte Kloster", "innewerden", "behufs", all of which hover as it were on the fringe between *Kanzleistil* and normal prose usage, are common in his works. Swiss expressions occur occasionally, too, but there is not a page in any of his works which is not perfectly comprehensible to any literate German reader. His older contemporary Gotthelf remains largely inaccessible to non-Swiss readers because of the excessive provincialism of his vocabulary. Keller was always determined to write in standard German; it could be tinged with Swiss emphases or show trifling deviations from North German usage, but an exclusively Swiss word is a rarity in his books and he always wrote for the whole German reading public.

A feature of Keller's style which strikes every reader is the occasional arrestingly original simile or metaphor. Thus in *Der grüne Heinrich* we read that the priest "baute seinen Scheiter-haufen aus Antithesen, hinkenden Gleichnissen und gewaltsamen Witzen, auf denen er den Verstand, guten Willen und sogar das Gewissen der Gegner zu verbrennen trachtete, seiner eigenen Meinung zum angenehmen Brandopfer". We are told that food-stuffs could not resist the attraction of Herr Amrain's belly, "sondern werden von dem Magnetgebirge des Bauches mächtig angezogen". Such comparisons, frequent in the earlier works, be-come rarer later on, and are almost completely absent from *Das Sinngedicht*. They disappear along with other aspects of the grotesque, which bulks large in works like *Die drei gerechten Kammacher* and *Ursula* but plays a diminishing role later on.

While Keller does not shun dialogue altogether he does not so frequently use it as a means of advancing his narrative as does Fontane, for example. In general, conversation figures less in his earlier works than in the later ones, and Salander contains more of it than any of the collections of short stories. Keller never com-pletely mastered the art of writing dialogue, and in this respect, though not in others, Fontane could have taught him something. Keller's humour ranges from the kindly to the fairly coarse slapstick, and he is also capable on occasion of savage satire. He hardly wrote a single work which is without humorous effects, although of course some stories are richer in these than others. On the whole the prevailing atmosphere of his work is relaxed and comfortable, and the author generally seems to have an ironical but kindly twinkle in his eye; in *Die drei gerechten Kammacher* farce assumes the upper hand, and there are moments of farce in other works, like *Ursula*, *Dietegen* and *Die arme Baronin*. Harsh satire is seen in, for example, *Die miß-brauchten Liebesbriefe* and *Das verlorene Lachen*.

Along with the sense of equilibrium provided by his humour goes a genuine awareness of the tragic and a lively sense of true pathos. *Romeo und Julia auf dem Dorfe* is an intensely moving work, even if by the coldly rational standards of today it is not easy to believe in the inevitability of the tragic outcome. Yet Keller does succeed in persuading us that whether Sali and Vrenchen *needed* to die or not they really did *choose* to die, and for the good reason that a shared future did not *seem* to them a possibility after Sali had injured Vrenchen's father. *Regine*—the only other completely tragic story which Keller ever wrote—also moves one intensely if one considers the contrast between Regine's timid and loving disposition and Erwin's obsessive anxiety that she should not let him down by committing some social gaffe. He is so obsessed with this by rational standards trifling worry that he is quite blind to Regine's misery when she is left in alien surroundings to face troubles which would be testing for the strongest disposition at the best of times. In other works, too, where tragedy does not predominate, Keller does not shun the representation of honest feeling, whether it be Figura Leu's tender affection for the man whom she will never marry, or Heinrich Lee's sad duty of helping the young joiner to make Anna's coffin, or Judith's sincere love for Heinrich, which he is at the time so incapable of appreciating at its true value.

If one were to attempt to sum up in a few words the atmosphere of Keller's works, one might say that they seem everywhere to reflect a conviction that the world is beautiful and life is good. Keller's eye is always responsive to beauty, whether in plants, animals, people, things or the works of man. A great joy in the world pervades all his writings.

Among his contemporaries, who are often known as Poetic Realists by German literary historians, Keller stands out for several reasons. He possessed a great deal of natural genius, and he shows a wider range of interests than any other German author of his day. Although the prevailing theme of all his writing remains the good life and how to live it, although a strongly pedagogical flavour is often manifest in his work, his stories are not only diverse in subject matter and technique but also cover a wide range of themes. *Der grüne Heinrich* while mainly concerned with the development of the human individual also deals with such questions as religion and church affiliations, the problem of evil and the whole matter of the artist and society. Everywhere in *Die Leute von Seldwyla* the idea of what constitutes the good individual and the good society is implicit, and *Pankraz, Spiegel* and *Die drei gerechten Kammacher* alike all raise the problem of how to behave properly towards one's fellows. From *Dietegen* and the *Züricher Novellen* we learn how much Keller knew of Swiss social and political history, and *Martin Salander* at least reveals an extensive familiarity with the world of business, law and cantonal administration.

Keller was by no means unaware of the factors which caused such men as Kleist and Hölderlin to despair of life and take refuge from it in suicide or insanity. Yet his reaction to disturbing experience was not to turn from it in despair but live through it and emerge strengthened and enriched. Behind all his work lies the profound conviction that life is good and has a meaning even if that meaning is not immediately apparent.

Fontane was Keller's greatest contemporary among German prose-writers. Each man possessed qualities which the other lacked. Fontane's range is narrower than Keller's, but on the other hand his technical competence was considerable even from the beginning. Fontane very skilfully represents the upper class Prussian social scene, but Keller ponders more deeply over the meaning of life. Fontane was a master of dialogue and brilliant at describing a social occasion. Keller could not do this as well as Fontane, but he saw modern life in truer perspective. Fontane uses the language more simply, more clearly, perhaps more elegantly; Keller's language is richer, more original, more creative.

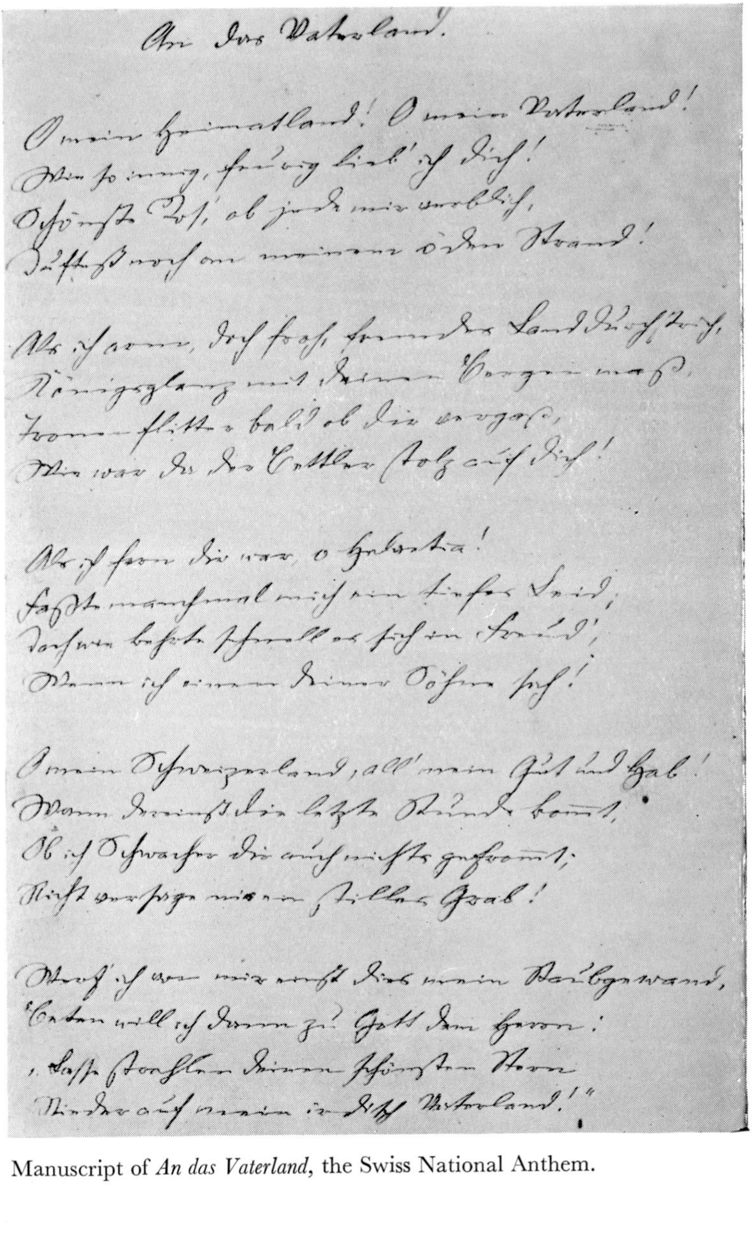

An das Vaterland.

O mein Heimatland! O mein Vaterland!
Wie so innig, feurig lieb' ich dich!
Schönste Ros', ob jede mir verblich,
Duftest noch an meinem öden Strand!

Als ich arm, doch froh, fremdes Land durchstrich,
Königsglanz mit deinen Bergen maß,
Thronenflitter bald ob dir vergaß,
Wie war da der Bettler stolz auf dich!

Als ich fern dir war, o Helvetia!
Faßte manchmal mich ein tiefes Leid;
Doch wie kehrte schnell es sich in Freud',
Wenn ich einen deiner Söhne sah!

O mein Schweizerland, all' mein Gut und Hab'!
Wann dereinst die letzte Stunde kommt,
Ob ich Schwacher dir auch nichts gefrommt,
Nicht versage mir ein stilles Grab!

Werf' ich von mir einst dies mein Staubgewand,
"Beten will ich dann zu Gott dem Herrn:
‚Lasse strahlen deinen schönsten Stern
Nieder auf mein irdisch Vaterland!'"

Manuscript of *An das Vaterland*, the Swiss National Anthem.

More fully than any other Swiss author Keller represents his country. Other German Swiss writers may exemplify individual aspects of Switzerland more completely and perfectly, but he remains its most natural and all-embracing representative. Rural German Switzerland lives in the pages of Jeremias Gotthelf, the Zurich patricians had their C. F. Meyer, but Keller was the literary spokesman, even the guardian angel of the whole country. Its landscape lives in the pages of *Der grüne Heinrich*, its political and educational ideals shine through the pages of *Das Fähnlein* and *Frau Regel Amrain*. Its social and religious history come alive again in the *Züricher Novellen*. Keller's love of Switzerland with all its strengths and weaknesses informs *Die Leute von Seldwyla* and his fears for its future colour the sombre pages of *Martin Salander*. He wrote his country's national anthem and many a now forgotten song for local, cantonal or national occasions of rejoicing. While he shunned chauvinistic self-assertion, he remained proud of his Swiss traditions, and, as he grew older, laid more and more stress on the poet's role as the spokesman of his people. That he could become this without the sacrifice of goodwill towards other Europeans and without succumbing to the intellectual provincialism common among German writers of his day is a true measure of the greatness of the man.

Keller's claim to be remembered is soundly based. Though he did not write a great deal, much of what he wrote is of good quality, and some of it can be measured by the highest standards and not found wanting. In two or three stories from *Die Leute von Seldwyla*, in his *Sieben Legenden*, in *Der Landvogt* and in *Das Sinngedicht* he has left some of the best examples of the *Novelle* in the German language. The last-named work constitutes a fitting memorial to this talented bachelor who knew so much about the respective qualities of man and woman. No better example of the use of the framework technque exists, and several of the stories within the framework are impressive *Novellen* even when read out of context. No other writer in Europe has performed this particular task of writing a cycle of stories on love and marriage with such distinction, and *Das Sinngedicht* alone would ensure Keller an honourable immortality.

SELECT BIBLIOGRAPHY

EDITIONS

Gottfried Keller, *Sämtliche Werke*, ed. J. Fränkel and C. Helbling, 24 vols., Berne, 1926–54 (the standard edition).

Gottfried Keller, *Werke*, ed. M. Zollinger and others, 10 vols., Berlin and Leipzig, 1935 (this edition has a useful register of proper names appearing in Keller's works).

Gottfried Keller, *Werke*, Atlantis, 8 vols., Zurich, 1942.

Gottfried Keller, *Werke*, ed. G. Steiner, 8 vols., Basle, 1947.

Gottfried Keller, *Sämtliche Werke*, ed. P. Goldammer, 8 vols., Berlin, 1958.

KELLER'S LETTERS

Gottfried Keller, *Gesammelte Briefe in 4 Bänden*, ed. C. Helbling, Zurich, 1954.

Emil Ermatinger, *Gottfried Kellers Leben, Briefe und Tagebücher*, 3 vols., Stuttgart and Berlin, 1915–16. (The first volume contains the life, based on Baechtold's original biography, vols. 2 and 3 Keller's letters and diaries. Vol. 1 was reissued in 1950; the other two volumes have now been superseded by the new critical editions of Keller's works and letters.)

Gottfried Keller, *Briefe Gottfried Kellers*, selected and edited by Carl Helbling, Zurich, 1940.

Paul Heyse und Gottfried Keller im Briefwechsel, ed. Max Kalbeck, Brunswick, 1919.

Keller—J. V. Widmann Briefwechsel, ed. Max Widmann, Basle, 1922.

Der Briefwechsel zwischen Theodor Storm und Gottfried Keller, ed. Albert Köster, 4th ed., Berlin, 1924.

Aus Gottfried Kellers glücklicher Zeit (letters to Marie and Adolf Exner), ed. Hans Frisch, Vienna, 1927.

AUTOBIOGRAPHIES

Keller wrote 3 autobiographies, none of them very substantial :

Autobiographische Skizze, 1847
Autobiographisches, 1876
Selbstbiographie, 1889

All are reprinted in vol. 21 of Fränkel's and Helbling's standard ed. of the works.

GENERAL WORKS ON KELLER

Emil Ermatinger, *Gottfried Kellers Leben, Briefe und Tagebücher*, 3 vols., Stuttgart and Berlin, 1915–16. Vol. 1 (the Life and Works) was reissued in 1950. This is the standard work, based on J. Baechtold's biography.

E. Ackerknecht, *Gottfried Keller, Geschichte seines Lebens*, Leipzig, 1939 and 1942. Along with Ermatinger this book offers the fullest available account of Keller's life, but unlike Ermatinger it does not deal with the works.

Ernst Alker, *Gottfried Keller und Adalbert Stifter; eine vergleichende Studie*, Vienna 1923.

Jakob Baechtold, *Gottfried Kellers Leben: seine Briefe und Tagebücher*, 3 vols., Berlin, 1894–97.

Fernand Baldensperger, *Gottfried Keller, sa vie et ses oeuvres*, Paris, 1899.

E. Bebler, *Gottfried Keller und Ludmilla Assing*, Zurich, 1952 (about Keller's friendship and correspondence with Varnhagen von Ense's niece).

Hans Ed. von Berlepsch, *Gottfried Keller als Maler*, Leipzig, 1895.

Hedwig Bleuler-Waser, *Die Dichterschwestern Regula Keller und Betsy Meyer*, Zurich, 1919.

Hermann Boeschenstein, *Gottfried Keller: Grundzüge seines Lebens und Werkes*, Berne, 1948 (an arresting and original book).

Emil Bollmann and Fritz Hunziker, *Gottfried Keller (Heimat und Dichtung)*, with drawings by E. B. and text by F. H., Frauenfeld, 1915.

Otto Brahm, *Gottfried Keller*, in *Deutsche Rundschau*, 1882.

Fritz Buri, *Gottfried Kellers Beitrag zu einer künftigen protestant-ischen Wirklichkeitstheologie*, Berne, 1944.

Fritz Buri, "Erlösung bei Gottfried Keller und Carl Spitteler" (in: *Jahrbücher der Gottfried Keller-Gesellschaft*, 14, 1945), Zurich, 1946.

Hans Corrodi, *Gottfried Kellers Weltanschauung*, Munich, 1932.

Richard Drews, *Gottfried Keller, Dichter, Politiker und Patriot*, Berlin, 1953.

Hans Dünnebier, *Gottfried Keller und Ludwig Feuerbach*, Zurich, 1913.

Robert Faesi, *Gottfried Keller*, Zurich, 1942.

Jonas Fränkel, *Gottfried Kellers politische Sendung*, Zurich, 1939.

Jonas Fränkel, "Gottfried Keller-Philologie", *Euphorion* xlvi, 3/4 (Fränkel's attack on Helbling for his alleged inadequacies as an editor).

Adolf Frey, *Erinnerungen an Gottfried Keller*, 3rd ed., Leipzig, 1919.

Adolf Frey, *Allerhand von Gottfried Keller*, Berlin, 1919.

Albert Gessler, "Gottfried Keller", in: *Allgemeine deutsche Biographie*, LI, 486 ff., Leipzig, 1905.

A. von Gleichen-Russwurm, *Gottfried Kellers Weltanschauung*, Philosophische Reihe, ed. Alfred Weber, 23, Munich, 1921.

E. F. Hauch, *Gottfried Keller as a Democratic Idealist*, New York, 1916.

Carl Helbling, *Arbeit an der Gottfried Keller-Ausgabe*, Berne, 1945.

Eduard Hitschmann, *Gottfried Keller. Psychoanalyse des Dichters, seiner Gestalten und Motive* (reprinted from *Imago*), Leipzig and Zurich, 1919.

Max Hochdorf, *Zum geistigen Bilde Gottfried Kellers*, Vienna, 1919.

Hugo von Hofmannsthal, "Unterhaltung über die Schriften von Gottfried Keller" (in: *Dichtung von Dichtern gesehen: Essays von Moritz Heimann, H. von Hofmannsthal und Oskar Loerke*), Berlin, 1929.

Ernst Howald, *Gottfried Keller, Schweizer, deutscher Dichter, Weltbürger, historisch-biographische Betrachtung*, New York, 1933.

Ricarda Huch, *Gottfried Keller* (Die Dichtung, IX), Berlin, 1904.

Albert Köster, *Gottfried Keller. Sieben Vorlesungen*, Leipzig, 1900.

Georg Lukacs, *Gottfried Keller*, Berlin 1946 (a Marxist view).

Fritz Mauthner, *Von Keller zu Zola: Kritische Aufsätze*, Berlin, 1887.

W. Muschg, *Gottfried Keller und Jeremias Gotthelf*, Frankfurt-am-Main, 1940.

Wolfgang Preisendanz, "Die Keller-Forschung der Jahre 1939–57" (in: *Germanisch-romanische Monatsschrift*), 1958, 144–178. A useful survey of recent work on Keller.

Edgar Neis, *Romantik und Realismus in Gottfried Kellers Prosawerken (Germanistische Studien*, 85), Berlin, 1930.

Thomas Roffler, *Gottfried Keller. Ein Bildnis*. Frauenfeld and Leipzig, 1931.

Paul Schaffner, *Gottfried Keller als Maler*, Stuttgart, 1923.

Paul Schaffner, *Gottfried Keller als Maler*, Zurich, 1942. (Though the text of the more recent work is less full, the illustrations are much better. This invaluable work gives an insight into Keller's capabilities and limitations as a painter. It also includes many portraits of Keller.)

Otto Schlaginhaufen, "Gottfried Kellers Ahnen- und Sippschaftstafel" (*Archiv der Julius Klaus-Stiftung*, IV, 1,), Zurich, 1929.

Otto Stoessl, *Gottfried Keller* (*Die Literatur*, X), Berlin, 1904.

Werner Weber, *Freundschaften Gottfried Kellers. Versuch über die Einsamkeit eines Genies*, Erlenbach-Zurich, 1952.

Louis Wiesmann, *Gottfried Keller, Das Werk als Spiegel der Persönlichkeit*, Frauenfeld, 1967.

Paul Wüst, *Gottfried Keller und Conrad Ferdinand Meyer in ihrem persönlichen Verhältnis*, Leipzig, 1911.

A. Zäch, *Gottfried Keller*, Berne, 1945.

A. Zäch, *Gottfried Keller im Spiegel seiner Zeit. Urteile und Berichte von Zeitgenossen über den Menschen und Dichter*, Zurich, 1952.

Charles C. Zippermann, *Gottfried Keller–Bibliographie, 1844–1934*, Zurich, 1935. (Neither as selective nor as well arranged as it might be; occasionally even confuses Keller with others of the same surname.)

W. Zolliger-Wells, *Gottfried Kellers Religiosität*, Zurich, 1954.

Max Zollinger, "Gottfried Keller als Erzieher" (in: *Jahrbücher der Gottfried Keller-Gesellschaft*, Zürich, 111), Zurich, 1935.

WORKS CONTAINING VALUABLE SECTIONS ON KELLER

E. K. Bennett (revised by H. M. Waidson), *A History of the German Novelle*, Cambridge, 1960.

Wolfgang Kayser, *Das Groteske in Malerei und Dichtung*, Oldenburg, 1957.

Johannes Klein, *Geschichte der deutschen Novelle*, 3rd ed., Wiesbaden, 1956.

Roy Pascal, *The German Novel*, Manchester, 1956.

KELLER'S POETRY

Paul Brunner, *Studien und Beiträge zu G. Kellers Lyrik*, Diss., Zurich, 1906.

Eduard Korrodi, *Gottfried Keller* (*Deutsche Lyriker IX*), Leipzig, 1911.

Eduard Korrodi, "Gottfried Kellers und C. F. Meyers Gedichte", in: *Hochland*, VIII, Kempten, 1911.

Gustav Müller-Gschwend, "Gottfried Keller als lyrischer Dichter", in: *Acta Germanica*, VII, 2, Berlin, 1910.

Emil Staiger, *Die Zeit als Einbildungskraft des Dichters*, Zurich, 1939. (Examines poems by various authors; offers an interpretation of *Die Zeit geht nicht*.)

Philipp Witkop, *Gottfried Keller als Lyriker*, Freiburg, 1911.

Philipp Witkop, *Die deutschen Lyriker*, Part II, Leipzig, 1921, pp. 225–244.

DER GRÜNE HEINRICH

Gottfried Keller, See vols. 3–6 and 16–19 of the Fränkel-Helbling ed. for comparison of the two versions, and especially the editorial comment by Jonas Fränkel in vol. 6, pp. 329 ff. and vol. 19, pp. 333 ff.

Gottfried Keller, *Green Henry*, translated into English by A. M. Holt, London, 1960

Fritz Hunziker, *Glattfelden und Gottfried Kellers Grüner Heinrich*, Diss., Zurich, 1911.

Franz Leppmann, *Gottfried Kellers "grüner Heinrich" von 1854/55 und 1879/80; Beiträge zu einer Vergleichung*, Diss., Berlin, 1902.

Paul Schaffner, *Der grüne Heinrich als Künstlerroman*, Stuttgart, 1919.

DIE LEUTE VON SELDWYLA

B. A. Rowley, *Kleider machen Leute* (an interpretation), London, 1960.

Benno von Wiese, "Gottfried Keller, *Kleider machen Leute*", in : *Die deutsche Novelle von Goethe bis Kafka*, Düsseldorf, 1956.

SIEBEN LEGENDEN

Gottfried Keller, ed. K. Reichert, *Galatea–Novellen* (the original version of the *Legenden*, planned as part of *Das Sinngedicht*), Frankfurt, 1965.

Albert Leitzmann, *Die Quellen zu Gottfried Kellers* Legenden, Halle, 1919. (Very useful work giving the sources and a critical text of the legends.)

ZÜRICHER NOVELLEN

Max Nussberger, *"Der Landvogt von Greifensee" und seine Quellen; eine Studie zu Gottfried Kellers dichterischem Schaffen*, Frauenfeld, 1903.

Max Wehrli, "Die Züricher Novellen. Rede". (*Jahresbericht der Gottfried Keller–Gesellschaft in Zürich*, 18), Zurich, 1949.

DAS SINNGEDICHT

Priscilla M. Kramer, *The cyclical method of composition in Gottfried Keller's "Sinngedicht"*, New York, 1939.

SOME RECENT ARTICLES OF SPECIAL INTEREST

Helen Adolf, "A mid-century duel : Gottfried Keller and Heine", *Germanic Review*, xxviii, 3, 1953.

L. W. Forster, "Gottfried Keller : Some echoes", *German Life and Letters*, x, 3, 177–182.

Mary E. Gilbert, "Zur Bildlichkeit in Kellers *Romeo und Julia auf dem Dorfe*", *Wirkendes Wort*, iv, 6. (Investigates the symbolical significance of colours and certain other ideas).

P. Goldammer, "L. Feuerbach und die sieben Legenden Gottfried Kellers", *Weimarer Beiträge*, 1958.

Ruth Heller, "Gottfried Keller and literary criticism", *German Life and Letters*, xii, 1.

H. W. Reichert, "Caricature in Keller's Grüner Heinrich", *Monatshefte für den Deutschunterricht*, xlviii, 1956.

J. M. Ritchie, "The place of Martin Salander in Gottfried Keller's evolution as a prose writer", *Modern Language Review*, lii, 2, pp. 214–22.

Paula Ritzler, "Das Aussergewöhnliche und das Bestehende in Gottfried Kellers Novellen", *Deutsche Vierteljahrsschrift für Literaturwissenschaft und Geistesgeschichte*, xxviii, 3, 1954.

Lionel Thomas, Introduction to *Gottfried Keller, Two Stories*, Oxford, 1966.

INDEX